The American
Energy Consumer

A Report to the Energy Policy Project of the Ford Foundation

The American Energy Consumer

Dorothy K. Newman
Dawn Day

Ballinger Publishing Company • Cambridge, Mass.
A Subsidiary of J.B. Lippincott Company

Published in the United States of America by Ballinger Publishing Company, Cambridge, Mass.

First Printing, 1975

Library of Congress Catalog Card Number: 75–4865

International Standard Book Number: 0–88410–339–0 HB
0–88410–340–4 PB

Printed in the United States of America

Library of Congress Cataloging in Publication Data

Newman, Dorothy Krall
    The American energy consumer.

    Bibliography: p.
    1. Energy consumption–United States.
I. Day, Dawn, joint author. II. Title.
HD9502.U52N48   333.7   75–486
ISBN 0–88410–339–0

Contents

v

List of Figures and Exhibits

Figures

List of Tables

Preface

The Energy Policy Project was initiated by the Ford Foundation in 1971 to explore alternative national energy policies. This book, *The American Energy Consumer,* is one of a series of special studies which the Project commissioned. It is presented here as a carefully prepared contribution to public understanding of how people, of various groups and income classes, use energy and what they pay for it.

It is our hope that each of the special reports in this series will stimulate further thinking and questioning in the particular areas it addresses. At most, however, each one deals with only part of the energy puzzle. The Project's already-published final report, *A Time To Choose: America's Energy Future,* attempts to integrate these parts into a comprehensible whole, setting forth our analysis, conclusions and recommendations for the nation's energy future.

This book, like the others in the series, has been reviewed by scholars and experts in the field not otherwise associated with the Project, in order to be sure that differing points of view were considered. With each book in the series, we offer reviewers the opportunity of having their comments published; one has chosen to do so with this volume (see page 305).

The American Energy Consumer is the authors' report to the Energy Policy Project, and neither the Project, nor its Advisory Board, nor the Ford Foundation assume the role of endorsing its contents or conclusions. The Project's views are expressed in our final report, *A Time to Choose.*

S. David Freeman
Director
Energy Policy Project

Acknowledgments

This book could not have been written without the help of literally thousands of people. They include the people who answered our questionnaires in almost 1,500 households and in 125 public utilities.

We have space to mention by name only a few of the many others who helped us. Reid Thompson, President of the Potomac Electric Power Co., and Paul Reichardt, President of the Washington Gas Light Co., helped us prepare the letter and design the questionnaire that we sent to the households' utilities. Their support and cooperation were responsible for the excellent response we received, and contributed greatly to the quality of our results.

Reuben Cohen, Executive Vice President of Response Analysis Corporation in Princeton, New Jersey, developed the sample design, and directed the household survey and tabulation of the results. We benefited greatly from his sampling expertise and his sage advice about the household questionnaire and tabulation format and content.

William J. Kruvant, research associate at the Washington Center for Metropolitan Studies, who wrote Chapter Six, "People, Energy, and Pollution," also made significant contributions to almost every chapter in this book.

William Beachy, research assistant at the Center, developed many of the analytical, statistical summaries required for clarity in writing. He contributed also to all substantive areas through careful and insightful research. He was a key member of the Center's energy research staff throughout the length of the project.

We are indebted to the research librarians of the Washington Center: first, to Mary Edwards, and after she retired, to Marion Shamu. They and their assistants, Mary Channon and Christine Miller, were immensely helpful in achieving breadth and accuracy in documentation.

Gratitude for work well done is due to Joanie Bagby, Rachel Coppock, Nancy Gaeta, Janice Outtz, and Nancy Rytina, who served at various times on the project. Sarah Browne assisted in an important way throughout, and helped in particular with the survey of households' utilities.

We are indebted to the Energy Policy Project staff for intellectual stimulation and technical contributions. We sought technical information from many who were generous with their time and helpful advice. Among them we owe particular thanks to staff at the National Bureau of Standards, especially Tamami Kasuda, and to David DiJulio, manager of the Air Quality Planning Programs of the Metropolitan Washington Council of Governments.

We are particularly grateful to the President of the Washington Center for Metropolitan Studies, Atlee E. Shidler, who gave us the kind of support that derives only from a generous, enlightened, and professional administrator.

Dorothy K. Newman
Dawn Day

Introduction

This book is for people who want to know about the part energy plays in their lives. It is for people who want to know how their personal use of energy differs from others, and how the production and use of energy affects them. The book is also for people who make the government or business policies affecting household energy use, and need facts to guide them in understanding the consequences of what they do.

American households[a] consume about one-third of the nation's energy each year directly in their homes and cars. Although households are major energy markets, most studies of energy have not been about household use or its effects on people. They have dealt chiefly with major issues of extraction, supply, production, conservation, and producers' costs. Also, they are often written for specialists, even when their significance for consumers is vital.

PROFILE OF THE STUDY

The purpose of this study, then, was first to find out about the relationship of energy use to people as consumers, and second to present the findings so that the public, and people who plan for the public, could understand and interpret them readily.

This approach to the study of energy was surprisingly difficult. We soon discovered that we were charting new ground by looking at individual household energy use nationwide and that we needed substantial help from physics, engineering, and architecture as well as from economics and the behavioral sciences to do the job.

Research that crosses disciplines is revealing, but it is hard to do and time consuming. Support for this study was generous, but time was wisely

[a]The term "household" as used in this study means the people living in a dwelling (house, apartment, etc.).

limited, since there is an urgent need for current information. The study, which began in October 1972, took 24 months to complete, including writing this book[b]. The energy crisis of 1973–74, which intervened, brought serious consumer shortages and sharply rising prices. This made clear the extent to which public policy then in the making would affect the public and the need for the facts we were assembling.[c] Many of the facts come from two surveys. One was a national sample survey of households[d] to find out about energy using characteristics of the households themselves and of their dwellings. The other survey was of the households' electricity and natural gas companies, made after receiving each household's consent. The utilities provided the actual amount and cost of the electricity and natural gas their customers used in the most recent twelve-month period.[e] The two sets of information (from households and their utilities directly) made it possible to match the exact amount and cost of electricity and natural gas used with each household's characteristics and the characteristics of their homes. Answers on the household questionnaire gave the basis for making similar—but less accurate—estimates of gasoline use.[f]

To analyze these data and add to general understanding of how energy use affects households, our research extended into a number of other areas, with primary focus on the cost of energy and the relationship of cost to households' means. We wanted to put numbers on the variations in energy use and cost among households of differing income and other characteristics. We also wanted to know how much households of all kinds depend on cars and gasoline for their transportation. We hoped to discover the main influences on household energy use. Of special interest also was the degree to which the fallout from energy use, in the form of air pollution, affects households of varying characteristics.

Wherever possible, we compared income groups, especially the poor with better-off households. The poor received special attention since we

[b]Financed through a grant from the Ford Foundation's Energy Policy Project to the Washington Center for Metropolitan Studies and from general support by the Ford Foundation to the Washington Center, with Dorothy K. Newman as director of the study.

[c]In response, the Energy Policy Project of the Ford Foundation issued a preliminary report early in the spring of 1974, *Exploring Energy Choices,* citing some of our early findings. In addition, we supplied information directly to the Federal Energy Office, the Office of Economic Opportunity, and to other agencies, committees, or commissions during the critical months of 1973–74.

[d]The field work was conducted in May–June 1973 by Response Analysis Corporation of Princeton, N.J., for the Washington Center for Metropolitan Studies. The questionnaire, households' responses, and details about the survey and the sample are found in the Appendix to this book.

[e]Most reports were for twelve months ending in May, June, or July 1973, after the spot heating oil shortage in the winter of 1972–73, but before the more widespread fuel oil and gasoline shortage of 1973–74. Details about the utility survey are found in the Appendix, including a list of the utility companies that assisted us.

[f]The methods for arriving at totals and average-per-household estimates for electricity, natural gas, and gasoline are described in the Appendix.

anticipated that the impact of shortages and costs weigh most heavily on them. We assumed that income was basic to our analysis, and it was. We could identify the extremes—those who could buy only necessities such as heat and light, and those who could afford luxuries such as central air conditioning and an outdoor gas light burning night and day.

The study provides two kinds of results: first, descriptions of what is true about energy consumption in households; and second, a basis for answering some key policy questions. Some of those questions are: (1) What role can households play in using energy more efficiently or in conserving it? (2) What role can other agencies—for instance, utilities, regulatory commissions, business, and government—play in helping households make more efficient use of energy? (3) What might the probable impact be of policies to conserve or allocate an energy source, or to improve air quality, on households of different kinds?

The book begins with a bit of history, showing how quickly we have become an energy devouring people (Chapter One). We follow with an investigative reporter's portrayal of how six households of widely different kinds have come to use energy as they do today (Chapter Two). Chapters Three and Four then present the basic background information—what uses most energy in homes and in transportation. These chapters analyze the implications of this and of recent trends in homebuilding and car production as well. The next two chapters get to the heart of household energy use: the amount and cost of the energy households consume and the air pollution effects for major income groups, emphasizing especially the difference between the poor, the almost poor and the better off[g] (Chapters Five and Six). Chapter Seven describes the energy situation of black households at varying economic levels, compared with whites at similar levels. In conclusion (Chapter Eight) we outline a few suggested energy policies for public discussion. These proposals are based on information in the previous chapters, and their object is to suggest ways to increase the efficiency of household energy use and thus help reduce rising consumption while improving the equity of energy distribution and costs among households. We think the proposals could also contribute to the growth and stability of the nation's economy and improve the American level of living.

HIGHLIGHTS

The main findings on which suggested policies are based are repeated in virtually every area into which the investigation reached. They show, without doubt, that the more money you have, the more energy you use at home and in your automobile. This is regardless of any other condition—climate; how and how far you commute to work; the size of your house; your age; number of people in

[g]The poor were defined using the federal government's criteria. The nonpoor in this book are divided as follows: lower middle (under $12,000 income); upper middle ($12,000–$15,999); and well off ($16,000 and over). See Chapter Five for details.

your household; and whether or not your house is protected from the weather by insulation, for instance. Paradoxically also, the better off you are, the more likely you are to have equipment that saves energy as well as a house and equipment that uses a great deal of energy.

Another key finding is that almost all households have a circumscribed choice, especially about the most energy related features of their house: the architectural design, the furnace, and the water heater. The structure and built-in equipment are there when almost every household buys or rents a dwelling. If you judge energy use on the basis of the number of major appliances in a home (as many do) you would be right, but only because the presence or absence of major appliances is a key indicator of total energy consumption and is linked chiefly with income. Appliances, which are usually bought separately and not built in, do not use much energy by themselves. Therefore, what one chooses and buys separately is less important to the energy consumed at home than are the basic features of the structure—about which a household has had little to say.

Limited choice is reflected also in the degree to which households use automobiles. Whether poor or rich, few workers felt they had a choice in how they commuted to their jobs. Either they used a car or had a time consuming, inconvenient struggle with public transportation. Therefore, almost all the chief breadwinners in American families use a car to get to work.

Lack of choice reaches far and deep. Exclusionary housing patterns affecting lower income and black households leave them even less choice than others in the dwellings they live in, and therefore in the energy using features of their homes. Automobiles are becoming heavier and more expensive, and the increases have been greatest among compacts that cost and weigh the least. Those who produce homes and the facilities in them that determine how much energy people use have been making their products more energy consuming and costly.

The costs are increasingly burdensome on those at the lower end of the income range, who have fewest options. They are least able to afford the sharply rising prices for every energy source. In addition, both electricity and natural gas prices are ordinarily higher the less you use. Low income households, who use least, pay more per unit (million Btu's) than the well off.

The inevitable conclusion is that households may be able to play only a modest role in energy conservation by themselves. Possible exceptions are the well off, who have most options. But even they are locked into a given housing stock and certain transportation alternatives. Conservation, then, is everybody's business if the public is to save energy. To a large extent the buck passes to commerce and industry; to state and local governments, which can modify land use, zoning, and building permit regulations; to various arms of the federal government that administer or enforce housing laws and utility and environmental regulations; and, finally, to the Congress. The Congress could provide legislation to remove some large remaining roadblocks that hinder free choice and energy saving alternatives in housing and transportation. If households had more choice, they would save energy. We found that people at all income levels were aware of how to save.

SOME NEXT STEPS

This study is a beginning—and just a beginning—in a large, complex field. Much is left to be done. Among the most important studies that should be undertaken soon is one that would show the impact of price changes for electricity and natural gas on different economic groups—that is, a rigorous, statistical analysis of the price elasticity of demand for households of different kinds.

Prices are rising rapidly now and apparently these increases will continue. Evaluating the effect of price change on demand could point to changes in the utility price structure for promoting customer equity, environmental protection, and energy conservation, while maintaining reasonable profits for public utility services. It could detect the households that contribute to demand peaks for electricity, and discover ways of discouraging their consumption at such times. Peak loads lead to brownouts and ultimately to construction of new generating facilities that use huge amounts of energy themselves, as well as contributing to pollution and other environmental problems.

Additional studies should go beyond our emphasis of associating energy use with income alone. We would have liked to have analyzed the effect on energy use of some key household characteristics, independent of income. Preliminary correlations indicate strong association with the number of persons in the household; this in turn is associated with the stage of the life cycle. When family earning power is at its peak, children are usually still at home; household size is greatest then, and so is energy consumption. We do not know how much influence to ascribe to number of people in the household alone or to stage of the life cycle, given the same house, climate, and kind of urban or rural location.[1]

While income remains basic, other household characteristics could play an independent role; for instance, the presence of more than one earner, a working wife, and residence in a very large metropolitan area compared with a small town. The question is how influential any one of the characteristics may be, apart from income.

Chapter Five, "The Energy Gap," discusses the shortcomings of income compared with wealth or economic security in assessing household consumption. Among influences on potential consumption, aside from current income, are ownership of property other than one's home, income from sources other than a job, education, and workers' benefits (such as private pension and medical and life insurance). All these could affect substantially the degree to which households feel free to spend their income and the kinds of things they spend it on, at varying stages of their life cycle.

The idea of the influence on consumption of a household's

perception of its "permanent" or future income (in a broad sense) was introduced by Milton Friedman in his famous *Theory of the Consumption Function,*[2] and has been studied, debated, and elaborated upon ever since.[3] Unfortunately in spite of attention economists have given to this concept, little has been done to incorporate its essential good sense into analyzing consumer behavior. Most studies about consumers, including this one, have used instead the much easier dimension of reported income. Here is a research challenge of substantial import—to assess the influence of economic security and the household's perception of its permanent and future income on energy consumption.

We began our work by saying it was about "life styles and energy." With great disappointment, we came to the conclusion quite early that we had neither the flexibility nor the time to develop a theoretical framework for relating an essentially qualitative phenomenon (life style) to one that, while partly qualitative, could still be quantified (energy use). To sociologists who wish to work quantitatively, life style has been a troublesome concept. We were optimistic that some of the criteria in the household questionnaire would help us, but the strictures of our study—budget, survey sample, time frame, questionnaire length, and requirements for developing energy estimates—proved too formidable. With particular emphasis on life style, we might have fruitfully followed the work of Susan Ferge and others who have collected and analyzed data on how individuals spend their time. We refer readers especially to *The Use of Time,*[4] a fascinating book about the daily activities of urban and suburban populations in twelve countries.

In analyzing social stratification in Hungary, Susan Ferge found she could demonstrate "the evolution of 'quantitative' and 'qualitative' differentiation: the gradual fading away of basic, quantitative differences and the growing importance of more subtle, qualitative ones."[5] She discovered more variety and enrichment in every component of the way of life with improved material conditions. These tendencies were accompanied by a search for conspicuous behavior that gave objects as well as attitudes a symbolic value that served to represent social standing.

Surely for Americans, the kind of house and car and their accessories—not to mention their number and, in the case of the house, its location—fits into this scheme. This has great relevance for energy use, but we must leave to others its deeper study.

The American
Energy Consumer

Chapter One

Household Energy—Past and Present

FROM FOOTCANDLES TO QUADRILLIONS OF BTU'S IN ONE GENERATION

The energy revolution in the twentieth century has transformed America within lifetimes. Twenty million older Americans remember reading by oil, gas, or candlelight, and splitting wood or carrying coal to feed the cook stove or potbellied room heater. They put ice cards in the window and stored perishables in the cool cellar or winter window box. They used tin basins and tubs, chamber pots and outdoor privies. Cooking, washing, cleaning houses, and doing farm chores were tedious, hard work.

In the country during the early 1900s farmers worked their land with muscle power—human and animal. Housewives scrubbed clothes on washboards, beat rugs with sticks or brooms, cooked in big pots over slow fires, and pumped water and plucked chickens by hand. Few town or city families owned even a horse, much less a carriage. Children walked to school, and after a few years they walked to work or to the store.[1] Motor buses were not common in cities until the twenties and trolley cars not until the thirties (see Table 1-1). To quote David Boorstin, "Streetcar tracks were rigid channels. A man in a streetcar had to go where it took him. And the streetcar, in almost any city, was likely to take him into the center; there were the great consumers' palaces."[2]

Even though electric power was a reality by the turn of the century, only a few households had it. True, electric lights illuminated the Philadelphia Centennial Exposition in 1876 and the Edison Electric Light Company was formed in 1878.[3] Even so, only 8 percent of all American houses were wired for electricity by 1907, and these were the homes of wealthy people living in big cities. Most people then were rural dwellers—60 percent in 1900. One-fifth of all other Americans lived in small towns.[4]

Table 1-1.   Public Transportation Passengers, by Type of Vehicle,
Selected Years, 1917–1972

Year	*Passengers (in millions)*		
	Railway (surface & subways)	*Motor bus*	*Trolley coach*
1917	14.5	a	a
1922	15.3	.4	a
1925	15.2	1.5	a
1928	14.5	2.5	b
1930	13.1	2.5	b
1935	9.5	2.6	.1
1940	8.3	4.2	.5
1945	12.1	9.9	1.2
1950	6.2	9.4	1.7
1955	3.1	7.3	1.2
1960	2.3	6.4	.7
1965	2.1	5.8	.3
1970	2.1	5.0	.2
1972	1.9	4.5	.1

[a]Not available or none.
[b]Less than 50,000.
Source: Prepared by Washington Center for Metropolitan Studies from U.S. Bureau of the Census, *Statistical Abstract of the U.S.: 1973*, p. 555; *Historical Statistics of the U.S., Colonial Times to 1957*, p. 464; and *Historical Statistics of the U.S. Continuation to 1962 and Revisions*, p. 65.

Only the rich could afford the new sources of energy. They had gas light and the first electric lights. The wealthy were very few and very rich and led conspicuously different lives from all the rest. The income and energy gap, which is still wide, was much wider in the early 1900s. A few people controlled most of the available energy either as owners or executives in the burgeoning railroads and new utilities, or in their personal lives. They had private railway cars, yachts, and the first automobiles. They also had the first coal furnaces for central heating.

Even among the rich, most of the energy was still muscle energy in the early years of this century. Horses pulled their carriages (for example, Alfred Vanderbilt had a team of beautifully matched greys to pull his sporting coach in 1910), and servants, who did the manual labor, slept in tiny bedrooms that filled the top floors of huge houses. The rest of the people led far simpler and more exhausting lives. Professionals, doctors, lawyers, and middling merchants—relatively few in number—had horses and buggies, one to a family. Their wives had "help," but the housewife herself still worked hard at household tasks. Beyond them were the great mass of farmers, artisans, factory workers, small shop keepers, bakers, butchers, barbers. They and their wives did their own work without the aid of the new energy conveniences.

The people in two of the stories told in Chapter Two, "The Way Some People Live," are about 60 years old—old enough to remember this style of life. Mr. and Mrs. M, for instance, began their housekeeping on one floor of an abandoned inn in a small town in West Virginia. It was within convenient walking distance of the mill where Mr. M worked. They paid $5 a month in rent, and although they had a good deal of space, they had no electricity, no indoor plumbing, and no central heating. The Ms, whom we call lower middle income (having less than $12,000 a year) now own a color TV, a window air conditioner, a plug-in electric heater, and a food freezer. They own a car too, and Mr. M has the daily use of his employer's truck. The Ms rent their apartment, and while the landlord pays the utility bills and owns the kitchen stove and refrigerator, the refrigerator is frost-free—the most energy consuming and labor saving type made. The Ms epitomize the results of the rapid spread of new forms of energy. They experienced a radical change in their style of life just within their adulthood.

A similar change took place in Mr. and Mrs. A's married life. They are living with Mrs. A's mother on Mr. A's social security pension, and are poor. They have no car, but they own their own small home in a busy city neighborhood. In their house they have a frost-free refrigerator, a washing machine, and a black and white TV. When Mr. and Mrs. A set up housekeeping about 35 years ago they rented a three-room house in a village near Richmond, Virginia. By a coincidence their rent was $5 a month, the same as the Ms'. The house had no electricity, no plumbing, and a wood stove. The As, though poor in terms of annual income, have prospered in terms of the energy at their command.

During the first few decades of the century almost all homes across the country were energy poor. Americans still burned kerosene for light, fathers and sons still split wood for the fire, and the family walked everywhere they needed to go. But technological change was so rapid that the difference between the rich and nonrich became less obvious year by year. Direct, cheap, available energy was making everyone's tasks easier, and leisure was no longer the monopoly of the leisure class. The spreading new energy sources were changing the shape of kitchens, of houses, of cities, of families, and of lives.

By 1925 over half (53 percent) of all homes were wired for electricty, mostly in urban or rural nonfarm places. (It was not until 1945 that half of all farm houses had electricity.) Natural gas became fairly common in the thirties (see Table 1-2). The number of passenger cars mushroomed from 181,000 sold in 1910 to almost two million in 1920.[5]

After President Wilson signed the Federal Aid to Roads Act in 1916, the common motorist came into being, with new styles, new words, and new cars chugging across blacktop roads. The first road census in 1904 reported

Table 1-2.   Growth of Residential Electric and Natural Gas Service, Selected Years, 1907-1973

	Percent of homes with electricity			Percent of homes with natural gas[a]
Year	Total	Urban & rural nonfarm	Farm	
1907	8	b	b	b
1912	16	b	b	b
1917	24	b	b	b
1920	35	47	2	b
1925	53	69	4	b
1930	68	85	10	b
1935	68	84	13	46
1940	79	91	33	47
1945	85	93	48	50
1950	94	97	78	51
1955	98	99	94	55
1960	99	b	b	58
1965	100	b	b	60
1970	100	b	b	61
1973	100	b	b	68[c]

[a]Computed using number of residential customers and total households.
[b]Not available.
[c]Households with natural gas, from Survey, see source.

Source: Prepared by the Washington Center for Metropolitan Studies from U.S. Bureau of the Census *Historical Statistics of the U.S., Colonial Times to 1957*, Series S 71-73, p. 510 and *Current Population Reports* P-20, No. 218, *Household and Family Characteristics March 1970*, Table 20, p. 85. American Gas Association, *1972 Gas Facts*, Table 58, p. 68; and for 1973, The Washington Center for Metropolitan Studies' Lifestyles and Energy Surveys.

154,000 miles of "improved" highway three-quarters of which was not hard surfaced.[6] By 1930 Americans had about 700,000 miles of highways on which to travel.[7] "Service stations" kept motorists from being stranded indefinitely with their "machines" when they took Sunday drives dressed in their "dusters," and had "blowouts." When it rained onto their open "touring cars" all hands went to the rescue by snapping on the isinglass "flaps."

Since 1930 the number of cars and taxis on the roads has jumped over four times, while the number of people who could drive or ride in them did not even double.[8] Now, four-fifths of all households depend on at least one automobile; there is a car in almost every homeowner's garage.

The rapidly increasing supply of all kinds of energy sources—electricity, natural gas, coal, and petroleum products—changed the way people lived enormously. It became practical to travel long distances to work or for pleasure, and to stay up late, with comfort, to read, study, visit, and listen to the radio.

Almost half of all households (46 percent) had a radio in 1925 compared with only 10 percent five years earlier. Many Americans living today remember sitting around the radio to hear FDR's fireside chats. The President during 1933 to 1945 addressed the nation by radio. There was no TV. But by 1973 virtually every home had television (Table 1-3). The electronic boom alone opened channels of communication from coast to coast and became a primary educator and advertiser.

Advertisers in the twenties used the wireless to sell proliferating electrical appliances and kitchen aids. A radio sales training feature of 1922, urging dealers to promote electrical appliances as gifts, used the slogan "many a June bride-elect hopes to become a wife electrical this year."[9] Small appliances were the only ones reaching many homes then—irons and vacuum cleaners, for instance.[10] Very few households had a refrigerator, an appliance that is in virtually every home now. Fewer than 8 percent had clothes washers in 1922, whereas almost 80 percent do today (Table 1-4).

By now, Americans know that the energy boom that revolutionized ways of living in a single generation has not been an unmixed blessing. It has caused blemishes on the land and shore, unhealthy air and water, paved the countryside and cities alike with highways, streets, and parking lots—all clogged with cars—and introduced us to brownouts and blackouts. Planning to avert these conditions has been delinquent and disjointed. But regardless of where the

Table 1-3. Percent of Households with Radio and TV, Selected Years, 1923-1973

Year	Radio	TV
1923	2	0
1925	10	0
1930	46	0
1935	67	0
1940	81	0
1945	88	a
1950	93	9
1955	96	64
1960	95	87
1965	100	92
1970	100	96
1973	100	97

[a]Less than 0.5 percent.

Source: Prepared by the Washington Center for Metropolitan Studies from U.S. Bureau of the Census, *Historical Statistics of the U.S., Colonial Times to 1957;* and *Continuation to 1962 and Revisions*, Series A242 and R 97–98; *Statistical Abstract of the U.S. 1972*, Tables 50, 803, and 1162; *1969* Table 1088, *1968*, Tables 743 and 1097, and *1965*, Table 729; and the Washington Center for Metropolitan Studies' Lifestyles and Energy Surveys for 1973.

Table 1-4.   Percent of Households Having Selected Major Appliances Available, Selected Years, 1922-1973

Year	Refrig-erator	Clothes washer	Dish-washer	Color TV	Clothes dryer	Home freezer
1922	a	8	a	0	0	b
1925	1	13	b	0	0	b
1930	9	24	b	0	0	b
1935	23	32	a	0	b	b
1940	46	44	b	0	b	b
1945	53	49	b	0	b	b
1950	77	67	2	0	1	6
1955	91	74	4	a	9	16
1960	96	84	7	a	19	23
1965	100	88	14	10	26	27
1970	100	92	27	43	45	31
1973	99	78	25	53	53	34

Note: The data for 1922-1970 are from *Merchandising Week* which reports sales and may not account for availability of more than one appliance in the home or for those discarded.

[a]Less than 0.5 percent.

[b]Data not available.

Source: Prepared by Washington Center for Metropolitan Studies using saturation of appliances data and estimates of wired homes from February 28, 1972 issue of *Merchandising Week*, applied to Census estimates of all households for the years shown. Census data are from *Historical Statistics of the U.S., Colonial Times to 1957*, Series A242, p. 15, and *Statistical Abstract of the U.S.: 1973*, Table 51, p. 40. 1973 data are from the Washington Center for Metropolitan Studies' Lifestyles and Energy Surveys.

responsibility lies for unsolved problems associated with a high energy using society, it is no wonder events have overtaken us. We are using almost twice as much energy per person today as in 1920 (see Table 1-5). Americans are the highest energy users among consumers of the industrialized western world. Only Canadians come even close: they use 83 percent as much per person as we do. Consumers in Sweden and West Germany are next, using energy at a rate about half that of Americans.[11] In total we consume a third of the world's energy, with only 6 percent of its population.[12] A Chinese delegate to a recent conference session on world resources is reported to have joked "the world can only afford one United States."[13]

HOW MUCH DO WE USE?

This book is about the energy that American households use directly, in their homes and in their cars.[a] In the year 1972-73 we used over 23 quadrillion Btu's

[a]Many of the tables in this book include simple percentages or percentage distributions, for easy reading and ready comprehension. The reader will find that percentages in percentage distributions do not always add exactly to the total. That is because we have left off tenths of points and rounded the figures to whole numbers.

Table 1-5. Energy Consumption in the United States, Selected Years, 1920-1973

Year	Total U.S. Energy Consumption[a] (trillions of Btu's)	Per Capita U.S. Energy Consumption (millions of Btu's)
1920	19,768	185.7
1930	22,253	180.6
1940	23,877	180.1 '
1950	33,992	223.2
1960	44,569	246.7
1970	67,143	327.7
1971	68,698	331.8
1972	72,108	345.3
1973[b]	75,561	359.1

[a]Includes coal, petroleum and natural gas and primary electricity. Firewood, animal wastes and most other non-commercial fuels are excluded.

[b]Preliminary.

Source: Energy Policy Project of the Ford Foundation, *Exploring Energy Choices: A Preliminary Report*, Washington, D.C.: Energy Policy Project, 1974, Table 1, p. 74.

of energy this way[b] (Table 1-6). Considering only electricity, natural gas, and gasoline, we consumed about 20 quadrillion Btu's, or not quite 350 million per household. Energy used only in the house itself is estimated at one-fifth of all U.S. energy, which in 1973 was about 76 quadrillion Btu's.[14] Another 10 percent of U.S. energy (7.3 quadrillion Btu's) is consumed by the gasoline in cars. Part of the rest—but only a part—goes to make and transport goods for consumers or to serve them.[c] A good deal of what industry makes, and wholesalers and retailers sell goes to federal, state and local governments for administration, for space exploration, and for military materiel (Table 1-7).

Succeeding chapters describe how American households use their millions of Btu's, and the wide variations that show up in use and cost. They bring history up to date.

This chapter explores one more question briefly: Has the energy revolution made housekeeping easier and less time consuming? Certainly home life is freer of the hard physical work and discomforts our parents and

[b]Includes electricity, natural gas, fuel oil and gasoline; excludes energy from wood, coal, kerosene, or bottled gas. All 1972–73 figures are from national surveys conducted under the direction of the Washington Center for Metropolitan Studies. Whenever information is from sources other than the Center's research, references appear in notes at the end of each chapter. The Washington Center's surveys were in two parts. The first asked a series of almost 150 questions of a stratified sample of 1,455 households nationwide about their dwelling and habits affecting energy use, and their opinions about the energy situation. The second asked 125 utility companies serving the sample households how much electricity and natural gas the households used and how much they paid for them during the most recent 12 months. Details of the surveys are found in the Appendix.

[c]See Chapter Five for a discussion of indirect energy use.

Table 1-6. Estimates of Annual Residential Use of Energy, by Source, 1972-1973[a]

Energy source	Btu's (in trillions)
Four energy sources—total	23,000
Electricity	6,400
Natural gas	6,600
Fuel oil	2,700
Gasoline	7,300

[a]See Appendix Tables A2-1 and A2-4 for the annual period covered for use of electricity and natural gas. All tables showing household use of these fuels cover a 12-month period in 1972-73. See also footnote a to Table 5-1.

Source: Washington Center for Metropolitan Studies' Lifestyles and Energy Surveys for all data but fuel oil. Data for fuel oil were derived from U.S. Bureau of Mines, *Sales of Fuel Oil and Kerosene in 1972, October 10, 1973*, Table 6, p. 4, using 90 percent of the sales of fuel oil No. 1 and 2, as advised by officials in the Division of Fossil Fuels of the U.S. Bureau of Mines.

Table 1-7. End Uses of Energy

Uses	Percent
All energy used in U.S.[a]	100
Personal energy use	34
In homes	19
In transportation	15
Cars[b]	10
Other[c]	5
Industrial, commercial and military	66

[a]Total refers to 1968, and total transportation is for 1970.

[b]Derived from 1972-73 data in Washington Center for Metropolitan Studies' Lifestyles and Energy Surveys which were applied to 1973 data from the U.S. Department of the Interior. See source below.

[c]Refers to air, rail, and taxi travel.

Source: Prepared by the Washington Center for Metropolitan Studies from the following: Eric Hirst, *Energy Interviews of Passenger and Freight Transportation Modes, 1950-1970* (Oak Ridge, Tenn.: Oak Ridge National Laboratory, April 1973), Table 10, p. 24. Stanford Research Institute, *Patterns of Energy Consumption in the United States* (Washington, D.C.: U.S. Government Printing Office, 1972), Table 13, p. 36. U.S. Department of Interior Release, "Energy Use Up Nearly 5 Percent in 1973," March 13, 1974, p. 1, and Washington Center for Metropolitan Studies' Lifestyles and Energy Surveys.

grandparents knew. It is free also of earlier generations' insularity. The great majority were bound by how far they could walk, ride a horse, or take a horse and buggy or a city bus or trolley.

Despite today's energy conveniences, however, it is debatable whether Americans have more leisure than a generation ago. While the paid work week for full time employees has declined, from 50 hours in 1920 to 43 hours in 1973,[15] these averages may be misleading. They include both straight time hours and overtime hours in the workplace. They do not take account of the work that women in the paid labor force do after business hours, such as housekeeping, shopping, and child care. Less than one-fourth of all women worked for pay outside the home in 1920, compared with about 45 percent currently. Relatively few married women were in the labor force early in the century compared with over 40 percent today (Table 1-8).

The official work week also does not take account of those men who moonlight (over 5 percent)[16] and an unknown but probably larger percentage of men who do repair and maintenance on their homes, gardens, cars, and other equipment, and sometimes help with household and child care tasks.

The time spent by women and men engaged in household tasks before or after their regular working hours is substantial. A number of studies about how people use their time show the surprising result that the proportion of strictly leisure time activities (sports, entertainment, visiting, pleasure trips, and so forth) has shrunk between the thirties and the mid sixties among both men and women, in spite of reduced working hours and sharply rising use of labor saving facilities at home.[17]

Traveling to and from work has eaten into some of the leisure time. A great surprise is that the time spent on housework has not changed in this century for nonemployed women, according to a recent study by Joann Vanek.[18] A shift has occurred from cleaning and cooking to household

Table 1-8. Percent of Women in the Labor Force, Selected Years, 1890-1973

	Percent in labor force	
	---	---
Year	*All women*	*Married women*[a]
1890	18	5 [b]
1900	20 [b]	[b]
1910		[b]
1920	23	[b]
1930	24	[b]
1940	26	15
1950	34	22
1960	38	32
1970	43	41
1973	45	42

[a]Civilian labor force.
[b]Not available.

Source: U.S. Bureau of the Census, *Historical Statistics of the U.S., Colonial Times to 1957*, Series D–20 and D–34, pp. 71–72 and U.S. Bureau of Labor Statistics, *Handbook of Labor Statistics 1974*, Tables 2 and 5, pp. 29 and 40.

management, shopping, and travel associated tasks, some of them in connection with family care. According to Vanek, employed women use less time for these tasks than nonemployed women. The present style of housekeeping has contributed to the vastly increased amount of energy used in the home.

Whereas the line between work and leisure may be difficult to draw, energy use can be clearly measured. Households today, whatever their economic situation, use much more energy than did households of the same relative economic position a generation or two ago.

Chapter Two

The Way Some People Live

Tom Kelly

These family vignettes provide a living frame for the facts and figures in later chapters. They tell the energy life story of different kinds of people of different ages, living in different places, under widely different circumstances.

This account of energy use from real life supplements the formal research findings in several important ways. First, people often think of their own experience as the norm, so it is important to illustrate how "other people" live. Yet, some people have unreal but firm ideas about "other people."[a] Since effective and equitable energy policy is crucial, it should rely on facts rather than beliefs. Statistics alone are often not enough to dislodge beliefs that are contrary to fact. Gunnar Myrdal has said, "Ignorance—like knowledge—is seldom random but is instead highly opportunistic, . . ."[b]

A statistical profile is not as clear or convincing to many people as a family profile. The following life stories bring into sharp focus many of the major findings: the huge leap some families have made from little but muscle power to run a home, to an energy filled household; the chasm in energy use even now separating poor and well off; and how energy using possessions often stem from necessity or lack of an alternative.

DAVID AND GLORIA M—INCOME $11,000 A
YEAR-PLUS—NEAR ALEXANDRIA, VA.

David and Gloria M, now both 60, have lived in a six-room apartment in a large complex of red brick buildings for twenty years. It is a mile north of Alexandria,

---

[a]The authors spoke with many people at all levels of income and education in the course of their research.

[b]Gunnar Myrdal, *Objectivity in Social Research* (New York: Pantheon Books, 1969, p. 99). Read this for a penetrating series of essays into how beliefs develop and are maintained; their relation to fact; and the role of research in bringing about change by informing.

11

Virginia and the Ms do not regard it as home. Home is in the Blue Ridge Mountains of Virginia.

Fairview, the apartment development where the Ms live, was built in the first years after World War I when there was an insatiable demand for homes. It was practical, economical, and reasonably attractive—the rectangular buildings have slate roofs and white "Colonial" pediments, the lawns were broad and green and young trees were budding by the quiet roadways. A small shopping center was across the principal road. Each of the 50 units held from four to eight families. It was clean and comfortable, but it had one major disadvantage—it was difficult to get from Fairview to Alexandria or any place, except by automobile. Bus service was nonexistent and the George Washington Memorial Parkway, the only accessible road, was a high speed thoroughfare not designed for walking or even crossing.

Most of the early settlers viewed Fairview as temporary, a place to stay until they bought their own homes. Most have long since left, but the Ms have not. The lawns are still neat, the buildings well kept, and the rents reasonable—and it is still almost impossible to get from Fairview to Alexandria or any place else without an automobile.

The Ms' apartment is compact. Two of the rooms, the living room and the dining room, are really one, ten feet by twenty-five, divided by an arched door almost as wide as the room. The furniture is as neatly arranged as the suites are in a furniture store display, and a thick green patterned rug covers the living room. Mr. M's green easy chair and matching hassock face the TV, a low sofa with doilies has its back against the wall, and a coffee table with a vase of artificial flowers is in front of it. The dining section has a heavily carved, mahogany-stained table and four matching chairs with red tapestry backs. It could be an illustration in a Sears catalogue except for one incongruous fact: a tall, white enamel freezer is jammed into the back corner of the dining room by the kitchen door. The freezer is there because Mr. M is a hunter, he needs to store his game, and there is no place else in the apartment for the freezer.

Mr. M works as a carpenter and maintenance man for a construction company that builds sprawling middle class housing developments in Northern Virginia. He keeps the houses in good repair until they are sold. He has a company truck to carry him on his rounds.

Mr. and Mrs. M own many things that consume energy—the most consumptive being a window air conditioner, a color TV, a plug-in heater, and a 1968 Chrysler Newport. Mrs. M uses the car (which they bought secondhand in 1969) to go shopping and to visit their grandchildren. The Ms are unusual in what they do *not* own—the landlord owns the gas stove and the electric frost-free refrigerator, and he also pays the utility bills.

Because of the central utility meters in their apartment building, no one—not the Ms, nor their electric and gas companies, nor their landlord—knows precisely how much energy David and Gloria M use. But their modest possessions suggest only a moderate level of energy consumption. Mr. and Mrs. M would like to have, but lack, a washer, a dryer, a humidifier, and a blender. Space and the awkward utility bills have curtailed their possessions; if they acquire anything beyond the basics they must negotiate an agreement with the landlord and then pay extra. The air conditioner costs them $29 a month and the freezer $40 a year. The arrangements with the landlord cause other small inconveniences. The apartment building is heated by a central oil furnace and the temperature in winter is seldom what the Ms would prefer: at night it tends to be too warm and when they wake up in the chill of morning it is too cold—hence the plug-in heater.

The Ms seem quite content with their lives—they are homebodies and family centered. They eat well, having meat two meals out of three, and they average only one TV dinner a week—but they never go out to restaurants or drive-ins. The Chrysler is used locally for utilitarian purposes and occasionally, twice a year, to take them back for a visit to the mountains. Neither David nor Gloria has ever ridden in a plane. Mrs. M finds that life in Fairview has its chronic imperfections—the neighbors are aloof and transitory; she would like, some day, to move back to the Blue Ridge or out west, to Arizona or Colorado (a son is stationed in Denver in the Air Force). But they are content. Like most Americans, they have, through the graces of God and technology, come a long way materially in a lifetime.

David was born in Hinton, West Virginia, a railroad center with 12,000 population. His father, a brakeman, died when David was 12 and the mother and children moved to a farm outside Covington, Virginia. Covington is in Alleghany County, deep in the mountains. It has a paper mill and a pervading smell of rotten eggs. David dropped out of school because the school was 13 miles from the farm and he had no horse and no car. When the family later moved to Callahan, a village six miles from Covington, David was working as a farmhand. The Callahan home was an improvement on the farmhouse. It had electric lights but no central heating and no indoor plumbing. Gloria's family lived on the edge of Callahan and their house was lit by kerosene and heated by burning logs. Heat was cheap: "the side of the mountain was full of wood," Gloria remembers.

By the late twenties the technological revolution had touched the Appalachian farms: the more prosperous farmers had tractors and Model T trucks and David had learned to drive them. He was driving one when he first came to Gloria's attention: "He was coming down the road in the truck and he near run me down!" They were soon engaged but Gloria was going to high school and they decided to wait until she graduated before marrying. She coveted the distinction.

When the Depression arrived a married man like David still had to have a job. He got one at the paper mill in Covington. He worked ten hours a day, six days a week, and he earned $34 every two weeks when the mill was working full time. "I make as much in a day now as I did in two weeks then," David says.

Transportation was a problem. Transportation—or the lack of it—was shaping (and would continue to shape) David's life. He had quit school because he had no way to get to the school house. Now he was in Callahan and the mill was six miles away. He found an expensive solution. A cab driver who lived in Callahan but who worked in Covington agreed to carry David and five other passengers back and forth for $3 apiece every week. It took twenty percent of David's pay.

David and Gloria decided it would be cheaper to move to Covington. There, they rented the entire floor of an abandoned inn on the outskirts of town within walking distance of the mill, for $5 a month. The new home was cheap but lacked refinements. The Ms had no electricity, no central heating, and no indoor plumbing. It was fine for newlyweds, but less so for parents—and a baby was coming. When she arrived they moved to Milo, a village on the other side of town but still within walking distance of the mill.

Milo was owned by one lady, the widow of a mill owner, who lived across the river in a "manor" house. The houses were all alike: four rooms, with electric lights, wood stoves, and outhouses. They rented for $12.50 a week. More children came—two in three years—and one died as an infant. The lady in the manor announced that the tenants could buy the houses. The price was fixed by a simple formula, 100 times the weekly rent, or $1,250.

The Ms bought their house and in time they installed indoor plumbing. Mrs. M remembers those years with affection. She had a large garden, flowers and vegetables, and congenial neighbors. The Ms bought their first car in 1936, a '31 Model A Ford, for less than $100. David soon traded it for a sports coupé. "The coupé was better than the sedan for getting around in the country. There wasn't much in the way of roads back then." Mrs. M got a refrigerator and a gas range. Mr. and Mrs. M were surviving nicely, the Depression was ending, and World War II about to begin.

When the war came David tried to enlist in the Air Force. He was 28, married and the father of two. The paper mill was running full-time but the pay was still low. With pay for dependents he would do better in the service, but the Air Force turned him down three times. In 1943 another son came, making his enlistment even less likely. (This son would follow his father's wishes but not his footsteps by making the Air Force his career.)

David found a new job. His brother was a skilled cobbler, specializing in orthopedic shoes. He had a small but steady business until the war came and shoe rationing began. Coupons were required for new shoes, but old shoes could be repaired and, as David recalls, "The law said that you could repair anything as long as you had some part of the shoe to begin with." Business boomed and the brother opened a second shop and put David in charge. He learned enough to put on a pair of heels and half soles. The brother did the harder jobs for both shops. David made more money than he'd ever made before. In the forties it was often easier to earn money than to spend it. There were no new cars, and old ones were extravagantly expensive. Other energy consumers, such as electrical appliances, were in short supply. David and Gloria were naturally thrifty and they saved; they had learned as children about rainy days.

In 1947 the war and the rationing ended and the second shop closed down. David was ready to move out in search of new opportunity. He bought a secondhand car and drove to Washington, D.C. where he'd heard home construction was booming. He knew a handsaw from a hawk, so he got a job as a carpenter's helper.

David was part of one of the great migrations of history—the movement from the countryside and the small towns of America to the big cities or, more accurately, to the suburbs of the big cities. It was a migration that depended on the automobile and on the country's ever-expanding industry. It had been delayed by the lack of cars during the war. Now, with new cars, new roads and new jobs the cork exploded from the bottle.

Most of the migrants were younger than David, men just out of the service, but many were middle-aged too. David was 34. He was able to expand his opportunities with an ease his father had never had. He could get a good job in northern Virginia because almost every family was a potential homeowner in those years of postwar economic recovery. David began commuting from Covington to the Washington suburbs, leaving home Sunday night and returning Friday. The automobile and the good roads made it possible. (He could have taken the bus but the journey would have been much more difficult.) The car was essential, but it cost him $15 to $20 a week.

David figured the building boom would last at least three years. In 1950 it showed no sign of diminishing, so David took another major step. The oldest child was about to graduate from high school and the youngest was about to start the first grade; it was the time to move. They sold their four-room house in Milo for $2,500 (exactly twice what they'd paid for it) and they moved to Fairview. Their first apartment there had two bedrooms, snug for five people, but it had its appeal—everything was shiny new. The kitchen was, by Covington standards, a marvel, with a new range and a new refrigerator; in the winter the heat was automatic, and there was indoor plumbing.

For Mrs. M there was also a new sense of isolation and loneliness. The car, which had been a convenience in Milo, became a necessity in Alexandria—Mr. M needed it to get to construction sites that were often twenty miles away, and Mrs. M needed it to shop in town. In the next twenty years the Ms would buy five cars, using Mr. M's shrewdly designed technique: "You buy a car when it's a year old. By then the price has dropped in half and if it has any bad faults they've shown up."

The children grew up and acquired homes, cars, appliances, and children of their own. The oldest, a girl, married an electrician and moved to nearby Maryland. The older son dropped out of high school and got a job loading luggage at National Airport, a few miles away. He was shortly promoted to the payroll department, and his ambitions grew—he enrolled in night classes in public speaking and salesmanship. In a few years he had established himself as a real estate salesman and had acquired a white Oldsmobile convertible. Ten years later he was the manager of a mortgage finance company and had bought a Lincoln Continental. His preference for a big, expensive car was explained to his mother: "He told me that he needed to have a big car for prestige," she said.

Mr. and Mrs. M seemed content with their possessions and their station in life. Mr. M in particular had the manner of a man who had worked hard and successfully making his way up in a difficult world. The Ms have come from kerosene lamps and wood stoves to color TV and air conditioning. Throughout this journey they have bought with care and hesitation. They have, for example, never bought a home in northern Virginia though they are saving people and they have now lived there for over twenty years. They have bought eight cars in 40 years, an average of one every five years, and they have never bought a new one. They now have a five-year-old Chrysler. Though Mr. M would have preferred a smaller car that consumed less gas and cost less to run, he deferred to Mrs. M, who explained that she insisted on a big car "because I am afraid of those bugs."

The Ms were asked what they would do if they suddenly had a $5,000 windfall. Mr. M said, without hesitation, "I'd put it in savings." Mrs. M said, "If someone gave me all that money I'd buy a stereo for my grandchildren and put the rest in savings." Then she thought some more and said, "I'd also buy a blender and then put the rest in the bank." There are a few things that Mrs. M would like in an ideal world—a humidifier, for example—but there are other things she wouldn't take at any price, like a dishwasher. "What good is a dishwasher?" she said. "You have to rinse the dishes off anyway so you might as well do the whole job." Mrs. M's daughter has a different view. "She insists that she couldn't live without one—she can't understand me."

When asked for their views about the energy crisis, Mr. and Mrs. M said that Congress is "mainly responsible for the fuel oil shortage." They said they would be willing to see a tax added to the cost of gasoline but only if "they used it on pollution, fine—but not if they used it for planning or for taking surveys." They believe that the fuel shortage can be resolved by "everybody being more thrifty and conserving."

EDWARD AND MABLE A—INCOME $3,000 OR LESS—MID-CITY, BALTIMORE, MARYLAND

Edward A was born around 1908. He is black and he lives with his 57-year-old wife and 80-year-old mother-in-law in Baltimore. Among those interviewed he had at least six distinctions: he was the oldest, the poorest, and the only one living mostly on social security. He had no car and he could not read nor write. He was the only one for whom the energy shortage had already arrived in mid 1973. Still he was more like than unlike the other older men and women—he, as much as anyone, had been caught in the updraft of mobility; he owned an automatic washing machine, an electric frost-free refrigerator, a gas stove, and a black and white TV.

Mr. A has lived in his present home for 22 years. The house is of great importance to him: it represents the efforts of a lifetime. Mr. A, like Dixon Avenue where he lives, is a symbol of the past. Dixon is a minor street near the center of the city, just off West Baltimore Street. Dixon follows its own meandering course, not the usual city grid. Once, perhaps, it was a cow path. The nineteenth century row houses, with flat brick fronts and three or four white marble steps ("stoops") in front, are in the Baltimore tradition. Once housewives who lived in such houses were expected to scrub down the steps with sand each morning. The stoops on Dixon street are still scrubbed and many of the houses have small yellow signs in the windows announcing that the people who live there are involved in the "Afro Clean Block" campaign, an annual refurbishing sponsored by local black newspapers.

Dixon Avenue, once all white, is now almost all black. One elderly white woman lives in Mr. A's block. "She don't bother no one and no one don't bother her," Mr. A says. As Mr. A sits on his stoop and talks, a peddler leads a horse and wagon filled with bananas down the hill, shouting as he goes. But there are signs also of modern times—the cars are parked bumper to bumper at the curbs and though many are battered, all are less than ten years old. There are TV aerials on many roofs and one house has a conspicuous electric burglar alarm beside its front door.

Mr. A's house is dim inside in the summer heat, for the shades are drawn and the lights are out. There is a sofa, a black leather chair, a rocker, a mirror on the wall and a marble-topped coffee table with a vase of artificial flowers. Mr. A and his mother-in-law have been watching the Senate Watergate hearings on TV. The lights are out to make the room cooler, to make the TV shine more clearly, and to save money. Mr. A receives a social security check each month and still works occasionally as a waiter for a catering service. He is a very saving man. During the winter he keeps his thermostat at 50° and his oil bill is only $63 a year. He believes the way to solve the energy crisis is for everybody to use less energy.

He was born in a village called Sawmill, not far from Richmond, Virginia. Sawmill, long since engulfed in Richmond suburban developments, consisted, appropriately enough, of a sawmill, a few houses, and a blacksmith shop. Mr. A's father was the blacksmith and the family lived in a three-room house by the forge. They had no electricity, no central heating, no indoor plumbing, and no running water. The house was basic shelter: walls, plank floors, a wood stove. The wood in the stove was scraps from the sawmill. The As were poor and Mr. A never went to school. "I can sign my name," Mr. A says. "Not very good, but I can sign my name."

In addition to his work in the "smithy," Mr. A's father did a little tobacco and corn farming. There were three children, but one, a girl, died as an infant. By the time Mr. A was a teenager, the blacksmith was becoming obsolete. "I never became a blacksmith because even back then the business was sort of fading away." Instead he got a job in the sawmill. Mr. A does not remember what it paid, but it cannot have been much since he quit it to take a job at the R. J. Reynolds Tobacco Company, in Richmond, at 30 cents an hour.

The As, father and son, had a total of three cars between them in their two lifetimes. The father bought the first, a used Tartan, some time in the twenties. He then bought a used Model T. The Model T lasted, in one form or another, for the rest of his life—he drove it until it could be driven no longer and then he converted it to a gasoline-driven power saw.

Mr. A married in his midtwenties. His wife, Mable, who had finished high school, found a job cleaning in the Richmond public schools. The young couple had a three-room house which they rented for $5 a month; it had no electricity, no plumbing, and a wood stove. Since they were both working in Richmond and living in nearby Catersville, they had to have a car. They bought a 1928 Chevrolet in 1933 and kept it for almost a decade.

The Depression years passed in grim routine; a daughter was born and they continued to live in the primitive three-room house until World War II. Mr. A could not read the newspapers but he heard about the war and some of its consequences on the radio. There were regular and—for people who'd reached maturity during the Depression—exciting reports about the booming defense industries. Mr. A heard they were paying big money. He went north to Baltimore, taking his wife and daughter with him but leaving the decrepit Chevrolet behind.

He got a job paying "more than $40 a week" in a plant making poison gas. Mr. A never understood the process; "I never asked no questions. All I know was that I unloaded sacks that were full of beans dyed dark red. That's all I know. It was hard work but it paid good." In Baltimore he didn't need a car. "I could get around pretty good on the bus."

He did want a house of his own, and with that in view he and his wife began saving every extra dollar. Mrs. A got a job in a clothing factory making uniforms, and their two jobs provided an enormous income relative to their past earnings. When the war ended, the jobs ended too, but they had money in the bank and Baltimore was clearly a better place to be than Catersville. "We didn't even think of going back. I didn't have no people down there any more and the work was better up here." Mrs. A returned to her first occupation, cleaning public schools. Mr. A got a job as a carpenter's helper. "I had to join the union and that meant they had to pay right good." In 1951 they made the down payment on the Dixon Avenue house.

In the early 1950s Mr. A, by then in his mid forties, found construction work too hard ("I couldn't stand being in the cold no more") so he changed occupations again, getting a job as a general kitchen helper in a catering firm. The daughter graduated from high school and got a job as a bookkeeper in a laundry. Mrs. A's mother moved in. They paid $50 on the mortgage every month. Their lives settled into a simple routine built around their jobs, their home, and their church. Mr. A stayed with the catering firm for twenty years, until he retired. In his final years he was a waiter, making as much as $120 a week. Mrs. A still cleans schools.

The As paid $168 between May 1972 and May 1973 for electricity and $184 for gas. The $352 total for both—plus $63 for heating oil—represents over 10 percent of their income, a large amount in view of their energy saving habits. Mr. A, as we have noted, has shunned many of the little conveniences of the age. He saves money and energy by keeping his thermostat at $50°$. He has eliminated the auto from his life, taking the bus to church, to visit friends, and to shop. "If there was no bus I'd walk. I walk half the time anyway. I get out and walk and it's a pleasure to me, looking in the windows and things. It's fun to me to walk."

He regards the world, the government, and the energy crisis with a jaundiced eye. He believes that President Nixon is responsible for the fuel shortage—Nixon and the fact that "they're burning it up in the air with them missiles. They burn it a lot faster than an automobile." Mr. A watches the big world from a distance and grapples with his own problems—the cost of food, taxes. He and his wife dry their clothes by hanging them in the back yard and they serve meat only five times a week. They do not go out to restaurants or carry-outs and they have taken no air or long auto trips, ever. They buy only dim light bulbs, 75 watts or less. Of all the modern conveniences, the one they would miss most is a TV. Since neither Mr. A nor his mother-in-law can read or write, it is their only channel to the outside world.

BILL AND SUSAN F—INCOME $100,000
A YEAR PLUS—MIDTOWN MANHATTAN

The Fs live over the store—but not in the manner of a Ma-and-Pa grocery. Bill is a handsome man of 42, tall, trim, and stylishly dressed. Susan F at 35 is a lady of delicate beauty—blonde and young looking below her years. They have four daughters; the oldest three—13, 15, and 17—are the children of Mrs. F's first marriage.

Bill F owns a large art gallery in the fashionable East 70s of Manhattan. It occupies the bottom two floors of a five-story brownstone; the Fs occupy the top three. Only the rich can afford to live in this style today, and the Fs are rich by any standard.

In addition to the brownstone, they own an eighteenth century refurbished stable in Oxford Village, Connecticut. Both homes are centrally air conditioned. They have their own elevator in town and they ride horses in the country. They have a male cook who lives in and a freezer full of steaks. They also have an automatic washing machine, dishwasher, an electric refrigerator, an electric clothes dryer, a gas stove, a sewing machine, and three color TV sets. They have fourteen rooms and six baths in town and as many in Connecticut. They serve meat or fish 21 times a week and they never eat frozen dinners.

Their homes are richly furnished with antiques and Renaissance paintings and have enormous fireplaces. Still, the Fs' consumption has not been as conspicuous as one might assume. Their town car is seven years old and they have recently and reluctantly bought a station wagon for the country. They also resisted buying a color TV until 1971, though once having acquired it they soon acquired two more. They feel somewhat burdened by their possessions.

They would prefer, for example, to own no car at all. The car in town is a Lincoln Continental, which gets nine miles to a gallon and which Mrs. F loathes to drive; but since large works of art must occasionally be transported across Manhattan, it is a convenience. Meanwhile, it lurks outside their house and their lives like a minor blackmailer, hitting them in the pocketbook. When the garage owner recently raised the monthly parking fee from $95 to $124, Mr. F was outraged and he began parking on the streets. This was not an ideal solution, since New York enjoys what is known as alternate street parking, which means it is illegal to park on one side of the street on Monday, Wednesday, and Friday and on the other on Tuesday, Thursday, and Saturday. The cook had to go out and move it at regular intervals. It was a burden and costly in traffic tickets, and one suspected that in time the Fs would succumb to the ease of the exorbitantly priced garage.

Meanwhile, the Fs—mother, father and four daughters—moved around Manhattan in taxis and in the country in a station wagon and on ten-speed bikes. The girls take cabs when they go more than three blocks. Mrs. F takes as many as five cabs a day. The family spends the entire summer in Connecticut, with Mr. F commuting. In the country, Mrs. F runs an antique store, which adds an incidental $10,000 a year to the Fs' very substantial income.

But in the summer of 1973, the Fs were not complacent about their way of life. The devaluation of the dollar, for one thing, had affected their businesses and for people living in midtown Manhattan, the problems of our times—pollution, energy shortages, and urban decay—were close at hand. When asked how in theory he would adjust to an America which suddenly had no air conditioning and no jet planes, Mr. F said without hesitation that he'd move to London.

The Fs have never been poor. Mrs. F was born rich at a time when the overwhelming majority of Americans felt they were on the brink of fiscal disaster. Her ancestors were Tories who moved from New York State to Nova Scotia during the American Revolution. This northeastern background has given her an inherent respect for thrift. She recalls with pleasure the times in her childhood when snows hindered oil deliveries and her father would build wood fires and the family would subsist on their own resources and stored supplies. She describes her father as "well off," but this phrase understates the facts since she estimates her father's annual income at $100,000 a year when she was a child during the early forties.

Susan grew up in the relatively rural atmosphere of Westbury on Long Island's North Shore, and learned to ride a horse, a bike, and a small "Farmall Cub" tractor before she was in her teens. She went to school at an Episcopal girls' school near Westbury and got her first car when she was sixteen. The car was wrecked almost immediately: when she was returning from school one day a pickup truck plowed into her side. At her father's farm there were more horses than cars, but they were thoroughbred racers, not work horses. There was no shortage of cars, either—she remembers a succession of autos before she was twenty: a Chevrolet, an Olds, a Ford, a Buick, a Lincoln. She never acquired a taste for them herself.

Susan went to Mount Holyoke, in Massachusetts, but dropped out to marry a young man in the Air Force. They moved first to Dayton, Ohio, and then to St. Louis, Mo. They had their three daughters and a life style somewhat less expansive than Susan had been accustomed to. She divorced her first husband in the mid sixties and married Bill F shortly thereafter.

Mr. F's early life was somewhat humbler than his wife's but hardly deprived. His father was a lawyer in Chicago, specializing in probates. He estimated that his father made between $30,000 and $40,000 a year in the late thirties and early forties when Bill was growing up. His father never bothered to own a car (although he got Bill a Ford coupé when he was sixteen). Mr. F, like his wife, has never become enamored of cars. He is essentially a big city person and driving a car in Chicago or New York has not been a pleasure since the days of the Stutz Bearcat.

Mr. F graduated from Yale and went to Harvard Business School where he dropped out before finishing. He worked in an insurance company briefly and then bought a seat on the New York Stock Exchange. After some years he left the Exchange and opened the art gallery. The gallery is designed in severely modern, austere style—white walls, indirect light, aluminum doors—but it specializes in eighteenth and nineteenth century paintings. Like most businesses in Manhattan, it is highly dependent on the technological age. By his own estimate, Mr. F has three or four phone conversations a day with London and he travels to England by jet an estimated fourteen times a year. (His wife goes abroad some eight times a year in search of antiques.) The gallery and the living quarters above are centrally air conditioned. Since the gallery has few windows, air conditioning is a necessity, for the clients as well as the paintings.

The elevator is a convenience if not an absolute necessity. Mrs. F suggested that it was not a necessity for the family, which prefers to use the stairs, but that it was for the business since paintings were stored in the attic and it was necessary to have the elevator when hauling them up or down. (Mr. F snorted at the idea that the elevator was a business necessity.)

The Fs can commute by available train to their Oxford home, 42 miles away. Still, independence from the automobile is more theoretical than real—the Fs use taxis in the city and Mr. F commutes to the country by auto rather than train, since he saves 55 minutes that way.

The Fs have strong opinions on the problems of the day. Mr. F believes that air and water pollution are major problems and the fuel crisis is a minor one. He believes that oil and gasoline shortages are the result of the machinations of the national oil companies. He believes, however, that everybody should be more thrifty and conserve electricity. He believes that a family using twice as much electricity as another should be charged "more than twice as much."

Mrs. F's attitudes are less sharply defined. She has a very clear image of the ideal life: it is, in essence, a duplication of the pleasant life she knew as a child, a life of luxurious thrift. The life is rural and it is static, with fixed social strata and fixed virtues. People are self-reliant; one grows much of one's own food. Those who have money should never be profligate. She recounted, with the amused approval of her daughters, various forms of home economies she now practices: they have a vegetable garden in the country; when the family returns to town, Mrs. F customarily empties the country refrigerator and puts all leftovers—potato salad and such—separately into little plastic containers and carries them back to New York. Susan F also has a habit of putting out electric lights in empty rooms.

"I hate waste," Mrs. F said. "I observe the rampant abuse of all our natural resources." She fears that the young do not realize the need for thrift. She has made constant efforts to teach her daughters to be self-reliant. Her own efforts to preserve a simpler way of life are often frustrated by circumstances. She economizes by stocking her deep freeze with meat and extra ice cubes but since steaks are always available they often have steak, though, she said, "not too frequently." ("Oh Mother," one daughter said, laughing, "what are we having tonight—steak, right?") It would seem that she has succeeded to some degree. Becky, the eldest, had a summer job as a mother's helper with a family in Delaware and she planned to tour Europe on her ten-speed bike, sleeping in youth hostels, before going to Yale in the fall. In Manhattan the younger ones, however, take taxis to a private school only a few blocks from home.

Their street is a handsome place with several art galleries a block from Central Park, but the Fs are as isolated as if they lived on a farm, since they know none of their neighbors. Despite her interest in thrift, it is difficult for Mrs. F to cope with the complexity and the finances of life in Manhattan.

Neither she nor her husband had an idea of the magnitude of the yearly fuel bill. Life in Manhattan, particularly among the affluent, makes great demands on time, and the use of time saving devices is inevitable. Mr. F estimates he works six days, 70 hours a week in the art gallery and that Mrs. F works six days, 30 hours a week. The Fs' extensive travel is always "work related."

The Fs are the richest family interviewed and the one most clearly dependent on the energy consuming accoutrements of the late twentieth century—planes, air conditioning, elevators, and autos (taxis as well as their own).

VERNON AND NORA Y—INCOME $30,000 PLUS —SUBURBAN LOS ANGELES

In spite of the exasperating disappointments, the anxieties, and the fatigue, the Ys are a couple whose dreams have come true. They have come a long way together in a relatively short time and they have a lot to show for it: a handsome house in a Los Angeles suburb (worth $75,000 at a minimum); four automobiles ranging from a Karman Ghia to a Cadillac (on which they put 45,000 miles a year); two sons and a daughter; a swimming pool; an automatic washing machine, electric refrigerator, gas stove, electric clothes dryer; automatic dishwasher; a color TV; central air conditioning; and a stereo.

The Ys, Vernon and Nora, are in their early forties and are affluent. They are city people. They own two houses, but their second home is rented out. Nora is involved in business and feels harassed. The Ys were born poor, and despite their achievements they are not in control of their daily routine. The Ys are concerned with the problems of the age and they have firm attitudes toward the energy shortage and pollution. They blame—with equal fervor—big business, the Congress, and the Los Angeles city government.

They have a feeling that something went awry with their carefully nurtured plan. Mr. Y is the director of nonfoods for the main grocery in a large chain. Mrs. Y remains in their suburban neighborhood where until recently she sold real estate. She stopped because "they wanted me to put real estate number one. I said, 'no, my family is number one.'" The two boys, Vernon, Jr. and Joey, go to college, one to UCLA and the other to a local community college. Both plan to be engineers. Their daughter goes to public elementary school.

Their house is in a subdivision of expensive houses. Theirs is the last on a dead-end street. It is a typical California house, one floor and spread out, with a two-car garage, lots of trees and shrubbery, and a large pool out back. The quiet street lined with palms is pleasant even on a hot midsummer day. The street lacks a prevailing sense of neighborliness. A few blocks away, Burbank Boulevard divides the rich from the poor; on one side of the Boulevard are $75,000 houses, on the other, $15,000 cottages. The palms are luxuriant on both sides.

The Ys are native Californians and they arrived in their neighborhood after growing up in San Diego and living in three other California cities as Mr. Y moved upward in the grocery business. Mrs. Y was born in 1934, close to the bottom of the Depression. Her father was a carpenter who did a number of other things as well. "He never did go on welfare," Mrs. Y said, proudly. She remembers that he had a little black Ford with a rumble seat in which he carried his carpenter's tool box. San Diego was then a small, cohesive city. She went to her neighborhood grammar school but when she reached high school she had to take the bus since there were only three high schools in San Diego and none of them near her house. "I took the bus because they'd already ripped out the street cars since they were too convenient," she said wryly. She was able to go to San Diego State College, a public institution where tuition payments were very small. There she met Vernon, who was majoring in journalism.

Vernon Y had been born as poor as Nora but his background had an exotic edge. His father had grown up in Shanghai, where Vernon's grandfather had a laundry business and his great-grandfather was an executive with the Dupont Company. His great-grandmother, a white Russian emigré, was a physician.

Vernon's father's childhood home was overrun with servants and languages; he learned, in lesser or greater degree, to speak Chinese, French, Russian, and English. Vernon's father was stationed in San Francisco and San Diego while serving in the Marine Corps. By the time his enlistment was up the Depression had arrived. He joined the San Diego Police Department where he remained, a patrolman, for 25 years.

In Vernon's own childhood home there was no money to spare. He began his working life as a teenager as a box boy at a grocery, a choice which shaped his future. When "the most fancy market San Diego had ever seen" opened, he got a job there and began moving up, to checker, to stock clerk, to receiving clerk. He kept his job after enrolling at San Diego State. He also bought a secondhand Studebaker and met Nora. They were children of their time; World War II was just over, the Korean War was about to begin, and the Depression was still vivid in their minds. They were determined to live better than their parents had, and they often talked about how they could get ahead.

"I remember one day Vernon took me out to the edge of town to look at some hills out there. He said land there would be a good investment, that it would be developed. He said he'd like to do it and he went down to city hall and they told him that the land was all public land and it couldn't be touched. Later we drove by and it was being developed. They had lied to him."

Vernon knew he'd soon be drafted and he wanted to get married. "Vernon wouldn't marry until we had a place of our own so we pooled our money. I had $1,000 and we bought a garage on a remote acre of land, halfway down a mountain. He quit school and we got married in December. He was drafted in March. We spent his last 30 days fixing the garage up as an apartment, painting it, laying tile, so we could rent it while he was away." He went into the Marines and he did very well. He had a high IQ and he could type so he was soon processing the papers for all the Marines in the West. He never did go to Korea. When he returned from the Marines they sold the garage apartment to the people who'd been renting it and Vernon decided to go back to school and get a business administration degree. Nora had a job as a secretary and he went back to working 40 hours a week in a market while going to school.

The Ys have always planned their life precisely. Nora worked until Vernon, Jr. was born. Vernon got his degree and remained in the grocery business. They moved rapidly ahead in terms of Vernon's job and in their possession of material things.

They had started low. "Vernon had a horrible Studebaker when we married. My father kept it running—my father can fix anything. We kept it until it fell apart and then we got another used car. I was working and we had to have transportation." In 1955 they bought their first new car, a Chevrolet, and a couple of years later they bought a second car, an old wreck that had belonged to Vernon's grandmother; its gearshift did not work in the lower registers and it had to be started each time with a push. Vernon took it to work, leaving the Chevy for Nora. By the time the second child arrived, the grandmother's car had lost all its gears. They traded the Chevy for a used Oldsmobile station wagon.

In 1961 Vernon had an opportunity to be a founding partner in a chain of supermarkets in the San Francisco area. The Ys bought a new Buick and moved to San Jose. Within a year Vernon was disillusioned. "He came home one day, much to my shock and said he was quitting. We had to move at once and we'd just bought a new house." Vernon moved to Sacramento with a new company. They sold the Buick and got an old station wagon. In his new job Vernon had the use of a company car.

The Ys spent what Mrs. Y calls the "happiest years of our lives" in Sacramento. They were not, she concedes, the "best career years for Vernon," but they lived in a big old house and the pace was relaxed. A daughter and another son were born. The son died in infancy. Then the neighborhood began to change; a superhighway was built through it, splitting off the most affluent part. The rest began to decay. Vernon got a new job and the Ys moved to Los Angeles in 1967. "One has to change companies to advance," Mrs. Y says, "but it was the hardest move of my life. We were all happy there." They've kept the house in Sacramento, which they rent out.

By the summer of 1973 the Ys were still pursuing their carefully planned lives but they were feeling the pressure of their upward mobile march. Their four cars are a necessity. Mr. Y leaves home at 4 a.m. each day and drives 35 miles to Los Angeles in his 1970 Buick Riviera. The car, which he bought second hand, gets ten miles to a gallon in the combination of freeway and urban driving. Mr. Y is not satisfied with that but he and Mrs. Y agreed that it is too dangerous to drive a smaller car on the freeway—"It's a gas eater but he needs it," she said. He leaves for work at dawn to avoid the rush on the freeway and to get all his paperwork done before the official office day begins at 8 a.m. He returns home at 7 p.m.

Mr. Y leads a striking example of the life of the modern successful man. He has little time to enjoy his swimming pool, the pleasant appointments of his home, the society of his family, or the soothing quietness of his neighborhood. Each of the Ys has a car, with the exception of the little girl. Mrs. Y's Cadillac is also a gas eater—getting ten miles to a gallon locally and thirteen long distance—but she felt she needed a new and expensive car for business reasons. "I was selling real estate and there's an aura about the real estate business. You need an impressive car."

Joey goes to UCLA and he needs a car to get there. Mr. Y bought a 1969 Impala for Joey. It gets twelve miles in the city and fifteen long distance. Vernon, Jr. goes to a junior college only a few miles from home, but there is no convenient way to get to school except by auto. There are no buses and one cannot bike or walk on a freeway. Vernon's 1969 Karman Ghia, bought in 1972, gets 22 miles on short hauls and 26 long distance. The boys are pursuing careers that reflect the Y's belief in detached planning. The Ys have concluded that a new engineering boom will supplant the recent slump, so by the time the boys get their masters degrees their skills will be in demand. They have noted that most engineering courses are now underenrolled.

The Ys are people who take life seriously and try hard. Energy and pollution problems are more obvious in the environs of Los Angeles than in most places, and the Ys are directly affected. They have discussed the problems with friends and among themselves and have touched on many different aspects—"conservation of natural resources, of air, of water, of trees; of the potential and threat of nuclear power; of alternate forms of heating; of recycling cans; of plastic milk containers." They believe that the unfortunate circumstances in which they find themselves are the result of the negligence or malice of the powerful. "Why can't the Detroit manufacturers meet the pollution standards? Why doesn't the government push research in solar heating? Why didn't Los Angeles start building a subway ten or twenty years ago?"

The Ys are examples of conspicuous success, yet they do not feel they are in control of anything. They feel manipulated by powerful, remote forces and they are bitter.

PAUL AND NANCY T—INCOME $15,000
—RURAL KANSAS

Paul T, 38, lives on his great-grandfather's homestead farm in Kansas, on Route 2, two miles north of Gordon, which is twelve miles from Mound City, which is 35 miles from Yoder. Gordon has a gas station. Mound City has two churches, a baseball field, a bar, and a Dairy Queen. Yoder is a sizable town, with a court house, a café, a supermarket, two motels, a bowling alley, a big public swimming pool, and a handsome tree-lined street where the gentry live. The movie house is open on weekends.

Nancy T is 35, and the kids are Tom, 12, Mike, 9, Peter, 8, and Jan, 4. Paul's parents and his grandfather live in a second farmhouse 25 yards away, so there are four generations living on the 520 acres. They raise cattle, hogs, row crops, and feed. They have two horses and a huge kitchen garden.

The young T family's house is frame and ramshackle, with four small rooms downstairs and four small bedrooms upstairs. The steps to the door are cinder blocks, the porch screen sags, and floors are plain unvarnished wood. In the kitchen there is a pink pushbutton wall phone next to the propane stove. In summer a flat, hassock-type electric fan cools the kitchen, which is the main family room.

Mr. T was the only person interviewed who was living in the very same place he was born. Moreover, his daily tasks and recreations are much the same as those of his father and his grandfather and his great-grandfather. The phone, the fan, the stove, the electric lights, and the black and white TV are new, but the Ts raise their own vegetables and slaughter their own meat. Paul T has a tractor and a 1964 Chevrolet station wagon in addition to his horses. In his opinion the technological changes which have occurred in his life are enormous, particularly those since World War II.

Paul was born on the farm but he spent his early childhood living with an uncle in Centreville, twenty miles away. When his grandfather retired they moved Paul and the Centreville house to the farm. Paul rode a horse to grammar school. The family got its first car, a 1935 Chevrolet, in the forties. Paul bought his own first car, a 1947 Plymouth, in 1951. He was then 16 and had never been out of Linn County. He dropped out of high school to work on the farm full time and he began exploring the towns and the people down the road. He met his future wife in nearby Anderson County.

Nancy's grandparents had been homesteaders. Her father was a part time farmer and an oil well driller. Nancy and Paul went to church socials together, and when Paul was 25 and she was 21 they married. By that time Paul was driving an old Pontiac. With marriage, the children came more often than the cars. In 1959 he replaced the Pontiac with a secondhand Chevy and in 1967 he turned in the Chevy for the 1964 station wagon he still has.

Time moves slowly on the farm. Mrs. T still works much as a farm wife did in 1900. She sows the big garden, weeds it, and harvests it. She puts up the surplus vegetables and gives some away to friends and relatives. Paul is preoccupied with his hogs and cattle. He feeds them and watches over their births, slaughters some and takes others to market.

The farm equipment has evolved as slowly as the rest. His father got a Farmall tractor with iron wheels in the forties. When electricity came to Linn

County in 1947 they put light in the barns as well as light in the house. The hand-cranked phone remained until 1968. The life style of the Ts surprises the outsider from the city. In prospect, at least, Mr. T is a wealthy man—the 520 acres are worth around $104,000. But a hand-run farm is not a particularly profitable investment. It is difficult for the Ts to put an accurate figure on the farm's net cash income, but they guess about $15,000. Whatever it is, it supports five adults and four children, and it allows for a few luxuries. Mrs. T has an electric refrigerator and a sewing machine. They have a big freezer full of meat. If wealth is measured by the control of energy, then the Ts are comparable to the As in Baltimore. Both have the same basic appliances and a house. The Ts eat better but Mr. A has more and better furniture. Mr. A has no car; the Ts have the old station wagon and a couple of horses, but Mr. A can use the bus.

The Ts are well off by the standards of Linn County but those standards are still the standards of another time. They live in a time pocket. Most families grow smaller, move a number of times in a lifetime, acquire time savers and labor savers, two or three cars, and bad air. But the Ts have never budged. The air is clean and little labor is saved on the farm or in the kitchen.

PETER AND SHELLY B—INCOME $8,000
—MID-CITY WASHINGTON, D.C.

Peter B is 25 and Shelly, his wife, is 24. Peter is a student at Georgetown University's School of Law, where for three years he has been rated "distinguished" in all but one course. He plans to practice criminal law. He has chosen summer jobs that have paid less but taught more: in the summer of 1973 he was an aide at the Criminal Justice Center. He has a pleasant wit, an amiable manner, and high ideals protected by an air of smiling cynicism. The cynicism is focused on the performance of the system rather than the failings of people. Although Peter is only five feet nine, he went through college on football scholarships.

Shelly is a pretty girl with a gentle, sentimental nature. She works with retarded children and finds the work rewarding in her association with the children and irritating in her association with the bureaucracy.

The Bs have strong feelings about the energy crisis and about pollution, and they try to conserve energy. Shelly does not turn the air conditioner on until Peter comes home.

The Bs have an uncertain income status that varies from relatively poor, when they are living on Shelly's salary alone, to relatively well off, when Peter is working in the summer. They will presumably become permanently comfortable when Peter graduates from law school, although his penchant for the less well paid fields of law may keep them from growing rich in a hurry. During their school years, Shelly and Peter have been subsidized to a great extent by Shelly's parents.

The Bs live in a pleasant basement apartment in a Capitol Hill townhouse, a few blocks from the Capitol building and a brisk walk from the law school. The apartment, with two large rooms, a kitchenette and a patio, is nicely furnished, largely with wedding gifts. Shelly's family gave them the living room furniture and the window air conditioner. They have an electric refrigerator, a gas range, a washing machine (which came with the apartment), a mixer, electric skillet, electric can opener, toaster, and iron. They have a stereo and a nine-year-old car. The car is also a gift from Shelly's folks.

To a limited degree at least, the Bs seem to have consciously rejected the values—or at least the symbols—of their parents' generation of Americans. They have no desire to own a home, a new and better car, or a variety of other symbolic possessions. Shelly is also notably disinclined to have children—she believes that today's problems can best be approached by "slowing down the population growth."

Shelly believes that what she regards as their indifference to material things is not particularly typical of her age group. She remarked that the people with whom she works, who have similar incomes, live less well in terms of food and entertainment, since they are more concerned with acquiring permanent possessions. Shelly's sister and brother-in-law (a Secret Service agent) have a home in nearby Maryland and have acquired a second house on Capitol Hill as an investment. Shelly regards her own life style and the contrasting life styles of others with a somewhat romantic eye.

Neither Peter nor Shelly was born into a household that was conspicuously well off. Peter's father has been slow to improve his lot. Shelly's father, on the other hand, moved up the ladder with what seems effortless ease. He was a bright Depression boy with a flair for mathematics. He advanced to a state normal school in Pennsylvania before he and the school authorities agreed that he did not have the temperament required to be a successful teacher (he was inclined to challenge authority). He went to work as a clerk at the Arcadia Insurance Company. Shelly's parents married young and had children rapidly. Shelly, the youngest of four, was born in 1949 in Washington, Pa., a working class town. Her father moonlighted by pumping gas at a service station after finishing a day's work at the insurance company.

Shelly does not remember a time when her family was not doing well and moving up: "I can't remember a time when we didn't spend the summer at the shore." They went from Washington to Oak Leaf Heights, to Glen Echo, and finally to Bethany, each neighborhood clearly better than the one before. Her father eventually became a partner in an actuarial firm. When the firm's owner died, he and four other actuaries bought the firm. Now one of the largest in the world, the firm handles (as Shelly noted with pride) 50 of the hundred biggest pension plans in the country.

Shelly's family somehow avoided acquiring some of the more obvious status symbols on the way up. "My mother still complains that we were the only ones on the block who had a wooden ice box and we always had crummy cars. The first nice car we got was the Chevrolet Impala in 1964." Shelly and Peter now drive the Impala. Shelly estimates that her parents' income is now in the neighborhood of $100,000 a year before taxes. Her father, despite his professional skills, pays half his income to government since he will not, as a matter of principle, seek out tax shelters. They live in a large and pleasant house but one less expensive than they could afford. Shelly's family does have a heated swimming pool and has spent great amounts over the years on travel, top quality foods, and other sources of life satisfaction. The parents take the children and their spouses to good restaurants, on excursions to the race tracks, and on vacation trips.

Peter's father stands in unfortunate contrast. Peter was born in a small town in South Dakota in 1949 and his father, like Shelly's, was selling gas. He had a station franchise. While remaining in rural South Dakota over the years, he moved from the station to a securities firm and then moved on to selling a wide variety of products, including slot machines. He dressed well and drove a new Buick or Hudson, since he felt a good car was "necessary in his profession" but he did not achieve any high level of success.

After leaving the securities firm he and the family moved to an 80-acre farm outside a very small town and Peter's mother took a job. Over the years the family has always had a second car, ten or fifteen years old, which she has driven to and from work. Peter and his two brothers always ate well since milk and eggs were cheap and the mother bought a side of beef at a time and kept the cuts in the freezer; but as Peter said, "we never had any money and never went on vacations." Peter went to State University on a football scholarship, but finding the athletic emphasis too strong there he transferred to Villanova in Pennsylvania (also on a scholarship), where he met Shelly.

Peter speaks of his father with a protective caution—he is painfully aware of his lack of achievements but he would like to think that he may yet succeed. "He's really getting into something good," Peter said. "At least it looks good."

Peter and Shelly are children of their time. Though born to clearly different families, in contrasting environments, they have nevertheless arrived at something of a common life view, believing the quest for possessions to be a feckless pursuit.

COMMENTARY

Despite differences in incomes and life styles, the six families interviewed had much in common. With the possible exception of Mrs. F in Manhattan, each couple interviewed was better off materially than their parents had been. In the twentieth century almost all Americans have been upwardly mobile and the possession of certain basic labor savers—electric irons, refrigerators, mixers, sewing machines, toasters, hair dryers and such—has become commonplace. Since this rise in affluence has been largely the result of cheap energy, the automobile has been the logical symbol of the age. Only one person interviewed did not own a car, and he had owned cars in the past. All were able to recall easily and in specific detail every car they'd ever owned. However, pride in car ownership is no longer unalloyed. The poorest family—Mr. and Mrs. A in Baltimore—were content to move around by taking buses and walking. The richest—the Fs in Manhattan—owned two autos but much preferred taking taxis for short trips and airplanes for longer ones. The Ys in Los Angeles were clearly the most car possessed: they owned four and they made it clear that they did so because they had no practical alternative—there was no available public transportation for the daily, long, necessary trips to work, to school, and to shopping areas.

The decades of cheap available energy have had secondary effects as important as the primary ones. Cars brought good roads and good roads allowed new concentrations of population and industry. Concentrations of power made the concentration and standardization of jobs practical, and almost everyone became mobile: people have moved across the country as easily as people once moved across town. Of the six families described only one, the Ts in Kansas, were living in the city or county in which they'd been born and only one other, the Los Angeles Ys, were living in the same state. The others had moved several times (some had moved thousands of miles) and almost all had moved for economic reasons.

The energy revolution of the twentieth century seems to have made Americans look and sound and think more nearly alike. We have become so similar in so many respects that we might tend to see ourselves as more nearly homogeneous than we are. The members of the six families we have studied make it very clear that we are individuals still.

Chapter Three

Energy in the Home

Save on heating fuel. Keep your home temperature lower than last winter. Don't leave the windows open. Pleas such as this from the government, business, or conservation groups can have an impact on energy use. The basic level of household energy use for heating, however, is determined by the climate and by the structure of the dwelling itself. Once location is decided, climate is virtually outside the household's control. The fabrication of the dwelling is usually outside the family's control as well, for most people live in homes built long before they moved in.[a] Even families buying a new house have little say about design. Their new home is more likely one of a dozen or more mass produced for sale by a developer rather than one they had built for themselves.[2]

Consumers have more discretion in appliance use, but even here they are limited by what is already in the home and by what additional or replacement appliances they can afford. Important also is the lack of information about appliance energy use.

This chapter is concerned with the role of consumer choice in home energy use. The following chapter deals with energy used outside the home in travel and the options people have in that sphere. Home energy use accounts for over half of all personal energy consumption. The remainder (46 percent) is consumed in travel.

Within the home, space heating is the most important energy user. Space heating accounts for almost a third of all personal energy use. Water heating is a distant second, using about one-tenth of all personal energy. Cooking and refrigerating each use about 3 percent. Other appliances and lighting account for the remaining 9 percent (see Table 3-1).

[a]Over half of all dwelling units (54 percent) were built 30 years before the 1970 U.S. Census was taken, and another fifth were built from 10 to 20 years before 1970.[1]

Table 3-1. Percentage Distribution of Personal Energy, by
Use, 1968

Use	Percent
All personal energy	100
Energy in the home	56
Space heating	32
Water heating	8
Appliances and other	15
Cooking	3
Refrigerating	3
All other	9
Transportation[a]	44

[a]Based on 1970 data. Personal transportation includes travel by air, rail and taxi in addition to travel in cars. Therefore the percentage of energy use in transportation reported here is greater than in the Washington Center for Metropolitan Studies data which cover only travel in households' cars.

Source: Prepared by the Washington Center for Metropolitan Studies from the following: Transportation: Eric Hirst, *Energy Intensiveness of Passenger and Freight Transportation Modes, 1950-1970*, Oak Ridge, Tenn.: Oak Ridge National Laboratory, April 1973, Table 10, p. 24. Other: Stanford Research Institute, *Patterns of Energy Consumption in the United States*, Washington, D.C.: U.S. Government Printing Office, 1972, Table 13, p. 36.

HOME HEATING

Energy use in home heating is influenced by the design of the dwelling, the climate, and the ways people use their homes.

Structure of the Home

A whole array of housing characteristics affect energy use, although some features are more important than others.[3] An important principle of energy conservation is that the more a dwelling is protected from the weather, the less energy it needs for heating. Thus—all other factors being equal—an apartment uses less energy than a row house (town house) of the same size, a row house less than a semidetached house, and a semidetached house less than a free standing single family home.

Insulation also serves to keep heat in and cold out. For example, an 1,800-square-foot house, located in the New York area and insulated according to current Federal Housing Administration (FHA) standards, could use as much as one-quarter less energy than it would have used if it were insulated according to FHA's earlier standards.[4]

A dwelling's foundation protects it from the chill that rises from the ground. A basement protects a dwelling most, a concrete slab less, and crawl space least—although with the addition of insulation, the protection afforded by a crawl space or slab is greatly improved.

An attic or crawl area above a dwelling helps prevent heat from escaping. An attached garage may afford some protection on one side of a house but, of course, is a heavy energy user in those uncommon instances when heated.

The larger the home, the more energy it uses, all other things being equal. The organization of space within the home can also make a difference. For example, a two-story house of 1,500 square feet has about 20 to 25 percent less exposed surface than a one-story house with the same floor area. Because it has less exposed surface, the two-story house also would use 20 to 25 percent less energy for heating.[5]

The type of heating system makes a difference. All other things being equal, an electrically heated home requires about twice as much fuel per unit of heat as a gas or oil heated home.[6] The presence of at least one thermostat or radiator valve is important in order to permit the family to control room temperature. More than one thermostat or valve is helpful, especially in large homes, permitting room temperatures to vary according to use.

The openings in a building, such as doors and windows, are places for heat to escape in the winter or to enter in the summer. The type of window also makes a difference. The most common type of window—double hung—is the most energy conserving. Casement and sliding windows are less energy conserving since they have more crevices and leaking areas for hot or cold air to move in or out. Wood frames provide better protection than metal; double glazed (thermopane) glass more protection than conventional (single glazed) glass. The larger the window, the more heat is likely to be lost. Storm windows, storm doors, and weatherstripping can reduce heat loss. (The relation of energy to dollar savings from storm windows is discussed later.)

Most of these structural characteristics that affect energy use are determined at the time of construction and may be impossible or at least difficult and expensive to change. This is true of square feet of floor space; size, shape, and number of windows and doors; degree of insulation; and type of roof and foundation. It is particularly true if the household lives in rented quarters, especially in an apartment.

The Average American Home

The average American home is a single-family house with five rooms plus bath. It has a furnace that burns natural gas and a thermostat or valve to control house temperature. It has insulation, an attic, and a basement. It has two entrances and a storm door. It has between 10 to 14 windows, some having storm window protection. In sum, it is a modest dwelling armed with some important energy conserving features (see Tables 3-2 to 3-7). The question of which households can afford more extravagant homes and which households have to make do with much less is considered in Chapter Five.

Table 3-2.   Type of Structure and Heating Fuel, by Heating
Degree Days, 1973 (number and percent of households)

Characteristics	All households	Heating degree days[a]		
		< 3500	3500– 5499	5500+
		Number		
All households (millions)	68.6	21.7	24.5	22.4
		Percent		
All households	100	100	100	100
All one-family homes	79	85	77	74
Mobile homes	4	3	4	4
Other one-family	75	82	73	70
Detached	68	78	64	62
Attached	7	4	8	7
All apartments	20	14	21	26
8 families or less	12	12	12	13
9 or more families	8	3	9	12
Unknown	1	1	2	b
Space heating fuel				
Natural/bottled gas	66	70	56	72
Oil	23	11	34	22
Electricity	9	15	7	4
Other	3	4	3	3
Thermostat or valve				
None	18	30	13	13
Some	81	70	86	87
1	65	55	66	72
2 or more	11	13	12	9
Unknown number	4	1	6	6

[a]The more heating degree days in a locality, the colder it is in the winter. See Appendix for further details.
[b]Less than 0.5 percent.
Source: Washington Center for Metropolitan Studies' Lifestyles and Energy Surveys.

Energy saving features are more important in colder parts of the country. Heating degree days[b] are an indicator of climate and more precise in that regard than the four census regions (Northeast, North Central, South, and West). The more heating degree days in a locality, the colder the winter. For example, Grand Forks, North Dakota has almost 10,000 heating degree days in an average winter while New Orleans, Louisiana has about 1,500. Figure 3-1 shows heating degree days for selected cities in the United States.

[b]Heating degree days are the number of degrees the average daily temperature is below 65 degrees summed over a year. The median number of heating degree days for American households is about 4,500. For a detailed explanation of heating degree days, see the appendix A2.

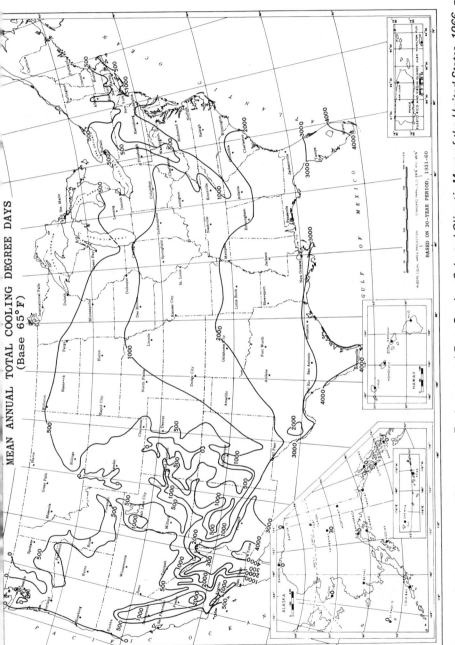

MEAN ANNUAL TOTAL COOLING DEGREE DAYS
(Base 65° F)

Source: U.S. Department of Commerce, Environmental Data Service, *Selected Climatic Maps of the United States, 1966,* p. 8.

Table 3-3.   Size of Home, by Heating Degree Days, 1973 (percent of households)

		Heating degree days		
Size	*All households*	*< 3500*	*3500–5499*	*5500+*
All households	100	100	100	100
Number of rooms				
1–3	11	12	10	11
4	18	16	22	16
5	24	28	19	24
6	22	23	23	20
7 or more	26	21	26	30
Square feet of floor space				
With estimate	60	64	57	58
Less than 1000	22	18	25	22
1000–1499	20	25	18	16
1500 and over	18	21	14	19
Without estimate	40	36	43	42
Size of living room				
With estimate	98	100	98	97
Less than 149	20	18	23	18
150–199	26	28	23	29
200–299	29	28	29	29
300 and over	23	26	24	20
Without estimate	2	a	2	3

[a]Less than 0.5 percent.

Source: Washington Center for Metropolitan Studies' Lifestyles and Energy Surveys.

Table 3-4.   Presence of Insulation, by Heating Degree Days, 1973 (percent of households)

		Heating degree days		
Presence of insulation	*All households*	*< 3500*	*3500–5499*	*5500+*
All households	100	100	100	100
With insulation	62	57	61	68
No insulation	22	25	25	15
Don't know	16	18	14	17
All single-family homes[a]				
With insulation	72	62	72	81
No insulation	19	26	21	10
Don't know	9	12	6	9

[a]Including mobile homes.

Source: Washington Center for Metropolitan Studies' Lifestyles and Energy Surveys.

Table 3-5. Foundations, Attics, and Garages, by Heating Degree
Days, 1973 (percent of homes)

Foundation type, attic, and garage	All households	Heating degree days		
		< 3500	3500– 5499	5500+
All single-family homes[a]	100	100	100	100
Foundation type				
Basement only	44	10	57	69
Crawl space only	31	53	27	12
Basement/crawl space	6	2	8	9
None of the above	19	35	9	11
Attic or crawl area above	65	69	62	65
Attached garage	36	36	31	41
Heated	3	1	5	4
Unheated	33	35	27	37

[a]Excluding mobile homes.
Source: Washington Center for Metropolitan Studies' Lifestyles and Energy Surveys.

Some energy related features, such as attics and double hung windows, are fairly common in all parts of the country. Other energy related features such as storm windows and doors, insulation, and basements are more common in colder areas (Tables 3-2 to 3-7).

Trend Toward More Energy Intensive Housing

Analysis of data from the U.S. Bureau of Census shows a distinct trend in the design of American dwellings leading toward more energy using characteristics. For instance, the single family home—the most energy using type of structure—has become more common, rising from two-thirds of all American households in 1940 to three-quarters by 1973 (Table 3-8).

Government reports on the characteristics of new single family homes indicate the energy related features of newly built housing. Between 1966-67 and 1971, the trend was toward an increasing number and proportion of energy using features: electric heating, central air conditioning, and slab foundations all became more common.[7]

The trends show sharp increases. They reflect a direction in residential building that means increasing energy consumption per home in the future. These features are built into the structures and thus are not likely to be changed soon, if ever. For instance, installation of electric heating in new one-family houses doubled during this period. This rapid growth meant that by 1971 electrically heated homes were almost one-third of all private one-family housing starts compared with one-fifth in 1967. Increases were greatest in the Northeast and South regions (see Table 3-9).

Table 3-6.   Characteristics of Doors and Windows, by Heating Degree Days, 1973 (percent of households)

Door and window characteristics	All households	Heating degree days		
		< 3500	3500–5499	5500+
All households	100	100	100	100
Number of doors opening to outside or unheated area				
0–1[a]	13	6	16	17
2	44	51	39	43
3 or more	42	42	45	40
Number of windows				
0–4	6	5	6	6
5–9	29	31	29	26
10–14	33	38	30	33
15–19	18	14	19	21
20 or more	14	10	16	14
Type of windows				
Double hung	69	64	76	65
Casement	11	11	7	16
Sliding	19	21	16	20
Other combinations	3	5	2	3
Number of extra large windows				
None	49	53	52	42
Some	50	46	48	57
1	26	25	22	30
2 or more	22	19	23	23
Number unknown	3	2	2	5

[a]An apartment with its only entrance through a heated hallway has no doors opening onto the outside.

Source: Washington Center for Metropolitan Studies' Lifestyles and Energy Surveys.

Gas heating in new one-family houses—still the most popular way of heating—rose also, but by less than the 33 percent increase in new one-family housing. (In some areas natural-gas companies, because of supply problems, will not take new customers.) The number of new single family houses with oil heat decreased.

Construction of one-family houses without basements and on slab foundations rose substantially in all regions. Slab construction predominates in the South and West where the increases were greatest. Even in the Northeast and North Central regions, however, where heating is more important and a basement could be of greatest help in conserving energy, the rate of slab construction in new homes increased at more than twice the general rise in new one-family homes. By 1971 new single family homes with slab foundations accounted for almost four out of ten new one-family housing starts, compared

Table 3-7. Protection on Doors and Windows, by Heating Degree Days, 1973 (percent of households)

Door and window protection	All households	Heating degree days		
		< 3500	3500–5499	5500+
All households	100	100	100	100
Door protection needed[a]	95	99	95	91
With protection	68	52	72	78
Storm doors	51	18	62	70
Weatherstripping only	17	34	10	8
No protection	23	41	20	9
Don't know	4	6	3	4
Protection not needed[a]	4	b	5	8
Presence of storm windows or insulating glass				
On all windows	34	8	40	52
On some	16	4	21	23
On none	50	88	40	24
With weatherstripping	12	22	10	5
No weatherstripping	32	54	27	15
Don't know	6	11	3	4

[a]If the door leads to hallway or lobby as in an apartment building, no protection is needed.
[b]Less than 0.5 percent.
Source: Washington Center for Metropolitan Studies' Lifestyles and Energy Surveys.

Table 3-8. Trends Toward Single Family Homes and Fewer Persons per Household, Selected Years, 1940-1973

Year	Percent of households in				Persons per household
	All homes	Single family	Apartment	Mobile homes	
1940	100	67	33	a	3.8
1950	100	66	33	1	3.4
1960	100	75	24	1	3.3
1970	100	69	28	3	3.1
1973	100	75	20	4	3.0

[a]Less than 0.5 percent.
[b]All year-round units.
Source: Derived by the Washington Center for Metropolitan Studies as follows:
Housing: U.S. Bureau of the Census, *Censuses of Housing 1970, 1960, 1950, and 1940.*
1970: *General Housing Characteristics*, Final Report HC(1)-A1, U.S. Summary, Table 3, p. 16.
1960: Vol. 1, *States and Small Areas*, U.S. Summary, Final Report, HC(1)-1, Table 5, p. 16.
1950: Vol. 1, *General Characteristics*, Chapter 1, U.S. Summary, Table 5, p. 3.
1940: Vol. 2, Part 1, *General Characteristics*, U.S. Summary, pp. 9–10.
Persons per household: U.S. Bureau of Census, *Statistical Abstract of the United States, 1973*, Table 2, 49, and 1167, pp. 5, 39 and 689. 1973 data: Washington Center for Metropolitan Studies' Lifestyles and Energy Surveys.

Table 3-9.   Change in Key Energy Using Characteristics of New
One-Family Houses Started, by Region, 1966-1971

Energy-using characteristic	U.S.	North-east	North Central	South	West
			Percent change		
All new 1-family houses[a]	33	7	15	40	65
Heating fuel used[b]	31	15	16	37	46
Electricity	99	114	73	113	64
Gas	19	-16	13	16	48
Oil	-6	35	c	-39	-50
Central air conditioning installed	93	44	77	94	119
Foundation					
Basement	4	-4	5	15	7
Slab	81	40	53	66	127
Crawl space	15	13	40	14	4
			Median square feet		
Floor space					
1966	1,460	1,520	1,480	1,385	1,570
1971	1,400	1,430	1,430	1,345	1,495

[a]Includes homes sold and contractor-built, owner-built, and rental homes started.
[b]Percent change for 1967-71.
[c]Less than 0.5 percent.
Source: Prepared by Washington Center for Metropolitan Studies, from U.S. Bureau of the Census, Construction Reports—Series C-25, Characteristics of New One-Family Homes, 1971, Tables 6, 10, 16 and 17, pp. 35, 52-57, and 91-104.

with less than three out of ten in 1966. Slab construction holds down building costs because it is cheaper than digging a basement.

Central air conditioning systems in new homes almost doubled. In the South and West, where central air conditioning is already most prevalent, the 1966-71 increases were greatest. But even in the Northeast and North Central regions, central air conditioning in new one-family homes grew twice as fast as single family housing starts. By 1971 central air conditioning was a planned feature in two-fifths of all new houses.

Homes Built for Sale Most Energy Intensive

In 1971 about two-thirds of all new single family houses were built on speculation for sale, usually in groups on large tracts of land. The trend toward more energy using characteristics is highest among these homes. Most are located in metropolitan areas where housing and energy demand are greatest, and energy loads at peak periods are likely to be a problem. For example, installation of electric heating more than doubled in houses to be placed on the market between 1967 and 1971, compared with a much smaller increase

Table 3-10. Change in Key Energy Using Characteristics of New One-Family Houses Started, by Type of Builder or Owner, 1966–1971 (percent)

Energy-using characteristic	All new 1-family homes	Built for sale[a]	Built for owner by contractor[b]	Built for owner by owner[c]
All new 1-family homes[d]	33	42	28	3
Heating fuel used[e]	31	37	37	-3
Electricity	99	149	76	26
Gas	19	20	27	-12
Oil	-6	-9	4	-11
Central air conditioning installed	93	108	63	63
Foundation				
Basement	4	2	4	3
Slab	81	102	65	-3
Crawl space	15	20	20	-5
Sq. ft. of floor space				
Median	-4	-7	-5	9

[a]Built by residential builders on their land and advertised for sale to prospective buyers.
[b]Built on the owner's land, to owner's specifications by a general contractor.
[c]Built on the owner's land, to owner's specifications, by the owner acting as his own general contractor but often subcontracting work to special trades contractors, such as electrical, plumbing, plastering, tiling, roofing.
[d]Includes homes sold and contractor-built, owner-built, and rental homes started.
[e]Percent change for 1967–71.
Source: Prepared by the Washington Center for Metropolitan Studies from U.S. Bureau of the Census, Construction Reports–Series C–25, *Characteristics of New One-Family Homes, 1971.* U.S. Dept. of Commerce, Washington, D.C., 1972, Table 6, 10, 16 and 17, pp. 35, 52, 91 and 98.

among houses built on the owner's initiative and to the owner's specifications (Table 3-10).

Trends in New Housing, 1971–1973

The trend toward more energy intensive characteristics in new houses continued into 1973. Between 1971 and 1973 new houses sold decreased by 5 percent. However, houses with central air conditioning increased by 19 percent; houses heated with electricity by 34 percent. (Natural gas hookups continued to be restricted in some areas.) The size of houses increased also. The only trend toward a more energy saving feature between 1971 and 1973 was in foundations. The proportion of new houses sold that had full or partial basements rose 7 percent[c] (Table 3-11).

[c]The housing construction data for 1966–71 are based on all new 1-family housing. The data for 1971 to 1973 are for new 1-family homes sold. Thus the two series are not directly comparable. However, 1-family homes built for sale were 64 percent of all new homes started for 1971–73.[8]

Table 3-11.   Percent Change in Key Energy Using Characteristics of New One-Family Houses Sold, 1971-1973

Selected characteristics	Change
All new one-family houses sold	−5
Heating fuel used	
Electricity	34
Natural gas	−24
Fuel oil	55
Other	−50
Central air conditioning installed	19
Foundation	
Full or partial basement	7
Slab	−7
Crawl space	−17
Square feet of floor space	
Average	5
Median	9

Source: U.S. Department of Commerce and U.S. Department of Housing and Urban Development. "Sales of New One-Family Homes Total 620,000 in 1973." Press Release dated June 10, 1974, and U.S. Bureau of Census, Construction Reports–Series C–25 *Characteristics of New One-Family Homes, 1971.*

While the June 1971 FHA standards increased the amount of insulation needed for new FHA insured houses, a declining portion of new houses must meet those standards. The proportion of the new housing market that had to meet FHA requirements dwindled to 17 percent by 1972.[9]

Even though the stock of housing changes slowly,[d] new housing is important because it will remain and influence household energy use for years to come.

Energy Saving Home Improvements

Home improvements are possible, but they can be expensive. From an energy conservation point of view, two important modifications are the addition of storm windows and insulation.

Storm Windows. Storm windows save substantial amounts of energy, but many families cannot afford them. A special analysis of dollar savings in natural gas fuel costs after installing a new storm sash on a common size of double hung windows shows that only in very cold climates such as Boston, will a storm window pay for itself in fuel cost savings in less than 10

[d]The 620,000 new one-family homes sold in 1973 represented only 1 percent of all the single family homes in the United States.

years.[e] The analysis was made for five cities—Atlanta, Boston, Chicago, Dallas, and New York (see Table 3-12). These savings are somewhat optimistic because they assume savings from both central air conditioning and central heating.[f] Most homes are not centrally air conditioned, and where they are not, it takes about an additional year for a storm window to pay for itself. The economics of storm windows could change dramatically if gas prices increase much faster than storm window prices, and already storm windows are an attractive investment for the 30 percent of homes using higher priced fuel oil or electric heat.

The period it takes to recoup the storm window cost in fuel savings is a particular problem because Americans change homes so often. About one-fifth of Americans move every year.[10] By 1970 only 54 percent of all household heads were living in the same homes as in 1965.[11]

Although the individual family may not save money by installing storm windows, the energy savings possible are high and could be very important to the country. The savings per window range from 1.7 million Btu's in Atlanta and Dallas to 2.7 million Btu's in Chicago, on the assumption that an average size dwelling unit is both heated and centrally air conditioned with natural gas. Consequently, a home with the average number of windows (12) would conserve over 20 million Btu's of natural gas in a year. This is the equivalent of 13 percent of the natural gas used by the average family who uses natural gas for heating (Table 3-13).

Insulation. Ceiling insulation can be added to the attic roof of an existing home. A program to take advantage of this has recently been approved by the Michigan Public Service Commission for two large Michigan natural gas companies. The companies are willing to install the insulation for a 20 percent down payment with the balance paid through the customer's fuel bill. If the customer pays all the insulation costs with the next three monthly gas bills, there is no interest or carrying charge. Payment over a more extended period carries a 1 percent per month (12 percent per year) interest charge. Initial calculations show that the average household in Michigan recoups the amount of the loan over only one year with lower gas bills. These calculations vary,

[e]A standard size window of 15 square feet was used for estimating purposes. Btu savings per square foot of insulated and uninsulated glass, and further savings from reducing seepage of cold and hot air, are based on methods suggested by the Center of Building Technology at the Institute of Applied Technology of the National Bureau of Standards and the American Society of Heating, Refrigerating and Air Conditioning Engineers. Storm sash prices are for moderately priced aluminum sash quoted by regional retail Sears, Roebuck and Company stores. Prices for steel storm sash are higher than for aluminum and were not considered. December 1973 natural gas prices for each city are from the Bureau of Labor Statistics. The initial price of the storm window and the cost of fuel were compounded annually at 5.5 percent.

[f]Only 15 percent of American households had central air conditioning in 1973; another 32 percent had window air conditioning.

Table 3-12.   Annual Cost vs. Savings for Installing One Storm Window, Five Selected Cities, December 1973[a]

	Atlanta			Boston			Chicago			Dallas			New York		
		Natural gas cost savings			Natural gas cost savings			Natural gas cost savings			Natural gas cost savings			Natural gas cost savings	
Years	Storm window cost	Heating & air conditioning	Heating only	Storm window cost	Heating & air conditioning	Heating only	Storm window cost	Heating & air conditioning	Heating only	Storm window cost	Heating & air conditioning	Heating only	Storm window cost	Heating & air conditioning	Heating only
1	$23.95	$1.92	$1.58	$30.63	$5.24	$5.12	$32.45	$3.24	$3.10	$23.99	$1.52	$1.00	$32.70	$4.38	$4.10
2	25.27	3.95	3.25	32.31	10.77	10.52	34.23	6.66	6.37	25.31	3.12	2.06	34.50	9.00	8.43
3	26.66	6.09	5.01	34.00	16.60	16.22	36.11	10.27	9.82	26.70	4.81	3.17	36.40	13.88	12.99
4	28.13	8.34	6.87	35.96	22.75	22.23	38.10	14.07	13.46	28.17	6.59	4.34	38.40	19.02	17.80
5	29.68	10.72	8.83	37.94	29.24	28.57	40.20	18.08	17.30	29.72	8.47	5.58	40.51	24.45	22.88
6	31.31	13.23	10.90	40.03	36.09	35.26	42.41	22.31	21.35	31.35	10.46	6.89	42.74	30.17	28.24
7	33.03	15.88	13.08	42.23	43.31[c]	42.32[c]	44.74	26.78	25.62	33.07	12.56	8.27	45.07	36.21	33.89
8	34.85	18.68	15.38	44.55	50.93	49.77	47.20	31.49	30.13	34.89	14.77	9.72	47.57	42.58	39.85
9	36.77	21.62	17.81	47.00	58.97	57.63	49.80	36.46	34.89	36.81	17.10	11.25	50.19	49.30	46.14
10	38.79	24.73	20.37	49.59	67.45	65.92	52.54	41.71	39.91	38.83	19.56	12.87	52.95	56.39[c]	52.78
11	40.92	28.01	23.07	52.32	76.40	74.67	55.43	47.24	45.21	40.97	22.16	14.58	55.86	63.87	59.78[c]
12	43.17	31.47	25.92	55.20	85.84	83.90	58.48	53.08	50.80	43.22	24.90	16.38	58.93	71.76	67.17
13	45.54	35.12	28.93	58.24	95.80	93.63	61.70	59.24	56.69	45.60	27.79	18.28	62.17	80.09	74.96
14	48.04	38.97	32.10	61.44	106.31	103.90	65.09	65.74[c]	62.91	48.11	30.84	20.29	65.59	88.87	83.18
15	50.68	43.03	35.45	64.82	117.40	114.73	68.67	72.60	69.47[c]	50.76	34.06	22.41	69.20	98.14	91.85
16	53.47	47.32	38.98	68.39	129.10	126.16	72.45	79.83	76.39	53.55	37.45	24.64	73.01	107.92	101.00
17	56.41	51.84	42.70	72.15	141.44	138.22	76.43	87.46	83.69	56.60	41.03	27.00	77.03	118.24	110.66
18	59.51	56.61	46.63	76.12	154.46	150.94	80.63	95.51	91.39	59.61	44.81	29.49	81.27	129.12	120.85
19	62.78	61.64	50.77	80.31	168.20	164.36	85.00	104.00	99.52	62.89	48.79	32.11	85.74	140.60	131.60
20[b]	66.23	66.95[c]	55.14	84.73	182.69	178.52	89.74	112.96	108.09	66.35	52.99	34.88	90.46	152.71	142.94

[a]December 1973 prices were used for storm windows and natural gas.

[b]Not computed after 20 years.

[c]The year when the storm window pays for itself.

Source: Derived by the Washington Center for Metropolitan Studies using the following method. Each storm window is assumed to be 15 square feet, the usual size of a double-hung window. Storm-window prices are for medium-priced aluminum sash sold at retail, and installed in each of the cities by Sears, Roebuck and Company. Natural gas prices are as of December 1973, from the U.S. Bureau of Labor Statistics. Storm window costs and energy cost savings are computed assuming a 5.5 percent interest rate, compounded annually. For the computation of Btu savings, see footnote to Table 3-13.

Table 3-13. Btu's Saved per Storm Window, Five Cities, 1972

City	Btu's (millions)
Atlanta	1.7
Boston	2.6
Chicago	2.7
Dallas	1.7
New York	2.3

Source: Estimated by Washington Center for Metropolitan Studies based on data from the U.S. National Bureau of Standards and the National Oceanic and Atmospheric Administration. The "air change" methodology used in the estimates was supplied by Stanley Glenn, Chairman of the ASHRAE Technical Committee 4.5.

however, according to the amount of insulation work needed, the type of house, and the effectiveness of the insulating materials.[12]

The focus so far has been on the limited choice a family has in how much space heating energy it uses. Climate is outside its control and so is the basic structure of the house. Even families moving into new homes have little control over important energy using characteristics, as these have already been determined by the developer who built the house for sale. Adding insulation and storm windows can save considerable amounts of energy, but does not always pay from the individual householder's point of view. Energy saving improvements may cost more than will be saved in fuel bills, unless the family plans to live in the same house a number of years—in fact, as long as a decade or more in warmer areas.

Life Style—The Family's Use of the Home

While the structure of the dwelling determines a basic level of energy use for heating, the family's style of living also makes a difference. For example, a family can influence its own energy use by adjusting a thermostat, opening windows, and plugging in electric space heaters.

Home Temperature. House temperature can be controlled after the structure is built, if the family has a thermostat or valve. About 80 percent of all households in the survey had a thermostat or valve. Those without temperature control include seven million households (mostly renters) who nonetheless pay for space heat.

The lower the indoor temperature in winter, the less energy is used. Households surveyed generally tended to keep their home temperatures between 70° and 72° during the day and below 70° at night (Table 3-14). (These temperatures were reported in May 1973, before government urging to "dial down.")

Table 3-14.   Indoor Temperature Control and Preference in
Winter, by Heating Degree Days, 1973 (percent of households)

Winter indoor temperature characteristics	All households	Heating degree days		
		< 3500	3500–5499	5500+
All households	100	100	100	100
With thermostat or valve	81	70	86	87
Temperature during day[a]				
Under 70°	12	12	14	10
70°–72°	52	51	51	56
73° or higher	33	34	33	33
Don't know	2	4	2	2
Temperature at night[a]				
Under 70°	45	51	49	38
70°–72°	35	30	33	41
73° or higher	16	13	15	19
Don't know	4	7	3	2

[a]For households with thermostats or valves.

Source: Washington Center for Metropolitan Studies' Lifestyles and Energy Surveys.

The reported daytime winter temperatures do not vary appreciably with climate, but the nighttime winter temperatures do. About 60 percent of all households in the coldest climate zone had indoor winter temperatures above 70 degrees at night (Table 3-14).

How much energy could be saved if people are persuaded to lower room temperature? Computer simulation research suggests that savings could be considerable. In Minneapolis there is an energy saving of about 3 percent for every degree the thermostat is set back over a 24-hour period. In Chicago the saving is about 4 percent, and in San Francisco it is almost 9 percent per degree of setback (Tables 3-15 and 3-16).

The percentage of saving is greater in warmer areas because the amount of fuel used is less overall, but the absolute amount of fuel saved per degree of thermostat reduction is greatest in the North. A family in Minneapolis reducing home temperature by one degree saves only a small percentage of its total energy consumption, but it saves more energy in absolute terms than does a family with the same home in San Francisco which also turns the thermostat down one degree.

For sleeping comfort many people prefer to open bedroom windows on winter nights to increase ventilation. Of course this tends to reduce indoor temperature and use more energy. Only a third of the households kept their windows open at night in the winter, however. Of those who did, almost half kept the bedroom door shut, thus containing the heat loss (Table 3-17).

Table 3-15. Estimated Percent of Heating Fuel Saved by Dialing Down Thermostat for 24 Hours, Selected Cities

City	*Approximate percent savings from 24-hour setback of*			
	1°F	*3°F*	*5°F*	*7°F*
Chicago	4	12	20	28
Columbus	4	13	22	30
Dallas	7	20	32	41
Denver	4	13	22	30
Des Moines	4	11	19	27
Detroit	4	13	22	30
Kansas City	5	14	23	32
Los Angeles[a]	11	34	47	61
Louisville	5	14	24	33
Madison	3	10	17	24
Minneapolis	3	10	16	22
Omaha	4	11	19	26
Pittsburgh	4	13	22	30
Portland, Oregon[a]	7	20	32	41
Salt Lake City	4	13	22	30
San Francisco[a]	9	26	39	51
Seattle[a]	7	20	31	40
Syracuse	4	12	20	28
Washington, D.C.[a]	6	17	27	36

[a]Savings figures for indicated cities have been adjusted to compensate for climate-introduced error; however, at higher amounts of setback, the percent savings shown may not be achieved.

Source: Honeywell, Inc., "Reducing Fuel Consumption by Dialing Down the Thermostat," Minneapolis, 1973 (pamphlet).

Electric Space Heaters. About 15 percent of all households use electric space heaters, either as supplements to a central heating system or as their only source of heat. Electric space heaters are somewhat less common in colder parts of the country (Table 3-17). This is fortunate, because electric space heaters are large energy users. According to an educational brochure sent from Consolidated Edison of New York to its customers, "most portable electric heaters are far less efficient than a central heating system, and most homes are not insulated properly for electric heat."[13]

Who Pays for Fuel? Families who pay their own fuel bills directly, rather than as part of their rent, are more likely to have a thermostat or valve to control room temperature. Perhaps because they have better temperature control than families whose fuel costs are included in the rent, families who pay their own fuel bills are somewhat less likely than others to open their bedroom windows on winter nights. They are also somewhat less likely to have supplementary electric space heaters (Tables 3-18 and 3-19).

Table 3-16.   Estimated Percent of Heating Fuel Saved from Night Thermostat Setback for Eight Hours, Selected Cities

City	Approximate percent savings from eight-hour night setback of		
	3°F	5°F	10°F
Chicago	4	7	11
Columbus	4	7	11
Dallas	7	11	15
Denver	4	7	11
Des Moines	4	7	11
Detroit	4	7	11
Kansas City	5	8	12
Los Angeles	9	12	16
Louisville	5	9	13
Madison	3	5	9
Minneapolis	3	5	9
Omaha	4	7	11
Pittsburgh	4	7	11
Portland, Oregon	7	9	13
Salt Lake City	4	7	11
San Francisco	8	10	14
Seattle	6	8	12
Syracuse	4	7	11
Washington, D.C.	6	9	13

Source: Honeywell, Inc., "Reducing Fuel Consumption by Dialing Down the Thermostat," Minneapolis, 1973 (pamphlet).

Table 3-17.   Electric Space Heaters and Window Opening Habits by Heating Degree Days, 1973 (percent of households)

Space heaters and window opening	All households	Heating degree days		
		< 3500	3500– 5499	5500+
All households	100	100	100	100
No electric space heaters	85	81	85	88
With space heaters	15	19	14	12
1	12	16	12	9
2 or more	2	3	1	2
Windows sometimes open at night during winter	33	38	30	32
Room door usually shut	15	16	12	16
Usually not shut	18	22	18	14
Windows almost never open	66	61	69	66

Source: Washington Center for Metropolitan Studies' Lifestyles and Energy Surveys.

Table 3-18. Winter Indoor Temperature Control and Characteristics by Whether Space Heat Is Paid For Directly, 1973 (percent of households)

Characteristics	All households	Pay for space heat	
		Yes	No
All households	100	100	100
With thermostat or valve	81	87	48
Temperature during day[a]			
Under 70°	12	12	14
70°–72°	52	53	45
73° or higher	33	32	38
Don't know	2	2	4
Temperature at night[a]			
Under 70°	45	45	49
70°– 72°	35	36	28
73° or higher	16	16	18
Don't know	4	4	4

[a]For households with thermostats or valves.
Source: Washington Center for Metropolitan Studies' Lifestyles and Energy Surveys.

Table 3-19. Temperature Controlling Characteristics by Whether Space Heat Is Paid For Directly, 1973 (percent of households)

Characteristics	All households	Pay for space heat	
		Yes	No
All households	100	100	100
No electric space heater	85	84	91
With space heater	15	16	8
1	12	13	8
2 or more	2	2	1
Windows sometimes open at night in winter	33	31	49
Room door usually shut	15	14	19
Usually not shut	18	16	28
Windows almost never open	66	68	50

Source: Washington Center for Metropolitan Studies' Lifestyles and Energy Surveys.

Furnace Pilot Lights. Turning off the pilot light of a natural gas furnace during the summer is a way of saving energy without causing a family any discomfort. In the summer before the energy crisis of 1973–74, about 13 million households saved energy by having their pilot lights turned off in the summer. Another 25 million left their furnace pilot lights on (Table 3-20). If

**Table 3-20.   Pilot Light of Natural Gas Furnace Off or On,
Summer 1972 (number and percent of households)**

Pilot light off or on	Number (millions)	Percent
All households with central gas heat	43.2	100
Pilot light off in summer	13.2	31
Pilot light on in summer	25.1	58
Not sure	4.9	11

Source: Washington Center for Metropolitan Studies' Lifestyles and Energy Surveys.

these 25 million households had turned off their furnace pilot lights, the country would have saved 58 trillion Btu's of energy, or about 1 percent of the total natural gas that households consumed in 1972–73.[14]

The dollar saving per household would have been under $5. This low dollar saving gives the consumer little incentive to have the pilot light turned off. Also there is the inconvenience of calling the gas company to turn the pilot light off in the spring and light it again in the fall. If the gas company charges the household directly for this, the charge could wipe out the dollar saving.

An ignition type of lighter that a customer could manage alone is now being developed. The production and the initial expense of buying and installing such a device should be investigated.

WATER HEATING

Water heating accounts for eight percent of all personal energy use (see Table 3-1 above). Most single family homes have natural gas water heaters; one-third have electric ones. Three percent of all households report having no hot running water at all (Table 3-21).

**Table 3-21.   Energy Source for Water Heating in Single Family
Homes, 1973 (percent of homes)**

Energy source for water heating	Percent
All single family homes	100
Natural gas	56
Electricity	31
Fuel oil	5
Bottled gas	4
Other and unknown	2
None	3

Source: Washington Center for Metropolitan Studies' Lifestyles and Energy Surveys.

Table 3-22. Trend in Energy Use of Water Heaters by Energy Source, Selected Years, 1950–1971

Energy source and year	Standard water heater
Electric	Btu's (millions)
1950	40
1959	43
1969	46[a]
Natural gas	
1960	24
1966	27
1971	32

[a]The quick recovery water heater used an estimated 52 million Btu's of electricity in 1969.

Source: Prepared by the Washington Center for Metropolitan Studies from unpublished materials from the American Gas Association, Arlington, Virginia, and the Edison Electrical Institute, New York.

Electricity is the most fuel intensive energy source, and the amount of energy needed to run electric water heaters has been increasing. In 1959 the average electric water heater used about 43 million Btu's annually. By 1969 its energy use had increased to 46 million Btu's, but a new, more energy intensive model was on the market as well—a quick-recovery electric water heater that uses 52 million Btu's annually. Energy used in natural gas water heaters has also increased, from an average of 24 million Btu's in 1960 to 32 million Btu's in 1971 (Table 3-22). Hot water is used for washing—dishes, clothes, and people. The amount used varies with the number of people in the household and the use of appliances that consume large amounts of hot water such as automatic dishwashers and clothes washers.

APPLIANCES

Cooking and refrigerating appliances account for about 6 percent of all personal energy consumption. Other appliances and lighting use an additional 9 percent (see Table 3-1 above).

Energy Use of Appliances

How much energy an appliance uses in a given year depends on how much energy it takes to run the appliance per second or per hour, as well as how much the appliance is used. For example, the average wattage (energy per second) of a microwave oven is 1,450. This is over four times the wattage of a 12 cubic foot frost-free refrigerator. Yet over a year, the oven uses less than one-fifth as much energy as the refrigerator, because the refrigerator is plugged in all the time while the microwave oven is used comparatively infrequently.[15] The estimated annual energy use for natural gas appliances and for major and minor electrical appliances is given in Tables 3-23 to 3-25.

Trends in Appliance Energy Use

All electrical appliances except stoves have increased in energy use per appliance since 1959–60. The situation with natural gas appliances is mixed. Gas stoves and gas clothes dryers with electric pilots have increased in estimated average energy use; air conditioners, gas lights, and clothes dryers with gas pilots have shown modest declines (Table 3-23). The largest increase in energy use among natural gas appliances—clothes dryers with electric pilot—went up 33 percent.

Increases of over 50 percent in energy use occurred among some electrical appliances in the decade of the 1960s. Energy use of regular refrigerators and automatic clothes washers increased most (over 70 percent). Only one electric appliance declined in energy use—the electric stove—but only by 4 percent (Table 3-24).

Energy use data on electric appliances are available back to 1950. From them it is possible to trace the rising level of convenience offered by appliances—and the rising energy use that has accompanied it. For example, in 1950 a prosperous homeowner could buy something called a "home freeze cabinet" (620 kwhr per year). By 1959 the freezer was on the market (860 kwhr

Table 3-23.   Trend in Estimated Annual Use of Natural Gas by Appliance, Selected Years, 1960–1971 (therms)

Appliance	1960	1966	1971	Percent change 1960–71
Range				
Apartment	a	74	88	19[b]
House	100	106	105	5
Refrigerator	120	a	a	a
Air conditioner				
(consumption per ton)	a	308	283	−8[b]
Clothes dryer				
Gas pilot	85	90	75	−12
Electric pilot	45	52	60	33
Gas light	a	183	181	−1[b]

[a]Not available.
[b]Percent change 1966–71.
Source: Prepared by the Washington Center for Metropolitan Studies from unpublished materials from the American Gas Association, Arlington, Virginia.

Table 3-24. Trend in Estimated Annual Electricity Use of Major Appliances, Selected Years, 1950–1969 (kwhr)

Appliance	1950	1959	1969	Percent change 1959-69
Stove	1,250	1,225	1,175	-4
Refrigerator				
Regular	345	420	728	73
Frostless	a	a	1,217	a
Refrigerator-freezer				
Regular	a	715	1,137	59
Frostless	a	a	1,829	a
Freezer				
Home freeze cabinet	620	a	a	a
Regular	a	860	1,195	39
Frostless	a	a	1,761	a
Air conditioner				
Room cooler	935	a	a	a
Window air conditioner	a	1,135	1,389	22
Laundry				
Clothes washers				
Nonautomatic	45	45	76	69
Automatic	a	60	103	72
Clothes dryer	520	910	993	9
Dishwasher	a	355	363	2
Television				
Black and white	290	325	362	11
Color	a	a	502	a

aNot available.

Source: Prepared by the Washington Center for Metropolitan Studies from unpublished materials from the Edison Electrical Institute, New York.

per year). By 1969 the thing to buy, if budget permitted, was a frost-free freezer (1,761 kwhr). The increase in size and convenience is undeniable, but so is the increase (180 percent) in energy use. Increases occurred elsewhere as well. The room cooler (935 kwhr) became the window air conditioner (1,389 kwhr). The wringer washer (45 kwhr) became the automatic clothes washer (103 kwhr). (See Table 3-24.)

These figures on appliance energy consumption are averages. Just as there are variations in design and purchase price among competing appliances, so are there variations in the amount of energy different appliances require to perform essentially the same task or service. For example, some room air conditioners are more efficient than competing models—i.e., they use less energy than others having the same cooling capacity.

Table 3-25. Annual Energy Requirements of Small Electric Household Appliances, 1973

Appliance	Average wattage	Estimated kwhr consumed annually
Food preparation		
Blender	386	15
Broiler	1,436	100
Carving knife	92	8
Coffee maker	894	106
Deep fryer	1,448	83
Dishwasher	1,201	363
Egg cooker	516	14
Frying pan	1,196	186
Hot plate	1,257	90
Mixer	127	13
Oven (microwave only)	1,450	190
Roaster	1,333	205
Sandwich grill	1,161	33
Toaster	1,146	39
Trash compactor	400	50
Waffle iron	1,116	22
Waste disposer	445	30
Comfort conditioning		
Air cleaner	50	216
Bed covering	177	147
Dehumidifier	257	377
Fan (attic)	370	291
Fan (circulating)	88	43
Fan (rollaway)	171	138
Fan (window)	200	170
Heater (portable)	1,322	176
Heating pad	65	10
Humidifier	177	163
Health & beauty		
Germicidal lamp	20	141
Hair dryer	381	14
Heat lamp (infrared)	250	13
Shaver	14	2
Sun lamp	279	16
Tooth brush	7	0.5
Vibrator	40	2
Home entertainment		
Radio	71	86
Radio/record player	109	109
Housewares		
Clock	2	17
Floor polisher	305	15
Sewing machine	75	11
Vacuum cleaner	630	46
Iron (hand)	1,008	144

Source: Electric Energy Association, "Annual Energy Requirements of Electric Household Appliances," New York, 1973 (pamphlet).

Air conditioners have been chosen by the National Bureau of Standards as the first appliance group to be labeled with energy efficiency information in their voluntary energy conservation labeling program. Ultimately other appliances will be labeled as well.[16]

Appliance Ownership

Not every household has all types of appliances. Refrigerators, stoves, and television sets are most common—almost 100 percent of households have them. Three-fourths of all households have clothes washers too, either wringer or automatic. About half of all households have clothes dryers, and one-third have food freezers (Table 3-26). The question of which household can afford the advantages of appliances is the theme of Chapter Five. For now, it is

Table 3-26. Households with Major Appliances, 1973 (percent)

Appliance	Percent
All households	100
Clothes washer	78[a]
Nonautomatic	10
Automatic	70
Dishwasher	25
Television	97[a]
Black and white	64
Color	53
Clothes dryer	53
Gas	16
Electric	38
Refrigerator (electric)	99
Must defrost	48
Frost-free	51
Refrigerator (gas)	1
Stove	97
Gas	52
Electric	46
Freezer	34
Gas light	4
Appliance index	
Less than 40	33
40 to 59	30
60 and over	38

[a]Does not add because households may own one or more of both types.
Source: Washington Center for Metropolitan Studies' Lifestyles and Energy Surveys.

Table 3-27.   Aspects of Air Conditioning by Cooling Degree Days, 1973 (percent of households)

		Cooling degree days	
Aspects of air conditioning	*All households*	*Less than 1,000*	*1,000 or more*
All households	100	100	100
No air conditioning	52	67	41
With air conditioning	47	33	58
Window	32	23	40
1 unit	22	17	25
2 or more	10	5	13
Central	15	10	19
Number of rooms cooled			
1-4	23	18	28
5 or more	22	14	29
Number unknown	1	1	1

Source: Washington Center for Metropolitan Studies' Lifestyles and Energy Surveys.

enough to point out that substantial differences exist among households in appliance ownership.

Air Conditioning

About half of all American households have air conditioning, two-thirds of which have window units. Whatever the type, air conditioning is naturally more common in warmer parts of the country. An indicator of summer climate more precise than region is the cooling degree day.[g] The more cooling degree days in a locality the hotter the summer (see Figure 3-2). For example, Grand Forks, North Dakota averages less than 500 cooling degree days, while New Orleans has close to 3,000.

About 60 percent of all households in areas with 1,000 or more cooling degree days had air conditioning of some kind. In areas with less than 1,000 cooling degree days only 33 percent of all households had air conditioning (Table 3-27).

The same structural features of homes which conserve heat in the winter help save "cold" in the summer. One of the ironies of air conditioning, from an energy point of view, is that its presence may cause a family to use more energy than the family would prefer. Consider the dilemma of the room with a single window. Installing a window air conditioner makes it impossible to open the window for ventilation or cooling even when outside weather invites it. A window air conditioner can also cause problems in a two-window room. With one window filled with an air conditioner, cross-ventilation is ruled out.

[g]Cooling degree days are the number of degrees the daily average temperature is above 65 degrees Fahrenheit summed over a year. The median number of cooling degree days for American households is over 1,000.

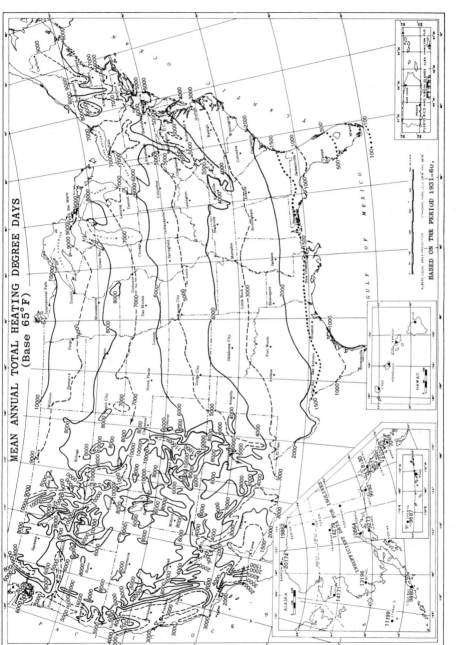

MEAN ANNUAL TOTAL HEATING DEGREE DAYS (Base 65° F)

BASED ON THE PERIOD 1931–60.

Source: U.S. Department of Commerce, Environmental Data Service, *Selected Climatic Maps of the United States, 1966,* p. 9.

An Estimate of Appliance Energy Use

A family with an automatic clothes washer, an electric clothes dryer, color television, frost-free refrigerator, and gas stove would use about 45 million Btu's per year for appliances, assuming average national use of each appliance. If the family had air conditioning, even more energy would be used, the amount depending on family preferences and climate. The median family in the WCMS surveys used an estimated 51 million Btu's of electricity and natural gas for appliances and thus probably had something close to the constellation of appliances noted, perhaps including air conditioning. The estimate of median appliance energy use is based on an appliance index.

Table 3-28 gives the average annual Btu's major appliances use, based on estimates made by the Electric Energy Association and the American Gas Association. These Btu estimates were used to create an appliance index. If a household reported having an appliance, the household was given points equal to the million of Btu's that appliance was estimated to use. The more appliances a household had, the more points it was given. Household scores on the appliance index ranged from zero (two survey households had no electricity at all in their homes) to 270.[17]

Households with low appliance index scores used relatively less electricity and natural gas than the average, and households with high appliance index scores used relatively more (see Table 3-29). As pointed out earlier, appliance use accounts for a fairly small proportion of total personal energy consumption. The reason the appliance index shows such a high association with total energy use in the home (including space heating) is because the families who have many of the major energy using appliances are also likely to be well off, and have spacious homes requiring large amounts of energy for heating. High energy use in all spheres and especially in appliances is associated with high family income.[h]

Consumer Choice

The purchase of appliances and water heaters is an area in which consumers may exercise considerable discretion, since the equipment is not usually part of the structure. But even here discretion is limited. An important limitation is cost; a family may not be able to afford the item, particularly if it would be only a replacement. A family trying to make ends meet would have little incentive to replace an electric water heater with a more energy conserving gas one. (See Table 3-22 above for the comparative efficiencies.)

A customer is also limited by what is available in stores. For example, virtually all refrigerators now sold at retail are the more energy intensive frost-free variety. Bearing this out, all refrigerators priced for the Consumer Price Index of the Bureau of Labor Statistics are frost free.[18]

---

[h]This theme is developed further in Chapter Five. The appliance index was developed by Dawn Day of the WCMS energy research group.

Table 3-28. Estimated Average Annual Btu's Used by Major Appliances

Appliance	Btu's[a] (millions)
Clothes washer	
Nonautomatic	1
Automatic	1
Dishwasher	4
Television	
Black and white	4
Color	6
Clothes dryer	
Gas	7
Electric	11
Refrigerator (electric)	
Must defrost	10
Frost-free	17
Refrigerator (gas)	12
Stove	
Gas	10
Electric	13
Freezer	13
Gas light	18
Air conditioners (range)	1-194[b]

[a]The conversion rate from kwhr's to Btu's was adjusted to include the energy expended in production and transmission of the electricity used in the home as well as the electric energy used in the home itself.

[b]The preliminary weight given to an air conditioner depended on whether the air conditioner was gas or electric, window or central. The preliminary weight was then adjusted for climate through the use of cooling degree days in the locality for each household. The adjustment factor was the cooling degree days for the respondent's locality divided by the mean cooling degree days for the whole sample.

Source: Developed by the Washington Center for Metropolitan Studies using estimates from: Electric Energy Association, "Annual Energy Requirements of Electric Household Appliances," New York: Edison Electric Association, 1973. American Gas Association. *Gas Rate Fundamentals.* New York, 1969, p. 55. American Gas Association, "Single-Family Residential Gas Appliance Usage," Arlington, Va., 1971 (Unpublished).

Customers are also limited by lack of information about energy use. For one appliance—the air conditioner—energy use is a particularly crucial variable, because air conditioners, more than other appliances, operate on highly varying amounts of energy.[19] The varying efficiencies of air conditioners are caused by differences in motors, heat exchangers (cooling coils), and fans. Using the Energy Efficiency Ratios (EER) of the National Bureau of

Table 3-29.   Average Btu's of Electricity and Natural Gas Used per Household, by Appliance Index Score, 1973

Appliance index score	Average Btu's (millions)	Btu index
All households	235	100
Less than 40	172	73
40–59	231	98
60 and over	293	125

Source: Washington Center for Metropolitan Studies' Lifestyles and Energy Surveys.

Standards, it is possible to judge how well different air conditioning models of the same cooling capacity perform. The EER is determined by dividing the Btu's-per-hour rating of a room air conditioner by the watts (power) it uses. Air conditioners with high EER ratings are relatively more efficient than those with low EER's. For a given cooling capacity, the more efficient models are less costly to operate.[20]

The EER labeling program is presently voluntary and not widely publicized. Would people take this information into account if it were made available to them in an understandable way? Respondents in the WCMS 1973 Lifestyles and Energy Surveys were asked this question:

> This exhibit shows costs for two different models of air con-ditioners. They look the same and work the same, but B costs $50 more to buy and $20 less per year to operate. Suppose you decided to buy an air conditioner and had to choose from these, which one would you buy?

About 85 percent of the respondents said they would be willing to pay $50 more to have the reduced operating costs and consequent energy savings. Most families purchase their air conditioning; only one-fourth of those with it say it came with their home (Table 3-30).

Knowledge about energy use might also affect consumer choice in television purchase. The quick warmup color television set is really "on" all the time, continuously using a small amount of current, which adds an extra 330 kilowatt hours per set annually. A similar black and white set uses an extra 200 kilowatt hours annually.[21]

Fluorescent lights are about four times more efficient than incan-descent lights and thus their use can save energy. Fluorescent lights last seven to ten times longer than incandescent lights, so they also save on replacement

Table 3-30. Type of Air Conditioning by Whether It Came With Home, 1973 (percent of households)

Air conditioning type	Total[a]	Came with home	Bought
All households with air conditioning	100	27	73
Window	100	18	82
Part of house cooled	100	14	86
Whole house cooled	100	23	77
Central	100	47	53

[a]Excludes unknowns.

Source: Washington Center for Metropolitan Studies' Lifestyles and Energy Surveys.

costs.[22] Consumer enthusiasm for fluorescent lights has been restrained by the lights' appearance. They look best in kitchen, bath, or utility room.

Outside gas lights use a lot of energy. These decorative lamps, burning day and night, collectively used 45 trillion Btu's in 1973. They create a pleasant atmosphere, but perhaps if the 2.5 million households that now have them knew how much energy they use, many might be willing to give them up.

HIGHLIGHTS

The householder trying to save on a fuel bill (or sharing national concern and trying to save energy) can do several things.

- Keep indoor temperature down in the winter
- Not open windows or doors unnecessarily
- Have the natural gas company turn off the furnace pilot light in the summer
- Avoid using electric space heaters
- Wash clothes in cold water
- Use fewer appliances and use them less
- Keep the lights off as much as possible

If a householder can afford to, he/she might add storm windows and storm doors, weatherstripping, and insulation. But basically the important factors affecting space heat—climate, type of structure and type of heating—are beyond the average household's immediate control.

The type of structure was settled when the home went up. This was determined by a complex interaction of building codes, building code enforcement, material costs, builder perceptions of consumer demand, and standards set by financing organizations, both public and private.[23] These considerations affect the characteristics of new homes and particularly those built by developers, who actually determine the design of most new housing today.

Until very recently, saving energy has not been a concern of those involved in any aspects of building, buying, and renting homes. The trend toward more energy intensive features in new homes described earlier in this chapter shows that energy saving was not of much concern even by 1973.

Once the structure is built, energy saving modifications are expensive and may not pay in terms of fuel bill savings. The experience in Michigan suggests that adding insulation to homes with attics in colder areas is economical within a year or two. Calculations by the WCMS show that the addition of storm windows does save energy, but the homeowner does not recover the cost of purchase and installation for several years, using the predominant heating fuel— natural gas. Of the five cities for which calculations were made, the storm window purchase and installation costs were recovered in fuel savings first in Boston and then only after seven years. The long cost recovery period is a problem in view of the high mobility of American families.

Turning off 25 million furnace pilot lights in the summer can mean considerable national energy savings, and this is important since natural gas is currently in short supply. At present, homeowners may be deterred from doing so by lack of knowledge about the energy savings possible, about how to do it, and by fees charged for this service.

Energy use in appliances is another area for energy conservation, even though reduced appliance use cannot save as much as reductions in space and water heating. At the moment, little information is available to the consumer to guide efficient and economical purchase. Even when such information is available, consumers are still restricted to what is for sale in the stores, by the cost of big items, and the stock of appliances already in the homes they move into.

DIRECTIONS FOR POLICY

Space heating is the single largest use of energy in the home. People need to be made aware of the characteristics of homes that influence space heating.[24] Ways need to be explored to provide information on heating costs to home buyers.

The greater energy use of electric heating compared to natural gas and fuel oil needs particular publicity, although the final choice of the furnace purchaser will be constrained not only by cost and energy conservation considerations but also by whether natural gas and fuel oil companies will accept new customers.

Ways need to be found to finance energy conserving modifications (storm windows, insulation) to homes, particularly in colder areas. Programs need to be large enough to make substantial changes in the housing stock in a year; and they should be financed so as to make energy conserving modifications attractive even to a family who plans to move in a relatively short period.

Home improvement loans or grants also need to be made available to households living in homes with particular heating system problems or in such poor condition that it is not possible to maintain a comfortable temperature. A recourse of some families in this situation—the electric space heater—is expensive and energy intensive.

Performance standards in housing with regard to heat loss need to be developed and incorporated into state and local building codes. Changes in building codes together with greater consumer awareness should slow or stop the present trend toward building new homes with energy intensive features. Legislation requiring "truth in energy" labeling of major appliances and water heaters is needed. Purchasers of major appliances should be aware of the operating costs of appliances as well as their initial purchase price. Generally, natural gas appliances are more efficient than electrical appliances.[25] Also, efficiency of energy use is known to vary among different models of a given appliance.

A way needs to be found to save the energy burned every summer by pilot lights on natural gas furnaces. Regulatory commissions could require that natural gas companies turn furnace pilot lights off and on without a separate charge, including this cost in their overall rate structure. An ignition type of lighter is being perfected. Its development and speedy installation in existing furnaces should be encouraged.

Regulations should be enforced to exclude persons with special interests from regulatory agencies that handle energy matters. To ensure improved service and understanding of consumer problems, more consumers, including women and minority group members, need to be included on energy regulatory agencies.

Chapter Four

Energy Use on the Road

Americans travel billions of miles each year, and for every mile they ride, they use energy. Transportation—cars planes, buses, trains, boats—uses up almost half of all the energy consumed by households (see Table 3-1, above). In terms of thousands of miles traveled, the car is the biggest energy user, accounting for almost 90 percent of all intercity passenger miles of travel (Table 4-1). In terms of the amount of energy used per passenger mile, the airplane uses the most energy with the car second[1] (Table 4-2).

Americans traveled an average of 6,000 miles per person between cities in 1971, and undoubtedly more miles per person since then, for the figure goes up every year. But average figures can be misleading; they imply an equality that does not exist. Some people travel a great deal; some not at all. Some stay at home by choice, others because they cannot afford to leave even for a short trip. A very important influence on personal travel is income. If a family has little money, even the cost of gasoline for a car trip is out of reach. About 65 percent of all household heads took an airplane trip or a rail, bus or car trip of 200 miles or more in 1972–73. Only 40 percent of all poor household heads did so.

Americans averaged about one and a third cars per household in 1973, but the cars were not equally distributed. Some 15 percent of all households had no car at all, while 10 percent had three cars or even more[a] (Table 4-3). Low income families are most likely to do without a car. Car use also is influenced by income; the more money a household has the more the household is likely to drive its car or cars for many thousands of miles every year. The effect of lack of money on car ownership and travel is explored further in Chapter Five, while this chapter focuses on the influences apart from

[a]The second car in many households is for the wife. Women are a rising proportion of all drivers: in 1940 one-quarter of all drivers were women; by 1972 almost half were women.[2]

67

Table 4-1.   Percent and Number of Passenger Miles per Person of Intercity Travel, by Transportation Modes, Selected Years, 1950-1971

Year	Total traffic volume	Private auto- mobiles	Airways	Buses[a]	Rail- roads	Inland waterways
			Percent			
1950	100	86	2	5	6	b
1955	100	89	3	4	4	b
1960	100	90	4	3	3	b
1965	100	89	6	3	2	b
1970	100	87	10	2	1	b
1971[c]	100	87	10	2	1	b
			Passenger miles per person			
1950	3,345	2,884	66	171	211	8
1955	4,338	3,859	139	151	176	10
1960	4,356	3,922	189	106	122	15
1965	4,754	4,227	300	124	93	16
1970	5,814	5,034	584	123	54	20
1971[c]	5,965	5,194	582	126	44	20

[a]Excludes school buses.
[b]Less than 0.5 percent.
[c]Preliminary.
Source: Prepared by the Washington Center for Metropolitan Studies from U.S. Bureau of the Census, *Statistical Abstract of the United States, 1973,* Tables 2 and 885, pp. 5 and 538.

rising income that have spurred the tremendous growth of American energy use in travel.

One element in the growth of energy use in transportation has been the shift from less to more energy intensive modes of travel. Since 1950 and even earlier the car has been the major means of intercity travel. The shift has been primarily from trains and buses to airplanes (see Table 4-1). The trend away from bus and rail travel can be seen in the changes in the distances over which service is provided. Between 1960 and 1970, the mileage over which trains provided passenger service declined by almost 50 percent. The mileage serviced by intercity bus increased by only 1 percent, while the mileage of service provided by airplanes increased by 60 percent. In urban travel cars have replaced buses trolleys and commuter trains. Between 1960 and 1970, urban bus route mileage increased only 2 percent. while railway, subway, and trolley routes declined 40 percent (Table 4-4).

Government action at all levels—local, state, and national—has been very important in shaping the options presented to would-be travellers. Zoning can affect how far it is to the grocery store and to work. Local government

Table 4-2. Comparison of Estimates of Energy Use for Various Means of Passenger Transportation

Transportation mode	Hirst intercity 1970	Hirst urban 1970	Makhijani and Lichtenberg 1968
	Btu's per passenger mile		
Plane	8,400	a	6,824
Car	3,400	8,100	5,016
Bus	1,600	3,800[b]	1,262
Train	2,900	a	1,979
	Index (car = 100)		
Plane	247	a	136
Car	100	100	100
Bus	47	47	25
Train	85	a	39

[a]Not available.
[b]Public transit.

Source: Prepared by the Washington Center for Metropolitan Studies from Eric Hirst, *Energy Intensiveness of Passenger and Freight Transport Modes 1950-1970*, Oak Ridge, Tenn.: Oak Ridge National Laboratory, April 1973, p. 27 and A.G. Makhijani and A.J. Lichtenberg, *An Assessment of Energy and Materials Utilization in the U.S.A.*, Berkeley, Calif.: Electronics Research Laboratory, College of Engineering, 1971, p. 30.

Table 4-3. Distribution of Households by Number of Cars Owned, Selected Years, 1960-1973 (percent)

Number of cars	1960	1970	1973
All households	100	100	100
None	25	20	16
One or more	75	80	84
2 or more	16	29	44
3 or more	a	5	9
4 or more	a	a	2

[a]Not available.

Source: Prepared by Washington Center for Metropolitan Studies from U.S. Bureau of the Census, *Consumer Buying Indicators*, Current Population Reports, Series P-65, No. 33, 40, Oct. 16, 1970 and May 1972. 1973 data from Washington Center for Metropolitan Studies' Lifestyles and Energy Surveys.

decisions create or fail to create commuter express bus lanes. Governments at all levels, when they build intercity roads, can choose whether to encourage bus travel or discourage it by prohibiting buses on parkways and other better roads. Low parking taxes (or none at all) encourage car commuters. Operating subsidies to public transit can keep fare increases down and encourage ridership.

Table 4-4. Transportation Mileage Operated, by Roads Used and
Transportation Mode, 1969 and 1970 (Intercity and Urban)

Roads used and transportation mode	Thousands of miles		Percent change 1960-1970
	1960	1970	
	Intercity		
Rural roads	3,116	3,170	2
Surfaced rural roads	2,165	2,411	11
Passenger miles served			
Intercity bus	265	268	1
Railroad	94	50	-47
Airplane	101	162	60
	Urban		
Municipal highways	429	560	31
Public transportation	114	115	1
Motor bus route miles, round trip	109	113	4
Railway, subway, trolley	5	3	-40

Source: Prepared by Washington Center for Metropolitan Studies from U.S. Department of Transportation, *1972 National Transportation Report*, July 1972, Washington, D.C.: U.S. Government Printing Office, p. 74, Table III-3 and p. 78, Table III-15 and U.S. Bureau of the Census, *Statistical Abstract of the United States 1972*, Table 879, 908, 916 and 932, pp. 538, 553, 557 and 567.

The federal government has played a major role in influencing transportation options. Land grants subsidized railroad construction in the nineteenth century. In the twentieth century, billions have been spent on highway construction.[3] Federal funds have also aided the construction of airports.[4]

Assistance from all levels of government to the air, rail, bus, and auto industries is a complicated subject that cannot be tackled in this book. Special attention needs to be given to how government decisions and government spending influence the transportation decisions of ordinary people. The outcome of present policies has been to encourage or at least not significantly discourage the American penchant for flying in airplanes and driving cars—the two most energy intensive ways to travel.

Energy intensiveness in travel (energy use per passenger mile) is the outcome of three factors: the amount of fuel needed to propel the vehicle, the vehicle's speed, and the number of passengers carried. Estimates of energy use per passenger mile differ, and a change in the estimate for one of these factors can alter the estimate of energy use per passenger mile considerably (see Table 4-2). For example, a city bus that is one-fifth full uses an estimated 3,800 Btu's per passenger mile. That same bus travelling with a full passenger load only uses 760 Btu's per passenger mile (Table 4-5). If all vehicles were driven only when every passenger seat was full, the energy intensiveness of each transporta-

Table 4-5. Actual and Minimum Possible Energy Use Per Passenger Mile, by Transportation Mode, 1970 (estimates based on seats used— Intercity and Urban)

Transportation mode	Actual		Minimum possible	
	Btu's per passenger mile	*Percent of seats used*	*Btu's per passenger mile*	*Percent of seats used*
	Intercity			
Bus	1,600	46	740	100
Railroad	2,900	37	1,100	100
Automobile	3,400	48	1,600	100
Airplane	8,400	49	4,100	100
	Urban			
Public transit	3,800	20	760	100
Automobile	8,100	28	2,300	100

Source: Prepared by Washington Center for Metropolitan Studies from Eric Hirst, *Energy Intensiveness of Passenger and Freight Transport Modes 1950-1970*, Oak Ridge, Tenn.: Oak Ridge National Laboratory, April 1973, Table 12, p. 27.

tion mode would fall, but the ranking would remain the same, with the airplane the most energy intensive followed by the car, railroad, and bus. In local transportation, public transit would still use much less energy than the car.

DECLINING CAR MILEAGE

Cars use a large amount of energy because there are so many of them. In addition, the passenger car has undergone a transformation toward greater energy usage per auto. The cars being produced today use more energy than those made in 1950. Increasing weight, higher speeds on freeways, and more energy-consuming equipment such as air conditioning, automatic transmissions, and emission controls have greatly reduced gasoline mileage (Table 4-6).

According to the U.S. Environmental Protection Agency, weight has the most important effect on gasoline mileage. A 5,000 pound auto has a 50 percent lower gas mileage than a 2,500 pound auto. In the United States, car weight (both for individual models and a weighted average for all sales) has increased significantly from 1962 to 1973.[5]

Households interviewed in the WCMS survey report better car mileage on older cars than on new ones. Almost half of all cars two years old and older get better than fourteen miles to the gallon in local driving. Less than two-fifths of the new cars do as well. The reported advantage in gasoline mileage for older cars is less in long distance travel, but still present: almost three-fourths

Table 4-6. Growth of Energy Using Characteristics of Cars
Selected Years, 1950–1971

Energy using characteristics	*1950*	*1960*	*1971*
Average gallons consumed per vehicle	603	661	723
Miles per gallon	15.0	14.3	13.7
Miles per hour[a]	48.7	53.8	62.0
Air conditioning–percent of new cars	b	7	61
Automatic transmission– percent of new cars	b	72	91
Average miles per car[c] (thousands)	9.0	9.5	9.9

[a]Based on actual speed of each vehicle recorded on tangent sections of main rural highways during off-peak hours.

[b]Not available.

[c]Includes taxicabs and motorcycles.

Source: U.S. Bureau of the Census, *Statistical Abstract of the United States, 1973*, Tables 898, 904, 909, 910, pp. 545, 549, 551.

of all older cars are reported to get fifteen miles or more to the gallon on the highway. Only about two-fifths of new cars do that well (Table 4-7).

Appreciable fuel savings could be made by shifting to lighter weight cars. For example, 1974 model cars weighing 2,750 pounds tested out at an average of just under nineteen miles per gallon.[6] If all cars owned by Americans in 1972–73 had gone the same distances but had the average gasoline mileage of 1974 cars weighing 2,750 pounds, gasoline consumption would have been reduced substantially. Table 4-8 lists the 1974 model cars that tested out at 18.5 miles per gallon or better.

The gasoline mileage loss from air conditioning, automatic transmissions, and emission controls is much less than the loss due to added weight. Losses from adding emission controls vary with car weight, with lighter cars showing much less and in some cases no efficiency loss.[b]

The trend toward falling gasoline mileage needs to be reversed or at least stopped. The individual consumer plays an important role in this when buying a car. Does he or she choose a lighter compact or a heavier, more gasoline

[b]The gasoline mileage loss from emission controls for 1973 vehicles, compared to uncontrolled (pre-1968) vehicles is 10.1 percent. The amount lost is highly dependent on the type of control systems the manufacturer has chosen to use, and varies by weight. Vehicles of less than 3,500 pounds show an average gain in gasoline mileage of 3 percent (due to carburetor changes made to control emissions), while vehicles of over 3,500 pounds show losses up to 18 percent.[7]

Table 4-7. Miles per Gallon Locally and Long Distance, by Age of Car, 1973 (percent of cars)

	All cars	
Miles per gallon	*Less than 2 yrs. old*	*2 yrs. old or more*
Miles per gallon locally[a]	100	100
Up to 14	62	51
15–19	19	33
20 or more	18	16
Miles per gallon long distance[b]	100	100
Up to 14	38	26
15–19	36	49
20 or more	26	25

[a]Excludes unknowns.
[b]Excludes unknowns and cars not used for long distance travel.
Source: Washington Center for Metropolitan Studies' Lifestyles and Energy Surveys.

Table 4-8. 1974 Model Cars for Sale in the United States Getting 18.5 Miles per Gallon or Better, by Manufacturer and Model

Manufacturer	*Model*
Alfa Romeo	2000 Berlina
	2000 GTV
American Motors General	Truck
	Utility Vehicle
Audi (Auto Union)	Audi Fox
Austin Morris BMC	MG Midget
	MGB Sports
BMW	BMW 2002
	BMW 2002 T11
Fiat	X1/9
	124 Special TC
Ford	Capri
	Comet
	E–100 Van
	Mustang
	Pinto
	Pinto Wagon
Fugi Heavy Ind.	Subaru Coupe
	Subaru Wagon
General Motors (Chevrolet)	Vega Hatchback
	Vega Kammback
	Vega Panel Express

(continued)

Table 4-8 continued

Manufacturer	*Model*
Honda	Civic
Isuzu	LUV Pickup
Lotus	Europa Europa Special
Mitsubishi	Dodge Colt Coupe Dodge Colt Station Wagon
Nissan	Datsun B210 Datsun 610 Datsun 710 Datsun Pickup
Opel	Manta Rallye
Porsche	911 T
Renault	12 Sedan 12 Wagon 17 Sport Coupe
Saab	Saab 97 Saab 99 Saab 99 LE
Standard Triumph	Spitfire
TVR	TVR 2500 M
Toyo Kogyo	Mazda 808 Coupe
Toyota	Corolla-1 Coupe Corolla-1 Sedan Corolla-2 Sedan Corolla-2 Wagon Mark II Wagon
Volkswagen	412 Station Wagon Convertible 15 Karman Ghia 14 (Coupe) Kombi-22 (Microbus) Super Beatle VW 181 (The Thing) VW Sedan 32 (Dasher) VW Station Wagon 33 (Dasher)

Source: U.S. Environmental Protection Agency, *1974 Gas Mileage Guide for Car Buyers*, February 1974.

consuming standard model? From an energy conservation point of view, smaller cars are desirable. From the consumer's point of view, totally apart from conservation, small cars are also advantageous because they are more economical to run. As gasoline prices rise, the circumstances seem ripe for a shift to smaller, more energy conserving cars.

In the face of this, auto manufacturers have raised car prices in a way that discourages the trend toward small cars. Price increases of compacts

Table 4–9. Average Price Increases[a] on New American Cars from April 1973 to June 1974, by Manufacturer and Type

Manufacturer	Full sized	Inter- mediate	Compact	Subcompact
	Average percent increase			
American Motors	2.1	5.2	10.7	18.3 [b]
Chrysler	10.8	11.8	16.6	
Ford	8.3	15.7	20.6	20.6
General Motors	7.8	11.4	11.6	19.7
	Average dollar increase			
American Motors	$ 98	$154	$266	$383 [b]
Chrysler	484	·388	427	
Ford	395	496	492	444
General Motors	421	380	300	422

[a]For all models produced by each company in 1973 and 1974.
[b]Not applicable.
Source: Automotive News, April 30, 1973, "Retail-Delivered Prices of '73 U.S. Models," pp. 40, 42; April 24, 1974, "Retail-Delivered Prices of '74 U.S. Models," pp. 44, 47; May 27, 1974, "Prices of '74 GM Cars," p. 20; June 3, 1974, "AMC, Chrysler Prices," p. 19, and Ford Motor Company, News Releases, Sept. 8, 1973; December 11, 1973; May 8, 1974.

and subcompacts averaged more than any other models during three price increases between April 1973 and June 1974. Compact and subcompact prices in this period went up 18 to 21 percent compared to increases of from 2 to 10 percent for full sized models (Table 4-9). Price increases that minimize the difference between small and large cars work to offset the otherwise strong consumer incentive to buy energy saving and money saving compacts. This is a good illustration of the basic point made throughout this book—energy conservation is not solely or even chiefly up to consumers: producers are key, and at times the chief decision makers.

LOCAL TRAVEL

Over three-fifths of all the miles driven by automobiles in 1969–70 were on trips of less than 30 miles. Over half the miles driven by automobiles were on trips of under 20 miles (Table 4-10). In energy terms this means a large portion of auto use occurs in stop-and-go local traffic that uses the most gasoline per mile and causes the most pollution.

Use of the car for local travel has become important because American cities are so spread out and because public transit is so inadequate in most places. The lack of public transit for most activities has forced people to buy cars. Once people have cars, they tend to use them for everything, even when public transit is available. Car ownership makes suburbs possible. Only

Table 4-10.   Annual Car Miles Driven, by Length of Trip, 1969-1970

Length of trip	Number (billions)	Percent	Cumulative percent
Total miles driven	777	100	
Under 5 miles	122	16	16
6–10	119	15	31
11–15	96	12	43
16–20	71	9	52
21–30	91	12	64
31–99	145	19	83
100 and over	133	17	100

Source: Unpublished data from U.S. Department of Transportation, Federal Highway Administration, *Nationwide Personal Transportation Study*, Washington, D.C.

with the car's flexibility can people live in spread-out areas beyond walking distance of stores and schools and beyond anything but feeder transit lines.

Early cities were walking cities. The streets were narrow; people lived close together, and they could find everything they needed within a few blocks. With the advent of public transportation, the trolley and railroad, cities developed along the transit lines and at transit stops. Much larger and more spread-out cities were now possible, but still people were clustered. It was only with the prosperity following World War II, the accompanying growth of car ownership, and the construction of superhighways that the auto and the suburbs became a part of the American scene. Now residential development was possible in all directions.

Suburban growth was not designed to encourage public transit use. Ridership began to decline, and with passenger decline came operating losses, increased fares, and decreased service. All this brought on further declines in passengers, further deficits, and a repeat of the cycle. As more and more people switched to cars, some of the pleasures and advantages of the car were lost. Instead of speeding to its destination, the car might get caught in a traffic jam. Instead of enjoying a fresh breeze the driver is more likely to wish for air conditioning to shut out the exhaust fumes from other vehicles.[8]

The impact of cities' historical development is evident today in the pattern of car ownership and use. It is least common in the central cities of metropolitan areas (Table 4-11). These are the most densely populated areas. Shops are fairly easy to reach on foot or by public transit. The relationship between population density, age of the city, and car ownership can be seen in the work of Lansing and Hendricks.[9] They distinguish between old and new central cities. Old central cities are Baltimore, Boston, Chicago, St. Louis, and Philadelphia. All had a population of over 500,000 in 1900. Lansing and Hendricks identify Cleveland, Detroit, Los Angeles, Pittsburgh, San Francisco,

Table 4-11. Number of Cars Owned, by Size and Type of Residential Location (percent of households)

Number of cars	Size of metro area[a] — Less than one million	Size of metro area[a] — One million or more	Location in metro area[a] — Central city	Location in metro area[a] — Ring	Outside metro area[a] — Urban	Outside metro area[a] — Rural
All households	100	100	100	100	100	100
None	16	19	29	8	15	11
1 or more	84	81	71	92	85	89
2 or more	48	40	29	56	40	47
3 or more	9	9	5	12	6	14

[a]Metro area (or SMSA) is an abbreviation for Standard Metropolitan Statistical Area and refers to a county or group of adjacent counties containing at least one city of 50,000.
Source: Washington Center for Metropolitan Studies' Lifestyles and Energy Surveys.

Table 4-12. Number of Cars Owned, by Type of Area and Family Income, 1963-1965 (percent of households)

Area and cars owned	Total	Income — Under $4,000	Income — $4,000-7,499	Income — $7,500 or more
Old central cities of 11 largest metro areas[a]	100	100	100	100
No car	54	85	46	14
One car	38	15	46	67
Two or more cars	8	[b]	8	19
New central cities of 11 largest metro areas[a]	100	100	100	100
No car	16	42	19	2
One car	62	58	76	53
Two or more cars	22	[b]	5	45
Smaller central cities	100	100	100	100
No car	20	52	12	3
One car	48	41	62	38
Two or more cars	32	7	26	59
All suburban areas	100	100	100	100
No car	4	16	3	1
One car	49	64	59	38
Two or more cars	47	20	38	61

[a]The 11 largest standard metropolitan statistical areas exclusive of the New York area have been divided into "old" and "new." The "old" cities are: Baltimore, Boston, Chicago, St. Louis, and Philadelphia. All had a population of over 500,000 in 1900. The "new" cities are: Cleveland, Detroit, Los Angeles, Pittsburgh, San Francisco, and Washington, D.C.
[b]Less than 0.5 percent.
Source: John B. Lansing and Gary Hendricks, *Automobile Ownership and Residential Density*, Ann Arbor: Institute for Social Research, June 1967, p. 16.

and Washington, D.C. as new central cities because these cities had not yet reached a population of 500,000 by 1900. The old central cities (those built up before the age of the automobile) have the highest number of households with no cars—almost 55 percent in 1963-65. In the new central cities only 15 percent reported having no automobile. In other words, the older cities were built to accommodate the walker, and to some extent they still do. Better public transportation lessens the need for a car in the old central cities as well. The relationship between age of central city and car ownership remain whatever the family income. (Table 4-12).

COMMUTING TO WORK

In 1960-70 commuting accounted for over 40 percent of all car miles travelled.[10] Throughout the 1960s, commuters turned to the automobile in increasing numbers. In 1960, two-thirds of all workers drove to work in cars; by 1970 that proportion had grown to over three-fourths.

The shift to cars occurred among workers living in both urban and rural areas.[11] The car continued to be the dominant commuter mode in 1973 when about 85 percent of all employed heads of households used private transportation, mainly the car, to go to work.[c] The privacy of those using private transportation was usually complete: over four-fifths traveled alone (Table 4-13). Some traveled considerable distances. Almost one-fourth reported going fifteen miles or more one way (Table 4-14). The use of the car and other private transportation, the absence of car pooling, and the fairly long distances involved all point to considerable energy use.

Why is public transit so little used? The main reasons given are either that it is not available at all, or if it is available, it is not convenient to home, work, or both. Commuters mentioned also the time it takes, needing a car for work, and the cost and discomfort of public transit (Table 4-15). The comparative disadvantage of public transit is obvious from data on commuting time. On the average, bus riders and other public transit commuters take twice as long to get to work as do car commuters.

Almost half the respondents who use public transit acknowledged, either implicitly or explicitly, that cost was an important factor in their choice. About 15 percent stated explicitly that public transit was cheaper for them than a car; another 30 percent reported they had no car or car pool available. The lack of a car is, of course, related to low income. Much smaller numbers of respondents cited other advantages of public transit such as being faster or more convenient than the auto (Table 4-16).

Most car commuters report that they do not have the option of public transit. Those who do were asked to compare cars and public transit on

[c]The men and women who were employed heads of households were about 60 percent of all employed persons in 1973.

Table 4-13. Means of Transportation to Work of Employed Heads of Households, 1973 (number and percent of employed household heads)

Transportation mode	Number (millions)	Percent
All employed heads	49.7[a]	100[a]
Private transportation—mode	42.2	85
Car	37.6	76
Truck	4.4	9
Motorcycle	.3	1
Taxi	.2	[b]
Public transit	3.8	8
Bus or streetcar	2.4	5
Subway, elevated train	1.1	2
Commuter train	.8	2
Walk or bicycle	2.3	5
Unknown	2.1	4
Private transportation—presence of others	42.2	100
Alone	35.0	83
With others	6.6	16
One other	3.7	9
2 or more	2.8	7

[a]Parts do not add exactly because some household heads used more than one means of transportation.
[b]Less than 0.5 percent.
Source: Washington Center for Metropolitan Studies' Lifestyles and Energy Surveys.

Table 4-14. Distance to Work of Employed Heads of Households by Means of Transportation, 1973 (percent of employed household heads)

Distance to work	Total	Private transportation	Public transit
All employed heads	100	100	100
Less than 5 miles	33	31	20
5–14	31	34	25
15 and over	24	24	45
No fixed place/unknown	13	11	10

Source: Washington Center for Metropolitan Studies' Lifestyles and Energy Surveys.

Table 4–15.   Percent of Employed Heads of Households, by Main
Reasons for Not Using Public Transit, 1973

Reason	Percent
All employed heads of households using private transportation	100[a]
Public transit is:	
Not readily available	71
Not available at all	57
Not convenient to work	10
Not convenient to home	7
Takes too long	9
Costs as much or more than private transportation	5
Uncomfortable	4
Need auto for work	6
Other	5
Unknown	11

[a]Does not add because some respondents gave more than one reason.

Source: Washington Center for Metropolitan Studies' Lifestyles and Energy
Surveys.

Table 4–16.   Percent of Employed Heads of Households, by Main
Reasons for Using Public Transit, 1973

Reasons	Percent
Employed heads of households using public transit	100
No car or carpool available	30
No drivers license	11
Public transit cheaper than auto	17
Public transit faster than auto	10
Convenience	16
Other	4
Unknown	11

Source: Washington Center for Metropolitan Studies' Lifestyles and Energy
Surveys.

time and cost. Some three-fourths of the car commuters who had a choice felt
that public transit would take more time; 40 percent felt that public transit
would cost more (Table 4-17). On the other hand, only about 15 percent of bus
commuters felt they were saving time over what it would take to drive in a car
(Table 4-18).

Table 4-19 illustrates how public transit ridership might be increased, given present routing and time schedules. The row titled "Public transit
users" gives the percentage of employed heads of households who presently go
to work by subway, bus or trolley. The row titled "Public transit users plus easy
switchers" gives the percentage of employed heads of households who presently

Table 4-17. Employed Heads of Households Using Private Transit: Comparison with Time and Cost of Commuting to Work on Public Transit, 1973

Time and cost	Percent
Employed heads of households using private transportation	100
Time by public transit would be[a]	
More	74
The same (within 10 minutes)	23
Less	3
Cost by public transit would be[b]	
More	40
The same (within $0.20)	36
Less	25

[a]Excludes unknowns. Distribution is presented for the 11.8 million heads of households for whom comparative data are available.

[b]The comparison is between the total cost of public transit and out-of-pocket car costs. Excludes unknowns. Distribution is for the 8.8 million heads of households for whom comparative data are available.

Source: Washington Center for Metropolitan Studies' Lifestyles and Energy Surveys.

Table 4-18. Employed Heads of Households Using Public Transit: Comparison with Commuting Time on Private Transit, 1973

Commuting time	Percent
Employed heads of households using public transportation[a]	100
Time by private transit would be	
More	16
The same (within 10 minutes)	33
Less	50

[a]Excludes unknowns. Distribution is for the 3.2 million heads of households for whom comparative data are available.

Source: Washington Center for Metropolitan Studies' Lifestyles and Energy Surveys.

use public transit plus those who could switch to public transit and not spend more time commuting. If all those who could switch would do so, the number of public transit users in the United States would increase from 3.8 million to 6.9 million—an increase of over 80 percent.

As can be seen from the table, the greatest potential presently for increasing public transit use is in the large metropolitan areas and in the central cities of metropolitan areas. In both, without increasing commuting time and

Table 4-19.   Present and Potential Users of Public Transit, by Size and Type of Area, 1973

Present and potential users of public transit	*Size of metro area*		*Location in metro area*		*Outside metro area*	
	Less than 1 million	*1 million or more*	*Central city*	*Ring*	*Urban*	*Rural*
	Number in millions					
All employed heads of households	15.5	20.2	15.7	20.0	6.1	7.9
	Percent					
All employed heads of households	100	100	100	100	100	100
Public transit users	4	15	13	8	0	2
Public transit users plus easy switchers[a]	12	24	24	14	1	2
Public transit users plus all possible switchers[b]	34	49	53	34	5	2

[a]Includes those private transit users who could switch to public transit and not spend more time commuting.
[b]Includes those who could switch but who then would spend more time commuting.
Source: Washington Center for Metropolitan Studies' Lifestyles and Energy Surveys.

given current routing and scheduling, public transit use could be increased by 10 percent and serve about one-quarter of all employed heads of households. Changes in routes, schedules and cost could probably attract more commuters in all types of locations.

SUBURBAN GROWTH AND COMMUTING PATTERNS

Suburban growth has been rapid over the decade of the 1960s. In 1960 one-tenth of all workers lived in suburbs of metropolitan areas of 100,000 or more; by 1970, over one-third of all workers lived in suburbs.[12] Suburban dwellers' commuting habits reflect their higher incomes and higher energy use patterns. Suburbanites are more likely than central city dwellers to use their cars for commuting and they are more likely to have to travel further to get to work (Table 4-20).

Most suburbanites do not work in the central city. Two-thirds of all workers living outside the central city (in SMSA's of 100,000 or more) in 1970 also worked outside the central city (Table 4-21). This means that a radial transit system geared to moving people from the suburbs to the central city cannot meet most suburban commuting needs.

For the third of suburbanites who work in the central city, radial

Table 4-20. Means of Transportation and Distance to Work by Size and Type of Area, 1973 (percent of employed heads of households)

Transportation mode and distance to work	Size of metro area		Location in metro area		Outside metro area	
	Less than 1 million	1 million or more	Central city	Ring	Urban	Rural
All employed heads of households[a]	100	100	100	100	100	100
Transportation mode						
Private transit	90	81	81	88	91	81
Public transit	4	15	13	8	0	2
Walk or bicycle	5	3	4	4	11	4
Unknown means	3	2	3	2	1	14
Distance to work[b]						
Less than 5 miles	38	25	43	22	69	42
5–14 miles	41	39	35	43	22	27
15 or more	21	36	22	35	10	31

[a]Parts may not add because some heads of households used more than one means of transportation.
[b]Excludes no fixed place of work and unknown distance.
Source: Washington Center for Metropolitan Studies' Lifestyles and Energy Surveys.

Table 4-21. Place of Work for Workers Living in Metro Areas of 100,000 or More, by Residence In or Outside Central City, 1970

Residence and place of work	Percent of workers
All workers in metro areas of 100,000 or more[a]	100
Live in central city	45
Work in central city	36
Work outside central city	9
In ring	7
Outside metro area	2
Live outside central city	55
Work in central city	18
Work outside central city	37
In ring	33
Outside metro area	4

[a]Excludes unknowns.
Source: Prepared by the Washington Center for Metropolitan Studies using data from the U.S. Bureau of the Census, Census of Population 1970, *Detailed Characteristics.* Final Report PC (1)–D1, U.S. Summary, Washington, D.C.; U.S. Government Printing Office, 1973, Table 242, p. 830.

systems linking a suburban parking lot to the central city can be encouraged and are being tried. Radial systems can also encourage downtown shopping and cultural activities. But for the two-thirds who both live in the suburbs and work there, and for the myriad other activities which take place between parts of the suburbs, a car or something like it is necessary. One energy-conserving possibility for the suburbs is small vehicle transit. Small vehicle transit means the use of car pools, group taxis, jitneys, employer vans, minibuses, and similar vehicles. The advantages of small vehicle transit for the suburbs have been elaborated by Colin Walters of the Washington Center for Metropolitan Studies.[13]

HIGHLIGHTS

Americans covered about 6,000 miles per person in intercity travel in 1971. They travelled an average of 580 miles per person in airplanes, and over 150 miles per person in buses and trains. Americans even managed to travel an average of 20 passenger miles per person on inland waterways (see Table 4-1). Not all people took trips, of course. As the data on trips by household heads shows, some people took several trips; others took none at all—including many persons from lower income families. Eighty-five households out of 100 now have at least one car; 45 households out of 100 have two cars or more. Half the poor have none.

The car and the airplane, the most common ways of getting places, are also the most energy-intensive. Over half of all car mileage is in short trips, which frequently involve stop-and-go traffic, the most energy intensive type of car travel.

Car miles per gallon have declined in recent years. This decline has been caused mainly by increasing car weight, but is also associated with new energy-using features such as air conditioning.

For many household heads a car is the only way available to get to work. For families living in less densely populated areas—suburbs and rural areas particularly—the car may be necessary to get to stores, medical care, swimming pools, private schools, and other social activities. The trends in travel all point toward increasing energy use. These trends include:

- The increasing weight of cars and the subsequent decline in gasoline mileage.
- The substitution of air travel (the most energy intensive mode) for bus and rail (the least energy intensive modes).
- The dispersion of the population to suburbs, where public transit service is inconvenient or not available and the car is the key to access to almost all activities.
- The increasing use of the auto for commuting to work, by all workers, regardless of place of residence.
- The increase in travel in general on the part of many (though not all) Americans.

DIRECTIONS FOR POLICY

With the new national awareness of energy as a scarce resource, the question is being raised about how the available transportation energy can be made to go farther. Air pollution in the cities—caused in large measure by cars—adds urgency to this question.

The general thrust of national energy transportation policy needs to be in the direction of encouraging bus and rail transportation between cities and within metropolitan areas, improving car gasoline mileage (or at least stopping the trend toward decreasing mileage), and discouraging excessive car use.

Possibilities for public transit are best in the cities, where people, shops, and other necessary services are clustered together. The need to reduce car use is also greatest in the central cities, for these are the areas which suffer most from auto-created air pollution. (This point is developed further in Chapter Six.)

The prospect for conventional public transit is least likely in suburban and rural areas because people live so far apart. An energy conserving possibility for the suburbs is small vehicle transit. Experiments to test the feasibility of the small vehicle transit need to be supported.

Those who presently have the option of using public transit need to be enticed to do so by better routing and time schedules, lower fares, and better cared for buses, subways, and trolleys. One way some communities have decreased bus commuter time is by creating special bus lanes during rush hours. Others have discouraged car commuters by increasing parking costs in the central city through parking taxes. Use of a mixture of these and other techniques should be encouraged. Bicycling could be fostered if safe bicycle commuter lanes were built and maintained.[14]

"Truth in energy" legislation is needed to provide all car buyers (of used as well as new cars) information about car weight and gasoline mileage.

Government programs aiding transportation should be redistributed with proportionately more funds to the energy conserving modes of travel—public transit, interurban and intersuburban transit and intercity bus and rail service. Additional funds for these purposes should be gotten from taxing cars by weight and from increased federal gasoline taxes. The proposals on cars are spelled out in greater detail in Chapter Eight.

Slowing the rate of growth of energy use in transportation depends in the long run on increasing the gasoline mileage of cars, making public transit more attractive and available, and decreasing dependence on cars. Much more thought needs to be given to how our urban areas can be designed and managed in ways that permit an attractive choice between cars and public transit for local trips.

Chapter Five

The Energy Gap—Poor to Well Off

Like the income gap, the energy gap poses significant public policy problems. Now that Americans have learned that fossil fuel energy, like all natural resources, is finite, they must consider distribution and pricing policies that will give all Americans a fair share of energy. Present maldistribution must be recognized, as well as the possibility of present and future shortages.

This chapter shows how poor, middle income, and well off families use energy. The poor use less; they pay higher prices for the energy they must have; and, more than any other group of Americans, they suffer from exposure to the noxious byproducts of energy consumption and production.

Energy use by the poor is almost entirely for essentials—space and water heating, cooking, food refrigeration, and lighting. When fuel supplies are limited and increasingly expensive, the wealthy can buy as much as they want, if price is the only obstacle. The poor, on the other hand, are inevitably deprived by rising costs. They are forced to forego some measure of pleasant or necessary life support—if not in heat and light or in gasoline for necessary transportation, then in the loss of amenities.

In 1972–73 poor households used an average of 207 million Btu's of natural gas, electricity and gasoline. The well off used more than twice as much. The middle income groups fell between. Figure 5-1 illustrates the stairstep pattern of energy consumption. The same stairstep pattern occurs for each fuel separately. The incline of the steps differs, however: as income rises, the increase in natural gas consumption is gradual, the increase in electricity is intermediate, and the increase in gasoline is sharp. The well off use almost one and one-half as much natural gas as the poor, over two and one-quarter as much electricity, and over five times as much gasoline. The well off use more of each than the middle income groups, but the differences are not as great, as Figure 5-1 shows.

Natural gas is used primarily for heating and cooking. It seems reasonable that, for these necessities, the less advantaged cannot reduce

Figure 5-1.   The Better Off You Are, The More Energy You Use

(Millions of Btu's per Household in 1972-1973)

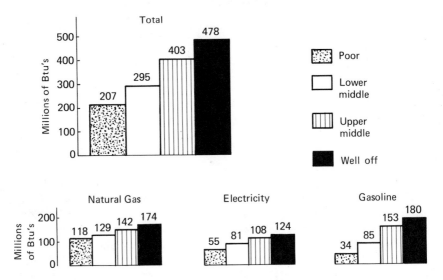

Source: Washington Center for Metropolitan Studies' Lifestyles and
Energy Surveys.

consumption much below that of the well off. Conversely, there would seem to
be little reason for the well off to increase their consumption greatly.

Electricity is used mainly in appliances and lighting, and thus is
part luxury and part necessity. Here, as with natural gas, there seems to be a
point when the well off prefer to spend their money for things other than
electricity using devices.

Gasoline is truly the fuel of both necessity and pleasure. Gasoline
may be necessary for shopping and commuting to work, but many gallons of
gasoline can also be consumed on family vacations, weekend excursions, second
cars, extra large cars, and so on. It is for these reasons that the well off use more
than five times as much gasoline as the poor and more than twice as much as the
lower middle group.

The energy gap reflects the income gap, but not precisely. From
available data, average Btu's used per household do not appear to rise as rapidly
as do average incomes, but this may be misleading. The energy gap might
increase if exact measurement of all the energy expended indirectly in supplying
households with various goods and services was possible. Fossil fuels and
energy are used to make home furnishings, clothing, jewelry, appliances,

recreational vehicles, and an almost infinite number of other things. It takes energy to produce, transport, cook, and serve the meals people eat outside the home; to manufacture and service the planes or rented cars they ride; to produce, transport, and use the materials and services provided in hotels; and to make, produce, warehouse, and transport the materials used in constructing or remodelling homes. It takes energy to make an aluminum pan, a nylon blouse, or a garden fence. Indirect energy use encompasses all of these ways of consuming fuel that can be attributed to households.

One way to think about indirect energy use is to think about all the possessions people have. Energy is used in creating virtually every item. The more a household has, the more energy has been expended in producing, transporting, storing, and selling those possessions and, consequently, the more indirect energy that household is using.

The Energy Policy Project of the Ford Foundation estimates that indirect energy consumption of the well off is about three times that of the poor[1] (Table 5-1). This estimate is useful as a beginning, but as the Energy Policy Project states, the estimates are very rough and leave a substantial part of indirect energy use (categorized as "other") to be identified and quantified. The estimate also incorporates the arguable assumption that government services are distributed equally among all income groups.

The purchase of energy depends on purchasing power, and a more realistic measure than current income of the ability to buy goods and services is needed, as well as an accurate measure of total energy the consumer actually buys. This would include accumulated wealth in the form of real estate, business equity, securities, and interest-bearing assets. Accumulated wealth is disproportionately greater among families with the highest incomes and then declines sharply. Middle income families have relatively little wealth; low income families virtually none.[2]

Lower middle and low income families also have less security that comes with employee benefits such as medical insurance, private pension plans and employer-paid life insurance. Therefore, the capacity of less advantaged households to use current income for buying expensive energy using goods or services is severely limited. This is especially true in the case of items that are costly both in the energy and capital required to produce them as well as the energy and cost to operate them.

Our inability to measure all the energy used in producing, transporting, warehousing, and selling goods and services, and to measure wealth as distinct from income, does not permit as much precision as we would like. If available, such information would give a much more accurate measure of the energy gap. Under the circumstances, we can only say that it stands to reason that households which have the wealth to command a wide range of costly goods and services use far more energy than those which are poor.

The average income of the well off is almost ten times that of the

Table 5-1. Indirect and Direct Energy Use, by Energy Source and Income, 1972-1973[a]

Energy use and source	Poor[b]	Lower middle	Upper middle	Well off
		Btu index (poor = 100)		
All households	100	150	220	280
Indirect	100	160	240	310
Direct	100	140	190	230
Natural gas	100	110	120	150
Electricity	100	150	200	230
Gasoline	100	250	450	530
		Average Btu's per household (millions)		
All households	560	844	1,234	1,573
Indirect	353	549	831	1,095
Direct	207	295	403	478
Natural gas	118	129	142	174
Electricity	55	81	108	124
Gasoline	34	85	153	180
		Households' mean income		
Dollars	2,500	8,000	14,000[c]	24,500[c]
Index (poor = 100)	100	320	560	980

[a]Families were asked their income for the previous year (1972), and thus the income groups are defined as of that year. In this and subsequent tables the date in the title refers to the year for household characteristics (1973) or the year for energy consumption data (1972-73).

[b]The definition of the poor takes account of both income and family size. For convenience and brevity in this and subsequent tables the poor are referred to as an income group only.

[c]The averages for the upper middle and well off are adjusted using unpublished data from the U.S. Bureau of the Census.

Source: Direct energy use derived from Washington Center for Metropolitan Studies' Lifestyles and Energy Surveys and indirect energy use from Ford Foundation, Energy Policy Project, *A Time to Choose: America's Energy Future*, Cambridge, Mass.: Ballinger, 1974, Chapter 5.

poor; the average wealth of the well off is even greater. Our expectation is that when more research is done and all the spheres of discretionary consumption of the well off are taken into account, the energy gap will begin to approximate the income gap, and the very rich will tower over all with their private yachts, executive jets, and multiple homes and cars.

This study takes a first step. It compares the consumption of fuels people buy themselves (their primary energy consumption) with their current income. The consumption figures are based on utility bills and the incomes from information supplied by the household. This approach avoids complex measurement problems, and at the same time provides necessary detail from a rich source of basic data. The results show that the more income a household has, the more energy it uses. This is true for space and water heating, the use of appliances and lighting, and for traveling.

Other research has pointed toward this finding, but usually the investigations have been limited to a single sphere of energy use, and have lacked precise electricity and natural gas data for individual households.[3]

CHARACTERISTICS OF INCOME GROUPS

Four income groups are used in this analysis: the poor, lower middle, upper middle, and well off. Families and individuals were defined as poor if their incomes fell below certain levels. The levels varied with size of the family and were based on the U.S. government's definition of poor and near poor for 1972.[a] In this study, the average income of poor households was $2,500.

The lower middle group includes all the nonpoor whose income was under $12,000 in 1972. (The average income of the lower middle households was about $8,000.) The upper middle group includes those with incomes between $12,000 and $15,999 in 1972, and the well off are those with incomes of $16,000 or more. The average income of upper middle households was $14,000, and of the well off, $24,500. The poor, upper middle, and well off each comprise about one-fifth of all households; the lower middle about two-fifths.[b]

The average household surveyed had three persons. Poor and lower middle income households were somewhat smaller, averaging 2.6 persons. Upper middle households averaged about 3.5 persons, and the well off 3.6 persons. The smaller households of the poor and lower middle groups are reflections of the life cycle position of the household heads. Disproportionately many are 65 or over and living alone (Table 5-2).

When the household head is under 45, poor and lower middle households are less likely than others to have children. Husband-wife households were least common among the poor, almost half of whom are elderly, and most common among the well off. The poor are the most likely to have no earners and the least likely to have two or more earners. The reverse is true of the well off.

The likelihood of the household head's being a professional or manager, having a college degree, owning a home, and owning property other than a home all rise with income. In general, the lower middle group is more like the poor, and the upper middle group is more like the well off (Table 5-2).

[a]The U.S. government's definition was modified for use with survey data for which income is reported within a particular range rather than a specific figure. The poverty thresholds are as follows: under $3,000 for one or two people; under $5,000 for three to four people; under $7,000 for five to six people; and under $9,000 for families of seven or more. See Appendix A2 for detail.

[b]The poor, lower middle, upper middle, and well off are 18, 42, 19, and 20 percent, respectively, of all households.

Table 5-2.   Household Characteristics by Income, 1973 (percent of households)

Household characteristics	Poor	Lower middle	Upper middle	Well off
All households	100	100	100	100
Life cycle				
Head less than 45	33	41	56	48
With children	26	28	47	39
Without children	7	13	9	8
45 to 64	21	34	38	47
65 and over	45	25	6	5
Persons in household				
1	37	21	4	1
2	19	36	22	22
3	14	17	20	21
4	9	14	29	26
5 or more	21	12	26	29
Household structure				
Husband/wife	41	66	90	93
Other	59	34	10	7
Number of earners				
None	56	25	3	2
1	33	53	47	42
2 or more	11	23	51	56
College educated household head	12	25	38	58
Head prof. or mgr.	7	20	34	56
Own home	47	62	76	89
Own other property	7	17	23	31
Head black	23	8	5	3

Source: Washington Center for Metropolitan Studies' Lifestyles and Energy Surveys.

Blacks are found disproportionately among the poor and disproportionately absent among the upper middle and well off groups.

HEATING HOMES

Keeping warm in the winter takes the most residential energy, and the poor use less energy for this purpose than other income groups do. This is true whether the space heating fuel is natural gas, electricity, or fuel oil. The difference between the well off and the poor is more marked with electric space heating than with natural gas. The well off use 40 percent more energy than the poor when heating with natural gas, and 100 percent more energy than the poor when heating with electricity (Table 5-3).

The WCMS comparison between income groups on the amount of fuel oil used is more indirect. The comparison is between those who spend less than $200 per year for fuel oil and those who spend more. About half the poor

Table 5-3. Amount of Natural Gas and Electricity Used for Space Heating, and Fuel Oil Cost, by Income, 1972-1973

Fuel used for space heating	*Poor*	*Lower middle*	*Upper middle*	*Well off*	*Number of households (millions)*
Average Btu's per household (millions)[a]					
Natural gas	132	142	154	184	41.3
Electricity	144	210	275	291	6.0
Btu index[a] (poor = 100)					
Natural gas	100	108	117	139	41.3
Electricity	100	146	191	202	6.0
Percent of households[b]					
Yearly cost of fuel oil	100	100	100	100	10.0
Under $200	49	40	40	32	4.1
$200 and over	51	60	60	68	5.9

[a]Only households using the fuel for space heating are included. The fuel probably is used by the households in other tasks (water heating, cooking) as well. The fuel consumed in these other tasks is included.

[b]Households paying for fuel oil and reporting the cost.

Source: Washington Center for Metropolitan Studies' Lifestyles and Energy Surveys.

spend less than $200 for fuel oil, while 40 percent of the middle income groups and only one-third of the well off spend so little.

One of three fuels—natural gas, electricity, or fuel oil—is the heating fuel for 85 percent of all poor households and about 95 percent of all other households. The other fuels used are propane, coal, wood, and in some cases, nothing at all (Table 5-4).

Influences on Energy Use in Heating

A variety of factors affect the amount of energy used for space heating, including climate, the structure of the house, and the family's style of living. Whatever the characteristic examined, the poor and lower middle income groups use less energy than others. The comparisons are made using household consumption of natural gas because natural gas is the most common space heating fuel, and therefore involves enough households to permit comparisons by both housing characteristics and income at the same time.[c]

[c]The comparisons of energy use by heating characteristics include all natural gas using households. About 90 percent of these households use natural gas for space heating and other uses; the remaining households use natural gas only for other purposes such as water heating or cooking. Because the latter group are such a small proportion of the natural gas using households, and because their use of natural gas is so small, it seems likely that their inclusion does not seriously affect the findings.

Table 5-4. Type of Space Heating Fuel Used, by Income, 1973 (percent of households)

Space heating fuel	Poor	Lower middle	Upper middle	Well off
All households[a]	100	100	100	100
Natural gas	54	62	62	61
Fuel oil[b]	23	22	22	28
Electricity	8	9	11	7
Bottled gas	9	5	4	4
Other and none	9	3	2	c

[a]The different fuels add to more than 100 because some households use more than one fuel for heating.
[b]Includes kerosene.
[c]Less than 0.5 percent.
Source: Washington Center for Metropolitan Studies' Lifestyles and Energy Surveys.

Table 5-5. Climate and Housing Characteristics, by Income, 1973 (percent of households)

Climate and structural characteristics	Poor	Lower middle	Upper middle	Well off
All households	100	100	100	100
Climate under 3,500 heating degree days	41	33	29	25
Apartment	32	26	13	8
Less than 5 rooms	47	35	18	8
Living room less than 200 sq. ft.	62	55	36	29
Less than 15 windows	82	73	67	45
No picture window	70	56	38	29
Some storm windows	31	49	54	63
Protected doors[a][b]	41	53	58	70
Basement in single-family homes	31	45	52	61
Insulation in single-family homes[b]	41	78	86	94

[a]Includes entrances with storm doors and doors opening on to apartment hallways and other heated areas.
[b]Excludes unknowns.
Source: Washington Center for Metropolitan Studies' Lifestyles and Energy Surveys.

Climate. Climate is an important influence on energy consumption. More poor households than others live in warmer areas (Table 5-5). However, even when climate is taken into account, the poor still use less energy than the well off (Table 5-6). In the warmer areas, the well off use about one and one-half times the natural gas of the poor. In the really cold areas (5,500 heating degree days and over), the well off use one and one-quarter times the natural gas of the poor.

Table 5-6. Index of Average Amount of Natural Gas Used per Household by Climate, Selected Structural Characteristics, and Income, 1972-1973 (Poor households = 100)

Climate and structural characteristics	Poor	Lower middle	Upper middle	Well off
All households	100	109	120	147
3,500–5,499 degree days	100	109	130	160
Single-family home	100	115	123	146
10–14 windows	100	107	115	128
Some storm windows	100	94	100	118
No storm windows	100	119	131	174
Foundation other than basement	100	121	124	139
No insulation	100	109	142[a]	[b]

[a]Results subject to substantial variation because of the small number of interviews in this group.
[b]Not reported because number of interviews too small for statistical stability.
Source: Washington Center for Metropolitan Studies' Lifestyles and Energy Surveys.

Structure of the Dwelling. The poor are more likely than other households to live in apartments, to have fewer rooms in their homes whether they live in single family homes or apartments, and to have smaller living rooms, fewer windows, and no large windows (Table 5-5). These are all characteristics of dwellings that work to conserve energy, although the structures usually were built without energy conservation in mind.

The features people add intentionally to conserve energy are least common in poor homes. Two-fifths or less of the homes of the poor have insulation and basements in single family homes, and storm windows and doors. Poor households very often cannot afford to buy storm windows or add insulation themselves when they are home owners. As renters (half the poor are tenants), they are not in a strong position to demand improvements.

The homes of some poor households are deficient in very basic ways. Some 15 percent of the poor do not have central heating; almost 10 percent share a bathroom with another family, or have no indoor toilet at all; and 8 percent have no hot running water (Table 5-7).

The homes of the well off are likely to have storm windows and doors, insulation, and basements—unobtrusive and desirable energy conserving features. From a structural point of view, an important part of the greater energy use of the well off can be attributed to spaciousness and other architectural features of their homes. The well off are more likely to live in single family homes, to have homes with five rooms or more, (including a large living room), and to have more than fifteen windows and a picture window. The upper middle income households are similar to the well off in most respects, and the lower middle suffer many of the disadvantages of the poor.

Table 5-7.   Selected Dwelling Characteristics, by Income, 1972–
1973 (percent of households)

Selected characteristics	Poor	Lower middle	Upper middle	Well off
All households	100	100	100	100
Central heating	85	94	95	96
Bathroom				
None or shared	9	1	a	a
One	82	75	58	30
Two or more	8	24	42	70
Water heating fuel				
Electric	31	28	26	22
Natural gas	42	54	57	59
Oil	2	5	7	12
Bottled gas	5	2	4	3
Other	a	1	2	a
None	8	3	1	1
Not sure	12	6	4	2

aLess than 0.5 percent.
Source: Washington Center for Metropolitan Studies' Lifestyles and Energy Surveys.

Income affects selection of the home. The well off can afford to choose what they want; the poor must take what they can get—which in housing means the homes with the least desirable combinations of features.

When households with the same housing characteristics but different incomes are compared for natural gas consumption, the poor always use less energy than the upper middle and well off and almost always use less energy than the lower middle (Table 5-6).

House Temperature Control.   Almost half of all poor households have no thermostat or valve to control room temperature: one-fifth of the lower middle group were in this position, 8 percent of the upper middle, and only 2 percent of the well off. In spite of their lack of room temperature control, most poor households (90 percent) reported that their homes were at the temperature they preferred. About 2 percent of all households felt the daytime temperature of their home was too high; 8 percent of the poor households (compared with only 1 percent of the well off) felt their home temperatures were too low. The most common room temperature during the day in the winter of 1972–73 was 70° to 72° for Americans in all income groups. The most common night temperature was 69° or under (Table 5-8). The poor were slightly less likely to have space heaters than were the other income groups.

The poor use less natural gas than other income groups when families having home temperatures of 70°-72° during the day are compared

Table 5-8. Aspects of Winter Room Temperature and Its Control, by Income, 1973 (percent of households)

Winter temperature control	Poor	Lower middle	Upper middle	Well off
All households	100	100	100	100
Temperature control				
Thermostat or valve	54	81	92	98
None	46	19	8	2
Daytime temperature choice[a]				
Actual same as preferred	90	93	94	97
Actual colder than preferred	8	5	4	1
Actual warmer than preferred	2	2	2	2
Usual day temperature[a]				
69° and under	17	14	14	13
70°–72°	49	52	53	55
73°–75°	23	24	24	26
76° and over	11	10	9	6
Usual night temperature[a]				
Less than 65°	36	20	13	13
65°–69°	21	31	33	33
70°–72°	28	34	36	38
73° and over	15	14	18	16
Bedroom window at night				
Open	31	36	29	35
Not open	69	64	71	65
Presence of electric space heaters				
None	87	86	85	81
One or more	13	14	15	19

[a]Excludes unknowns.
Source: Washington Center for Metropolitan Studies' Lifestyles and Energy Surveys.

Table 5-9. Index of Average Amount of Natural Gas Used per Household by Winter Room Temperature and Its Control, by Income, 1972-1973 (Poor households = 100)

Temperature characteristics and control	Poor	Lower middle	Upper middle	Well off
All households	100	109	120	147
Usual day temperature				
70°–72°	100	120	134	162
73°–75°	100	83	85[a]	113[a]
Usual night temperature				
Less than 65°	100	90	115[a]	145[a]
Bedroom window at night				
Open	100	126	160	175
Not open	100	109	112	146

[a]Results subject to substantial variation because of the small number of interviews in this group.
Source: Washington Center for Metropolitan Studies' Lifestyles and Energy Surveys.

(Table 5-9). Families having home temperatures at the extremes show less consistent patterns of natural gas consumption. These differences may be related to differences in the family's ability to control room temperature. The poor and lower middle income households use less natural gas than do the upper middle and well off groups, whether or not they keep their windows open at night during the winter.

APPLIANCES AND LIGHTING

Virtually all households have a stove, refrigerator, and television. Beyond these three appliances, ownership varies considerably by appliance and by income (Table 5-10). The refrigerator is necessary for storing food, and the stove for cooking. Television has probably become a universal household appliance because it is a relatively inexpensive form of entertainment and information (free except for electricity costs after purchase) and because it is always available. With roughly the same amount of money, a family of four can either go to the movies once a month for a year or buy a television set and see movies every day (if they are so inclined) for a number of years.

As would be expected, the poor are the least likely to have the most energy consuming or the fancy versions of the basic appliances. For example, one-quarter of the poor have color television while three-fourths of the well off

Table 5-10. Households with Selected Appliances, by Income, 1973 (percent)

Appliance	Poor	Lower middle	Upper middle	Well off
Stove	95	97	99	98
Refrigerator	98	100	100	100
Manual defrost	74	51	39	30
Frost-free[a]	24	48	60	69
Freezer	23	30	38	47
Clothes washer	62	73	89	91
Wringer	18	9	5	1
Automatic[a]	44	64	84	90
Clothes dryer	24	45	70	80
Dishwasher	3	13	39	55
Television—any type	94	96	98	98
Color	27	48	63	74

[a]Households which reported having both versions of the appliance are included in this group only.

Source: Washington Center for Metropolitan Studies' Lifestyles and Energy Surveys.

do. One-quarter of the poor have frost-free refrigerators compared with over two-thirds of the well off. The higher energy use of the frost-free refrigerator is not well known, but if a poor household had known this and, trying to make ends meet, had tried to buy a regular refrigerator instead of a frost-free model, it probably could not have, for in recent years, only the frost-free model has been available in most retail stores.

Poor households generally use less energy for lighting. They have fewer rooms lit in the evening. They are less likely than other households to keep a light on all night, and they are more likely to buy bulbs which use 75 watts or less (Table 5-11).

Laundry Equipment

The poor lag considerably behind the well off in laundry equipment. Nine-tenths of the well off have washing machines and eight-tenths have dryers. Less than two-thirds of the poor have washers and only one-quarter have dryers. Three-fourths of the lower middle have washers and nearly half have dryers.

The washing machines of the well off are virtually all automatic. Of the poor who have washers, about two-thirds have an automatic and one-third have the old-fashioned wringer type.

For households without washers of any type, the laundromat is obviously an important institution. For households without cars (almost half of the poor), a distant laundromat could multiply the time and human effort necessary to clean clothes.

Dishwasher and Food Freezer

The dishwasher and the food freezer are the least common major appliances among the well-off, only about half having them. These appliances are

Table 5-11. Household Home Lighting Habits, by Income, 1973 (percent of households)

Home lighting habits[a]	Poor	Lower middle	Upper middle	Well off
All households	100	100	100	100
Number of rooms lit in the evening				
0–1	63	53	38	32
2	24	31	35	31
3 or more	13	16	27	37
Lights on all night	30	35	41	42
Buy bulbs of 75 watts or less	70	61	50	46

[a]Excludes unknowns.

Source: Washington Center for Metropolitan Studies' Lifestyles and Energy Surveys.

even more uncommon among the other income groups: one-quarter of the poor have freezers and only 3 percent have dishwashers.

The automatic clotheswasher, clothes dryer, frost-free refrigerator, food freezer, and dishwasher are all time savers. With them, the mother's time (or the time of others in less traditional families) is freed for rest, leisure, and for activities which can enrich the family's life, either culturally or financially.

Air Conditioning

Air conditioning is one of the major energy users. Residential, commercial, and industrial air conditioning combined are responsible for summer peak loads and brownouts.

As with other appliances, the poor are less likely to enjoy air conditioning than are other income groups. One-fifth of the poor have air conditioning compared with two-thirds of the well off (Table 5-12). When poor households have air conditioning, it is almost always a window unit. Among the well off with air conditioning, about half have window units; the other half have central air conditioning.

The majority of households in all income groups reported a willingness to buy air conditioners which would cost $50 more initially but $20 less a year to operate. The percentage of respondents agreeing with this statement went from 70 percent among the poor to 93 percent among the well off. Poor households are the least likely to buy air conditioners at all. Thus as the likelihood of the household's actually purchasing an air conditioner rose, so did the likelihood of that household's being willing to take into account long term operating costs.

Appliance Index

The appliance index described in Chapter Three included all the major appliances with weights according to average energy use as estimated by the Edison Electrical Institute and the American Gas Association. The higher a family's score on the appliance index, the more energy using appliances that family had in its home.

Poor households had low scores and well off households had high scores. Almost two-thirds of the poor had scores of less than 40; only about one-tenth of the upper middle and well off had such low scores. Lower middle income households were more like the poor; about two-fifths of them had appliance index scores of less than 40 (Table 5-13).

The low appliance index scores of most poor households mean that the poor are doing without many of the work saving appliances other households have and enjoy.

Table 5-12. Air Conditioning Characteristics, by Income, 1973

Air conditioning characteristics	Poor	Lower middle	Upper middle	Well off
		Percent		
All households	100	100	100	100
Air conditioning	22	45	58	64
Window	18	34	39	33
Central	4	10	19	32
None	78	55	42	36
All households living in area with less than 1,000 cooling degree days	100	100	100	100
Air conditioning	9	27	42	51
None	91	73	58	49
All households living in area with 1,000 cooling degree days or more	100	100	100	100
Air conditioning	31	58	71	76
None	69	42	29	24
All households with air conditioning	100	100	100	100
1-3 rooms cooled	56	44	28	26
4 or more	44	56	72	74
All households	100	100	100	100
Buy air conditioner that:				
Costs $50 *less* and $20/yr *more* to operate	15	8	7	5
Costs $50 *more* and $20/yr *less* to operate	70	86	93	93
Don't know/No answer	16	6	1	2
		Btu index (electricity; poor = 100)		
All households	100	147	196	225
Air conditioning				
Some	100[a]	124	143	157
None	100	123	188	221

[a]Results subject to substantial variation because of the small number of interviews in the group.

Source: Washington Center for Metropolitan Studies' Lifestyles and Energy Surveys.

Table 5-13. Percent of Households, by Appliance Index, by Income, 1973

Appliance index	Poor	Lower middle	Upper middle	Well off
All households	100	100	100	100
Less than 40	65	39	13	10
40-59	21	30	40	26
60 and over	14	31	47	64

Source: Washington Center for Metropolitan Studies' Lifestyles and Energy Surveys.

AT THE GAS PUMP

Cars take people to work, to school, to parties, to supermarkets, to doctors, and to many other places. A car can be used for weekend excursions, long trips, or just local driving. How much a car is used for these activities—in fact, whether the household has a car at all—is strongly influenced by family income. Money or good credit is necessary to buy a car in the first place. Money is also necessary for repairs, insurance, licenses, and gasoline.

The poor use less energy in travel than does the rest of the population. The poor have fewer cars and use less gasoline in the cars they have. They take fewer long trips. When they do take long trips, the poor are less likely to use an airplane (the highest energy user). Lower middle income households also use comparatively little energy in travel.

Cars

Comparatively few of the poor and lower middle households have cars. The position of these less advantaged households with respect to car ownership improved during the 1960s, but was still dramatically lower than the more advantaged groups. Over the 1960s, an important change among the more advantaged groups was the increase in the number of households having two or more cars. For the lower middle and poor, there was a modest increase in the number of households having two or more cars, but the more striking point is that so many households remained without any car at all. Almost half the poor and one-sixth of the lower middle still had no car in 1973 (Table 5-14).

The poor have older cars than others and they buy more used cars. Seven-tenths of the cars owned by the poor were five years old or older, while less than four-tenths of the cars owned by the well off were that old (Table 5-15). About three-fifths of all cars are standard models. About one-fifth are compacts and subcompacts. The rest are vans, pickup trucks, and luxury cars. The van or pickup is somewhat more common among the poor, and the compact is somewhat more common among the well off (Table 5-15).

At first glance, it may seem extraordinary that the well off own proportionately more compacts than the poor. This seeming anomaly occurs because few of the poor own two cars or more compared with over three-fourths of the well off. The second or third car of a well off household is often a compact. Looking at the ratio of cars per hundred households, this becomes clearer. Poor households average fourteen compacts per hundred households while the well off average over 50. The poor average 42 standard cars per hundred households, while the well off have 115—an average of more than one per household (Table 5-16).

The more advantaged households have more cars and use much more gasoline than do less advantaged households. Well off and upper middle income

Table 5-14. Percent of Households, by Number of Cars Owned, and by Income,[a] 1960 and 1973

Income and car ownership	1960	1973
Poor	100	100
No car	65	47
One car	32	37
Two or more	3	16
Lower middle	100	100
No car	26	16
One car	64	52
Two or more	9	32
Upper middle	100	100
No car	8	4
One car	72	35
Two or more	20	61
Well off	100	100
No car	5	1
One car	56	21
Two or more	39	78

[a]For 1973 the income groups are defined as in other parts of this study. For 1960 the group defined as poor is the lowest fifth of the income distribution and the lower middle is defined as the second and third fifths; the upper middle and well off are the fourth and highest fifths respectively.

Source: Prepared by the Washington Center for Metropolitan Studies from U.S. Bureau of the Census, *Current Population Reports*, Series P-65, No. 18, August 11, 1967, "Special Report on Household Ownership and Purchase of Automobiles and Selected Household Durables: 1960-1967," Table 1, p. 5 and 1973 Washington Center for Metropolitan Studies' Lifestyles and Energy Surveys.

families together constitute two-fifths of all households, but they consume three-fifths of all the gasoline (Table 5-17). The poor consume the least gasoline. The poor (some 18 percent of all households) use only 5 percent of the gasoline, thus the gap between the poor and other income groups is greater with gasoline than with either natural gas or electricity.

Gasoline consumption was estimated for each household by multiplying the reported miles traveled times the miles per gallon reported for local driving for each car and summing over all cars. (See Appendix A2.) This method of estimating gasoline consumption is not as precise as the methods used for estimating natural gas and electricity consumption, but it was the best method, given the resources available, and yields plausible as well as significant results.

The low gasoline consumption of the poor and lower middle income households who have cars reflects both the fewer miles their cars are driven each year and better gasoline mileage.

Table 5-15. Car Characteristics, by Owner's Income, 1973
(percent of cars)

Car characteristics	Poor	Lower middle	Upper middle	Well off
All cars	100	100	100	100
Type of car				
Standard	61	62	62	58
Compact/subcompact	20	22	20	26
Luxury	4	4	8	7
Van or pickup truck	15	12	10	9
Age of car (model year)				
One year old ('72–'73)	8	16	21	26
2–4 years old ('69–'71)	23	28	34	37
5 years or more ('68 and older)	69	56	46	37
Bought				
New	26	45	47	63
Used	74	55	53	37
Miles per gallon locally				
Less than 14 miles per gallon	31	50	54	62
15–19	47	32	30	24
20 and over	22	17	16	14
Miles per gallon long distance				
Less than 14 miles per gallon	22	23	32	34
15–19	46	49	46	44
20 and over	32	29	22	22

Source: Washington Center for Metropolitan Studies' Lifestyles and Energy Surveys.

Gasoline Mileage

The poor get better gasoline mileage primarily because their cars are old, and older cars get better gasoline mileage than new models that tend to be heavier and more extensively equipped with energy using accessories (see Table 5-15). (See also Chapter Four for more detailed discussion of the mileage of old versus new cars.)

Over two-thirds of the cars used by the poor are reported to get over fifteen miles per gallon in local driving. Less than two-fifths (38 percent) of the cars used by the well off get mileage that good. Mileage on long distance travel improves for all income groups, but cars used by the poor are still reported to get somewhat better mileage than those of the more advantaged.

Miles Driven in 1972–73

The better gasoline mileage of cars of poor households is not the whole story. The poor (and lower middle too) use their cars much less than others. This is partly because they have fewer drivers and cars per household, take fewer long trips, and are more likely to live in central cities. All these conditions are associated with having less money.

Table 5-16.   Cars per 100 Households[a] by Car Characteristics and
Income, 1973

Car characteristics	Poor	Lower middle	Upper middle	Well off
All cars	71	122	167	198
Type of car				
Standard	42	75	102	115
Compact/subcompact	14	27	34	51
Luxury	3	5	13	14
Van or pickup	10	14	17	17
Age of car (model year)				
One year old ('72–'73)	6	19	34	51
2–4 ('69–'71)	16	34	55	71
5 or more ('68 and earlier)	48	67	75	72
Bought				
New	18	55	78	123
Used	52	66	86	73
Cars used for long distance driving	50	100	135	163

[a]Includes households without cars.

Source: Washington Center for Metropolitan Studies' Lifestyles and Energy Surveys.

Ownership of few cars or no cars at all among the lower income groups is a major factor in the gasoline energy gap between them and others. Averaging gasoline consumption over all households, the well off use over five times as much gasoline as the poor. Even the lower middle group uses considerably more gasoline than the poor—about two and one-half times as much (see Table 5-17). If the comparison is confined to households with cars, the differences between income groups are reduced; but a considerable gap still remains.

Another element in household gasoline consumption is the number of drivers. The more drivers in a household, the more a car is likely to be driven. Poor households, more than others, have only one driver. Looking only at households with cars, almost three-fifths of all poor households have only one driver. This contrasts with two-fifths of all lower middle income households, and a tenth or less of all upper middle and well off households (Table 5-18).

An important way poor and lower middle households keep down their car use is by not taking long car trips. Three-quarters or more of all upper middle and well off household heads reported taking at least one auto trip in the past year of 200 miles or more. About one-half of the lower middle households reported such trips. Among the poor, such trips were even less common (Table 5-19).

Another factor associated with car use is where you live. Households living in the central cities use their cars less than households living in the

Table 5-17.   Distribution of Households, Cars and Gasoline, and Gasoline Consumption by all Households and by Households with Cars, by Income, 1972–1973

Households—total and with cars	*All house- holds*	*Poor*	*Lower middle*	*Upper middle*	*Well off*
	Percentage distribution				
All households	100	18	42	19	20
All cars	100	9	38	23	30
All gasoline	100	5	32	27	33
	Average gasoline Btu's per household (millions)				
All households	106	34	85	153	180
All households with cars	127	63	101	160	181
	Btu index (gasoline; poor = 100)				
All households	312	100	250	450	529
All households with cars	202	100	159	252	286

Source: Washington Center for Metropolitan Studies' Lifestyles and Energy Surveys.

suburbs. The poor are disproportionately located in central cities (Table 5-18). But it should not be inferred from this, that the poor living in central cities need cars less than do other households. It is more likely that they are doing without things they need, instead.

As stated earlier, the restraining effect of poverty on car use is a powerful one. Only about half of all poor households have cars in the first place. The modest consumption of gasoline by the poor compared to other income groups holds even when controls for other important influences are introduced, such as residential location, number and type of car, and number of drivers (Table 5-20).

Considering just households in the central city, the low gasoline consumption of the poor is apparent. In central cities, the well off use double the gasoline of the poor. The comparatively low gasoline consumption of the poor is even greater when comparing households living in the suburban ring: in the suburbs the well off use almost three times as much.

Income also has an impact regardless of the number of cars and the number of drivers. Whether comparing households with one or two cars, or households with one or two drivers, the outcome is the same—upper-middle and well off households consume from one and four-fifths to three times as much gasoline as the poor.

Getting to Work
The vast majority of employed heads of households who are poor commute to work by car. They go to work by car almost as frequently as the well

Table 5-18.   Cars, Drivers, Residential Location, and Car Mileage by Income, 1972-1973

Cars, drivers, location, and mileage	Poor	Lower middle	Upper middle	Well off
	Percent			
All households	100	100	100	100
Cars				
No car	47	16	4	1
1	37	52	35	21
2	14	25	51	58
3 or more	2	7	10	21
Drivers				
None	34	12	2	1
1	43	39	13	7
2 or more	23	50	85	92
Drivers all households w/cars				
None	2	1	a	1
1	57	41	11	7
2 or more	41	58	89	92
Residential location				
Inside metro area	56	68	71	82
Central city	39	39	24	24
Ring	17	29	47	58
Outside metro area	44	32	29	18
Miles driven in past year[b]				
Less than 10,000	64	39	15	12
10,000-14,999	17	27	18	15
15,000 or over	20	35	67	72
	Median miles			
Miles driven in past year	8,000	12,000	18,000	20,000

[a]Less than 0.5 percent.
[b]For all cars owned 12 months or more and for which mileage was reported.
Source: Washington Center for Metropolitan Studies' Lifestyles and Energy Surveys.

off do—84 percent of poor heads of households compared to 91 percent of the well off. The poor are more likely to live closer to work; 63 percent of poor household heads compared to 48 percent of the well off live less than ten miles from their place of work. On the other hand, as large a percentage of poor heads of households as middle income and higher income household heads have to travel 20 miles or more each way to their job—about one-fifth (Table 5-21).

On balance, employed poor heads of households use less energy commuting to work than employed household heads who are not poor. The poor use less energy in two ways: one is through somewhat greater use of public transit, an energy saving mode of travel; the other is through living somewhat

**Table 5-19.   Long Distance Travel, by Income, 1972-1973
(percent of household heads)**

Long distance trips	Poor	Lower middle	Upper middle	Well off
All household heads	100	100	100	100
One or more—any travel mode[a]	43	62	80	86
Auto[b]	34	56	74	80
Airplane	11	19	27	46
Railroad or bus[b]	9	9	2	6
Work related—employed household heads				
One or more	13	13	28	39

[a]Does not add because some heads took a trip on more than one mode of transportation.
[b]One hundred miles or more one way.
Source: Washington Center for Metropolitan Studies' Lifestyles and Energy Surveys.

**Table 5-20.   Gasoline Btu Index for All Households with Cars by
Residential Location, Car Number and Type, Number of Drivers,
and Income, 1972-1973 (Poor households = 100)**

Location, car number and type, drivers	Poor	Lower middle	Upper middle	Well off
All households with cars	100	159	252	286
Residential location				
Inside metro area	100	145	222	262
Central city	100	116	218[a]	202[a]
Outside metro area	100	168	287[a]	285[a]
Number and type of car				
One car	100	171	245	255[a]
Standard type	100[a]	194	291[a]	303[a]
Two or more	100[a]	133	181	188
Number of drivers				
One	100	194	269	b
Two or more	100[a]	128	182	203

[a]Results subject to substantial variation because of the small number of interviews in the group.
[b]Not reported because the number of interviews is too small for statistical stability.
Source: Washington Center for Metropolitan Studies' Lifestyles and Energy Surveys.

Table 5-21. Characteristics of the Commute to Work, by Income, 1973 (percent of employed household heads)

Means, miles, and minutes to work	Poor	Lower middle	Upper middle	Well off
All employed household heads[a]	100	100	100	100
Means of transportation				
Car	84	87	89	91
Alone	70	74	71	75
With others	13	13	16	15
Public transit	8	7	9	8
Walk or bicycle	10	6	5	1
Miles to work				
Less than 10	63	61	59	48
10 to 19	15	23	22	32
20 or more	22	17	20	20
Minutes to work				
Less than 16	54	49	50	46
16–30	27	34	31	32
31 or more	19	17	19	22

[a]Excludes no answers. May not add due to rounding and because some people use more than one means of transportation.
Source: Washington Center for Metropolitan Studies' Lifestyles and Energy Surveys.

closer to work so that less energy is needed to get there, whatever the means of transportation used.

The main reason why employed heads of household (whatever their income) use cars to go to work is because they report no other choice. Over 70 percent of all employed household heads commuting by car say public transit is not readily available either at home, at work, or both.

LONG DISTANCE TRAVEL

Poor heads of households are much less likely than others to have taken any long distance trips during the previous year. This is true for all modes of travel taken together and for the two most common and most energy intensive means of travel—the airplane and the automobile. Poor heads of households are slightly more likely than others to have chosen to take a long trip by bus or train, the most energy conserving modes of travel (Table 5-19).

In long distance travel, as well as other activities discussed in this chapter, the poor use less energy. Their conservation is probably not voluntary. If low cost travel were more available, it seems likely that the poor, like the better off, might choose to spend a vacation away from home, to visit an ailing relative, or to enjoy a holiday with distant friends.

PUBLIC TRANSIT

Since poor households are much less likely than others to have a car, the question arises, how do they get around? The answer is that they car pool, they use public transit, and they miss doing things. The most common uses of public transit by the poor are for shopping and medical care, with social activities coming third (Table 5-22).

Studies of public transit show that the poor and lower middle income families use it most. For example, a recent study of the bus system in metropolitan Washington, D.C. shows that the average bus rider makes between $3,000 and $6,000, has no choice but to travel by bus, must transfer once, and uses the bus primarily to get to and from work.[4]

Do family members miss activities because of lack of transportation? Most families of all incomes reported having no problems (Table 5-23). However, the poor are disproportionately hurt: over a fourth of all poor households report having a problem of some kind. Only one-tenth of the middle income families and one-twentieth of the well off report any such problems. The most severe problem of the poor is in the constriction of their social lives—their inability to visit friends and relatives. Another important transit problem of the poor is their isolation from less expensive stores. This is particularly important because it means that the few dollars the poor have cannot be stretched as far as possible. Thus the poor suffer disproportionately from lack of transportation.

Carl Stokes, the former mayor of Cleveland, put it this way:

> As a society we have opted for an automotive society which has conferred vastly improved access and mobility on the majority who

Table 5-22. Households Using Public Transportation During the Past Month by Purpose and Income, Spring 1973 (percent)

Transportation purpose	Poor	Lower middle	Upper middle	Well off
All households	100	100	100	100
Shopping	20	12	9	7
Groceries	16	4	1	3
Clothes	14	10	9	7
Things for home	11	6	4	3
Visiting a doctor or dentist	18	9	4	4
Socializing	15	10	8	6
Visiting friends	12	7	5	1
Visiting relatives	12	7	5	3
Other social activities	7	4	3	4
Going to a religious service	10	2	1	1
Going to school	4	3	5	8

Source: Washington Center for Metropolitan Studies' Lifestyles and Energy Surveys.

Table 5-23. Activities Missed in Past Year Because of Inadequate Transportation, by Income, 1972-1973 (percent of households)

Activities missed	Poor	Lower middle	Upper middle	Well off
All households[a]	100	100	100	100
No problem	74	89	90	95
Unable to				
Visit friends and relatives	19	4	5	2
Shop at less expensive stores	15	4	4	2
Go to doctor or dentist	9	5	3	2
Attend a religious service	9	3	3	b
Apply for a particular job	4	2	2	2
Take a particular job	3	2	4	3
Number of areas in which household reports problems				
None	74	89	90	95
1	9	6	5	2
2	9	3	1	1
3 or more	7	2	3	2

[a]Items do not add because some respondents reported problems in more than one area.
[b]Less than 0.5 percent.
Source: Washington Center for Metropolitan Studies' Lifestyles and Energy Surveys.

could take advantage of it. In the process, however, we have ignored the problems automotive civilization creates for those who cannot own or drive a car. The poor, elderly, and those too young to drive must pay more for transportation, while having fewer and fewer places they can reach by public transit.[5]

Ironically, the poor also suffer more from traffic congestion caused by the autos of others. Respondents were asked:

About what percentage of the traffic on this street or road is caused by trucks, buses, and cars of persons not living on this street?

Over 50 percent of the poor report that they believe over half the traffic on their street is caused by vehicles of persons not living on their street. Only one-third of the middle and well off households report this situation. (The air pollution problems of the poor are discussed in detail in Chapter Six.)

LOWER MIDDLE INCOME AMERICANS

Many Americans, while not poor, still do not have a comfortable income. Authors who have discussed this group point out that the lower middle income households constitute a present and serious problem. Although not poor, many could easily become so. They have few accumulated assets, and many have no pension to look forward to except social security.[6]

Do these families have different patterns of fuel use? The answer is "yes," as the previous discussion has shown. The lower-middle-income group compared to the upper middle and well off generally have less money and are more conserving of fuel regardless of the kind of dwelling they have. Their homes are truly modest, with only a few more conveniences than those of the poor. In all climates, they use less energy than average.

This group—about two-fifths of all households—is the largest segment of all households and all workers. Their lives are disadvantaged by accepted American standards. For instance, they have fewer cars than the average, they travel less for pleasure, but they use their cars as much as the average since they must often drive considerable distances to and from work.

From evidence about their housing also, the rising concern about households below the comfortable middle appears justified. Although they practice the work ethic and the frugality of "waste not, want not," lower middle income households have not acquired the solid security that produces the levels of consumption that many call the American way of life.

DIFFERENT KINDS OF HOUSEHOLDS
AND ENERGY USE

Households differ widely. One household is a single individual, another a family with or without children, a third several adults sharing a home. Some households have only one earner, others have two or more (the latter usually including a working wife). Some households are headed by a college educated professional, others by someone who did not complete high school. Some own; some rent.

Whatever the characteristic, if the household is well off, it uses about twice the energy of a poor household with the same characteristic. The amount varies somewhat of course; but there is no question that the well off use more energy than other households and that the poor use the least. This is true of households with one earner, of households with heads under 45, of households with a college educated head, and of households who own their own homes. (For details, see Table 5-24.)

RISING ENERGY PRICES

Energy prices rose sharply during 1973–74, the year of the "energy crisis." What is not generally realized is that energy prices already were rising steeply before that. Between May 1969 and May 1974, consumer prices for each of the fuels (electricity, natural gas, fuel oil, and gasoline) increased more than for any other major item in the Consumer Price Index, except food (Table 5-25). The increases were 40 percent for electricity and gas, 58 percent for gasoline, and a whopping

Table 5-24. Btu Index (Electricity, Natural Gas and Gasoline) by Household Characteristics and Income, 1972-1973 (Poor households = 100)

Characteristic	Poor	Lower middle	Upper middle	Well off
All households	100	142	194	230
Age of household head				
Head under 45	100	152	186	215
45-64	100[a]	118	160[b]	196[b]
65 and over	100	126		
Household structure				
Husband-wife	100	128	164	192[b]
Other	100	128	168[a]	[b]
Employment status of household head				
Not employed	100	123	[b]	[b]
Employed	100	137	173	205
Wife not employed	100	120	158	184
One earner	100	138	181	217
Head fore., crafts., oper.	100[a]	92	119	127[a]
Education of household head				
High school or less	100	141	202	237
College	100[a]	130	163	201
Tenancy				
Own	100	141	181	210
Rent	100	124	195[a]	186[a]

[a]Results subject to substantial variation because of the small number of interviews in the group.
[b]Not reported because the number of interviews is too small for statistical stability.
Note: The Btu data on which this table is based represent the average per household using the fuel for natural gas and the average per household (regardless of whether the fuel is used) for electricity and gasoline. This was done because, generally speaking, there are no substitutes for electricity and gasoline, and the household not using these fuels is probably doing without.
Source: Washington Center for Metropolitan Studies' Lifestyles and Energy Surveys.

100 percent for fuel oil. Food prices rose 49 percent. Overall, the Consumer Price Index rose 34 percent.

Price increases have fallen most heavily on the poor, who have no money to spare. They have no "discretionary income" as the economists call it—money they can either spend or save for extras.

Only about one-fifth of all households use fuel oil for heating. Fuel oil use is concentrated geographically, however. It is especially prevalent in the North, where winters are most severe. The extraordinarily sharp rise in fuel oil prices—100 percent in five years—must have worked a special hardship on the

Table 5-25.   Increase in Consumer Price Index for Selected Items and Fuels, May 1969 to May 1974 and May 1973 to May 1974 (percent)

Item	May '69–'74	May '73–'74
All items	34	11
Food	49	16
Services	34	9
Medical care services	35	9
Services less medical care	33	9
Utilities and public trans.	33	8
Public transportation	31	2
Private transportation	28	13
Durable commodities	20	6
New cars	10	3
Used cars	17	1
Appliances (incl. radio and TV)	5	2
Nondurable commodities (less food)	29	13
Fuel and utilities	44	19
Fuel oil #2	100	65
Gas and electricity	40	14
Gas–all types	38	11
Residential heating gas	42	14
Other (total)	34	8
Electricity (total)	43	18
Gasoline	58	43

Source: Prepared by the Washington Center for Metropolitan Studies from published and unpublished data from the U.S. Bureau of Labor Statistics.

more than two million poor households who use it. How does a family shift its expenditure for necessities when nothing is left over to shift?

Gasoline prices have also been rising rapidly—58 percent over the five-year period ending in May 1974. Such a large increase creates severe problems in the already strained budgets of low income households. This is especially true of the almost one million poor household heads who drive thirty miles or more round trip each day to get to work. And rising gasoline prices are not the only factor. Adding other costs for operating a car such as maintenance, parts, tires, insurance, tolls, parking fees, and taxes—all of which are increasing in price also—the cost of operating a car is a sizeable part of the poor and lower middle income household's budget.[7] These costs affect decisions about where to work and what kinds of jobs to hold. The decisions workers make about jobs have serious implications for their employers as well.

The problem of needing a car for the journey to work could be solved partly if the working poor had a choice of housing; but their housing alternatives are severely limited. Vacancy rates are low in standard dwellings; rents and the selling price of houses are high and rising; and little additional subsidized or public housing will become available under current legislation or government plans. Furthermore, housing that poor households can afford is unwelcome in many areas. The particular housing problems of black families are discussed in Chapter Seven.

Lack of choice in housing is a serious handicap which, along with inadequate or inconvenient public transit, makes it impossible for the poor to avoid transportation costs and heating bills that are disproportionately large relative to their income.

Raising prices as a means of reducing energy use was not a popular policy alternative with respondents even back in May 1973, before the latest upward spurt. Half the respondents felt that the best way to handle an electricity shortage would be for households to be more thrifty; 45 percent thought that the supply of electricity should be increased, and only 2 percent favored increasing its price. If expansion of supply were linked directly to rising prices (as it is in fact), presumably even more respondents of all income groups would have chosen the first alternative. The well off (and big users) were more likely than other income groups to favor increasing supply (Table 5-26).

Even though soaring prices of energy—particularly fuel oil and gasoline—have fallen most heavily on the poor, families with incomes which lift them only a short distance above the poverty level are hard hit also. Poor households spent an average of 15 percent of their incomes for electricity, natural gas, and gasoline in 1972-73. Lower middle income households spent 7 percent, and the well off about 4 percent (Table 5-27). This is the continuation of a pattern. Throughout the twentieth century, low income families have paid a higher proportion of their income for household energy than others.[8]

An important finding of the Lifestyles and Energy Surveys is that in addition to paying a sizeable portion of their family budget for household

Table 5-26. Policies Favored to Prevent a Hypothetical Electricity Shortage Over the Next Decade, by Income, 1973 (percent of households)

Policies favored	Total	Poor	Lower middle	Upper middle	Well off
All households[a]	100	100	100	100	100
Increase supply	45	41	45	39	52
Be more thrifty	50	48	50	54	47
Slow population growth	9	5	8	11	11
Increase price	2	3	1	1	4
Other and no answer	4	7	4	3	2

[a]Do not add because some respondents gave more than one answer.

Source: Washington Center for Metropolitan Studies' Lifestyles and Energy Surveys.

Table 5-27. Amount, Price, and Cost of Energy, by Energy Source and Income, 1972-1973

Energy source	Average annual Btu's (millions) per household	Average price per million Btu's	Average annual cost per household	Percent of average income[a] spent on energy
All three energy sources[b]				
Poor	207	$1.83	$379	15.2
Lower middle	295	1.94	572	7.2
Upper middle	403	2.06	832	5.9
Well off	478	2.08	993	4.1
Natural gas				
Poor	118	1.24	147	5.9
Lower middle	129	1.19	153	1.9
Upper middle	142	1.17	166	1.2
Well off	174	1.15	200	.8
Electricity[c]				
Poor	55	2.38	131	5.2
Lower middle	81	2.07	167	2.1
Upper middle	108	1.97	213	1.5
Well off	124	2.11[d]	261	1.1
Gasoline				
Poor	34	2.96	101	4.0
Lower middle	85	2.96	252	3.2
Upper middle	153	2.96	453	3.2
Well off	180	2.96	533	2.2

[a]The average income of the poor, lower middle, upper middle and well off are $2,500, $8,000, $14,000 and $24,500 respectively. The averages for the upper middle and well off were adjusted using unpublished data from the U.S. Census Bureau.

[b]The data for gasoline and electricity are for all households, since households have no substitue for the basic uses made of them. The data for natural gas however, are only for households using it and are presented in this way to reflect household energy, use for heating generally.

[c]As elsewhere in this book, electricity consumption is given in terms of the amount of fuel consumed at the power plant in order to produce the electricity used by the consumer. Presented in terms of the consumption and cost of electricity in the home, the figures are as follows:

Electricity				
Poor	17	$7.71	$131	5.2
Lower middle	25	6.68	167	2.1
Upper middle	34	6.26	213	1.5
Well off	39	6.69	261	1.1

We are indebted to Joseph R. Rensch, President of Pacific Lighting Corporation for suggesting that we illustrate this point.

[d]Well off households pay a higher price for electricity than lower and upper middle because a smaller proportion of the well off have electric heat—7 percent compared with 11 percent of the upper middle and 9 percent of lower middle households. Electric companies offer special low rates to homes with electric heat.

Source: Price of gasoline at 37 cents per gallon from *1973 Platts Oil Price Handbook and Oilmanac*, New York: McGraw-Hill, 1974, p. 125. Consumption and other price data supplied by utilities for the Washington Center for Metropolitan Studies' Lifestyles and Energy Survey.

energy, the poor also pay more per unit for electricity and natural gas than do more prosperous households. Indeed, as we move up the income scale, the higher the income the lower the price per unit paid. In 1972-73, the poor paid $2.38 per million Btu's of electricity, a rate 13 percent higher than that paid by the well off. Poor households paid $1.24 per million Btu's of natural gas, a rate 8 percent higher than that paid by the well off.

Not only do the poor pay more per unit of natural gas and electricity, but their comparative disadvantage as consumers of small amounts of energy has increased over the years. Between 1963 and 1971, the price of 250 to 500 kwhr of electricity per month (relatively low consumption) rose 12 to 13 percent. The price of 1,000 kwhr of electricity per month (relatively high consumption) rose only 10 percent (Table 5-28).

Between 1952 and 1972, the monthly price of 9,000 cubic feet of natural gas (relatively low consumption) rose 45 percent, while that of 14,000 cubic feet (relatively high consumption) rose 43 percent[d] (Table 5-29). Thus the gap between low and high levels of consumption of both electricity and natural gas has increased slightly. Economically speaking, the small user has been discriminated against in terms of price by being forced to pay higher unit prices. The discrimination has worsened slightly as prices paid by small users have increased more than for others.

The price per unit of electricity and natural gas is higher at lower consumption levels because of the pricing system for the two fuels. This system is based on rates by consumption level and is called "declining block rates." Prices decrease according to the amount bought. The more you buy, the less you pay per unit. The rates, known as promotional rates to utility decision makers, are designed to encourage consumption and are effective in this respect among the well off. This pricing system, however, penalizes the poor who can afford only small amounts that are used almost entirely for necessities.

The present system of promotional rates for electricity and natural gas developed at a time when energy seemed abundant, when air pollution was unheard of as a serious problem, and when energy cost per kilowatt hour fell as the amount of electricity generated rose. Now energy is no longer abundant; air pollution is a serious problem; and the cost per kilowatt hour increases as the amount of electricity generated rises.[e]

[d]This discussion of trends in electricity and natural gas prices is based on the work of William Kruvant of the WCMS energy research group.
[e]Research now shows that electric power plants are responsible for about half of all the sulfur oxides, and a quarter of the nitrogen oxides and particulates in the air. (Natural gas is the truly clean fuel, yielding almost no air pollutants when it burns.) The air pollutants from power plants, when concentrated, can cause illness and even death.[9] Most of the deaths from heavy air pollution in the past forty years have been attributed to a combination of sulfur oxides and particulates. Less dramatic, but also serious, are the chronic respiratory diseases caused by sulfur oxides, including emphysema, bronchitis, and bronchial asthma. (For further discussion of air pollution problems and how they affect the less advantaged, see Chapter Six.)

Table 5-28.   Price and Annual Consumption of Residential
Electricity by Monthly Amount Used, 1953, 1963, 1971

Monthly residential electricity use (kwhr)	Cents per kwhr			Percent increase		Annual consumption (millions of Btu's)[a]
	1953	1963	1971	1963-71	1953-71	
100	3.82	4.03	4.51	12	18	13
250	2.84	2.97	3.34	12	18	33
500	2.05	2.12	2.40	13	17	65
750	b	1.93	2.15	11	a	98
1,000	b	1.89	2.07	10	a	131

[a]Monthly residential use converted to annual consumption in millions of Btu's for the convenience of the reader.

[b]Not available.

Source: Prepared by the Washington Center for Metropolitan Studies from Edison Electric Institute, Statistical Yearbook of the Electric Utility Industry for 1972, New York, 1973, Table 61S, p. 67.

Table 5-29.   Price of Residential Natural Gas by Amount Used,
1952, 1962, 1972[a]

Monthly residential natural gas use	Cents per 100 cubic feet			Percent increase		Annual consumption (millions of Btu's)[b]
	1952	1962	1972	1962-72	1952-72	
4,000 cubic feet	10.22	13.35	15.89	19	56	50
9,000	8.87	11.02	12.85	17	45	111
14,000	8.27	10.19	11.79	16	43	173

[a]Data are for the 29 largest private companies that served about half of all residential natural gas customers in 1972.

[b]Monthly residential use converted to annual consumption in millions of Btus for the convenience of the reader.

Source: 1972 price data prepared by the Washington Center for Metropolitan Studies from the American Gas Association. American Gas Association Rate Service. Arlington, Va., using the latest appropriate issues. Data for 1952 and 1962 were supplied by individual gas companies at the request of Washington Center for Metropolitan Studies. Customer data are from Brown's Directory of North American Gas Companies, Duluth, Minn.: Harcourt and Brace, 87th ed., 1973.

Since increased electricity production now means increasing costs per kilowatt hour, economist Barbara Epstein points out that there is presently no cost justification for a rate structure incorporating a declining energy charge with increased electrical use.[10]

Utilities have been concerned that each customer should pay that household's share of the fixed costs of installing electric lines, gas mains, reading meters, processing payments, and so forth.[11] This is a reasonable concern; but all aspects of the situation need to be explored. Service costs are probably not the same for all customers. Residential density could play a role; more meters can be read in less time in high density areas; and the length of service lines and pipes used per customer are also shorter in high density areas. The poor are more likely to live in such areas while upper income customers are more likely to live in suburbs. This suggests that if costs of service were carefully measured, the central city poor would be helping to pay for the service costs of suburbanites.[12]

Restructuring utility rates can result in a more equitable system for customers and help utilities as well. By cutting the growth of consumption, there will be less pressure to expand plant and equipment. This should be particularly helpful when interest rates are high.

Utilities are legal monopolies regulated by state and local utility commissions. As such, their rate of maximum profit is fixed, so that changing prices for classes of residential customers can change the source of their income, but ultimately not the mandated profit rate.

Finally, equalizing rates among residential consumers will eliminate the revenue erosion that takes place as more customers move out of a higher rate schedule into lower-rate blocks. As customers increase their consumption—causing the utility to build new plant at ever increasing cost—the amount of revenue per kilowatt actually falls. This leads to the anomalous situation of declining average revenues and increasing average costs—a widening gap which erodes the utilities' revenue position, causing them to seek ever increasing rates to cover the gap. Equalizing rates would help eliminate this problem by making people pay the same rate per unit as consumption rises. It would also probably end the present necessity of raising rates at the lower end of the scale and penalizing poor customers who are not responsible for the increasing costs in the first place.

Respondents in the Lifestyles and Energy Household Survey were asked, through an example, whether they endorsed the declining rate structure. Only 23 percent did. Most respondents (60 percent) recommended that everyone pay the same price regardless of consumption. Ten percent recommended that the high volume consumer pay more per unit, and 5 percent had no opinion.

Residential vs. Industrial and Commercial Users

Thus far the focus has been on reducing differentials among residential users. Residential, commercial, and industrial rates also need to be compared. In 1972, residential users paid, on the average, twice as much as large industrial users for their electricity, and over two and one-half times as much as industrial users for their natural gas (Table 5-30). Can the price differential between residential and industrial energy users be reduced or eliminated? Since 1952, there has been a trend in this direction in both electricity and natural gas. This trend needs to be accelerated.

Table 5-30.   Index of Price of Electricity and Natural Gas by Size and Type of User, 1952, 1962, 1972 (Large volume users = 100)

Type of user	1952	1962	1972
Electricity			
Commercial & industrial			
Large light and power	100	100	100
Small light and power	251	247	204
Residential	274	251	210
Natural gas			
Industrial	100[a]	100	100
Commercial	308	227	201
Residential	405	289	264

[a]1950.

Source: Prepared by the Washington Center for Metropolitan Studies from Edison Electric Institute, *Statistical Yearbook of the Electric Utility Industry, For 1972*, New York, November 1973, Table 45S, p. 53. American Gas Association. *1972 Gas Facts: A Statistical Record of the Gas Utility Industry in 1972*. Arlington, Va., 1973, Tables 64 and 79, pp. 78 and 98.

In general, new cost-justified structures that reflect the costs of providing energy should replace the promotional block type of rate structures now in use. With electricity, such a pricing system also needs to be geared to peak period use, as is now the case in France.[13] Such a pricing system would eliminate or at least greatly modify the present rate system, which causes the poor to pay more per unit of energy than others. Such a reformed rate system would also slow the growth in residential consumption generally, thereby easing possible energy shortages and the air pollution created by the fuel additional electric generating plants would burn. By slowing the rate at which plant must be expanded, such a reformed rate system would give utilities opportunities to find ways of eliminating the pollutants given off into the air by their existing plants.

Advertising

With air pollution and energy shortages as immediate concerns, the need for advertising by energy companies is being challenged. The head of the Federal Energy Administration recently sent a stinging letter to the presidents of twenty major oil companies calling on them to stop the "hard-sell tactics in gasoline."[14]

Increased prices rather than decreased profits pay for most energy advertising. With utility advertising, there is little question that the cost is paid by the consumer, because promotional activities are usually considered part of the operating expenses by the utility regulatory commissions. Thus utilities are allowed to pass these costs on directly in their rates.[15] Some regulatory commissions are beginning to restrict promotional advertising by utilities.[16] This trend needs to be encouraged. Efforts to discourage oil company advertising should also continue.

HIGHLIGHTS

The Lifestyles and Energy Surveys have established the basic facts of the energy gap. The poor use less fuel to heat their homes, less for lighting and appliances, and when they have cars, less gasoline. The poor can afford little energy for extras. Lower middle income families are also strapped. More affluent families are able to buy some conveniences beyond necessities and, occasionally, a luxury item. Rich Americans simply buy the fuel using conveniences they want and have a great deal of money left over.

Energy in the Home

Poor and lower middle income households use less fuel for the essentials of heating, lighting, and cooking because they are forced to be thrifty, and because their homes are modest. They are more likely to live in apartments or homes with only a few rooms and a few windows.

Half the poor and one-third of the lower middle households are dependent upon a landlord for repairs and any major energy conserving improvements. Some poor households do without what is common in others. About 15 percent of the poor do not have central heating; almost 10 percent share a bathroom with another family or have no indoor toilet at all; 8 percent have no hot running water.

Almost half of all poor households have no thermostat or valve to control room temperature; one-fifth of the lower middle group were in this position. Virtually all poor households have a refrigerator, a stove, and a television. The refrigerator and stove are unquestionably necessities, by American standards; the television provides an economical form of entertainment. With any particular appliance, the poor are less likely to have the more energy intensive model. For example, the poor are less likely than other households to have a color TV or frost-free refrigerator. Aside from the refrigerator, stove and TV, poor households are much less likely than others to have and enjoy the convenience of major appliances.

Energy on the Road

The energy gap is greatest in gasoline use. The well off are two-tenths of all households, own three-tenths of all cars, and use over three-tenths of all gasoline. The poor, also about two-tenths of all households, own slightly less than one-tenth of all cars, and use about 5 percent of the gasoline. The lower middle are closer to the poor, using less gasoline than their proportion in the population, while the upper middle are more like the well off.

Poor and lower middle households use less gasoline because they go fewer places and because their cars get better gasoline mileage. They get better mileage because the older cars these groups own tend to weigh less than newer models, and are without such gasoline consuming extras as air conditioning and power steering.

Over four-fifths of all household heads, regardless of income, commute to work by car. The poor are only slightly more inclined than other heads of households to use public transit or to walk. For the majority of all household heads, public transit is not available either at home or at work, or both.

Almost half of all poor households and over 15 percent of all lower-middle-income households have no car. To get to distant locations within the city, they use mass transit, a taxi, or don't go. The result is that low income households use public transit more than others. However, public transit is often not available, and about one-fourth of all poor households report missing activities because of inadequate transportation.

The Cost of Energy

Energy prices have risen rapidly in recent years. Between May 1969 and May 1974, the individual prices for electricity, natural gas, fuel oil, and gasoline increased more than for any other major items in the Consumer Price Index, except food.

While all people except the very rich feel the impact of these rising prices in their family budgets, the poor suffer most. By 1973, poor households were spending almost 15 percent of their incomes for electricity, natural gas, and gasoline. Lower middle households spent about 7 percent; and the well off, 4 percent.

Ironically, the poor also paid more per unit of energy for electricity and natural gas. In 1972-73, they paid 13 percent more per unit for electricity than did the well off, and 8 percent more for natural gas. The poor pay higher unit costs precisely because they use less energy—electricity and natural gas prices are structured that way. Looking back over the past twenty years, the evidence indicates that price differentials between low and high users of electricity and natural gas have even increased slightly.

The rate structure of the utilities encourage energy consumption. Electric generating plants are a major source of sulfur dioxide—one of the most dangerous of the air pollutants.

Utility regulatory commissions now permit utilities to include advertising as a production cost. This means that the cost of advertising is paid by the consumer and is not taken out of profits.

Industrial and commercial users of electricity and natural gas pay less than half as much per unit of energy than residential customers.

IMPLICATIONS FOR POLICY

Chapter Three emphasized how important storm windows and insulation are to energy conservation. The data in this chapter show that storm windows and insulation are most frequently absent from the homes of poor and lower-middle-income households. Ways need to be found to provide funds for families in these income groups who are homeowners so that they can make improvements. Incentives also need to be made available to landlords to add these items. The problem is particularly great in colder areas and in situations where the landlord controls the thermostat but the family pays the fuel bill. Funds are also needed to improve the deteriorated and low quality housing of some poor families so that their housing will be made better at the same time energy conserving features are added.

Over two-thirds of all households, whether poor or not, said they would be willing to purchase a more expensive air conditioner if it cost less to run. Information on the energy use of major appliances and cars needs to be made available to buyers so that it can become a factor in their decisions.

Chapter Four brought out the need for low cost, well routed public transit to attract people away from their cars. This chapter puts the need for better public transit in more immediate terms. The poor especially suffer from the lack of transportation (half have no car at all); convenient public transportation could help them greatly.

Chapter Four also pointed out that public transit is best adapted to expansion in the central cities, where people live most closely together. For all the areas where public transit does not now exist, and perhaps never can, ways need to be found to help the poor. One way, which is presently being explored, is through transportation stamps that are good for all types of transportation, including taxis, buses, trains, and airplanes.[17] At present, without some kind of assistance the poor family without a car and without good public transit is truly isolated; the better off take the line of least resistance, an attractive, expensive alternative—the personal automobile.

Rationing

Rationing a fuel by giving equal amounts to all households would hurt the well off more than the poor because the well off consume so much more. Rationing a fuel to a percentage of previous consumption levels leaves the poor in their usual disadvantaged position—at the bottom of the energy gap. Since their consumption is already at a very low level, the poor are hurt even more when they must cut. For example, the affluent family with a large home can cut its fuel oil consumption if it shuts off an extra room. A poor family already living in cramped quarters cannot do this; it must instead lower room temperature, perhaps to an uncomfortable level.

If gasoline were rationed by the number of drivers, the poor would be at a disadvantage also, because there are fewer drivers in poor households, and therefore they would get less gasoline. Any gasoline rationing scheme should include a special ration for workers who live a long way from their jobs. One-fifth of all employed heads of households travel more than 40 miles to work and back every day. This means they are each traveling over 10,000 miles a year just to get to work. The special rations would need to extend to those who take new jobs, too; otherwise labor mobility would be affected.

Present Utility Pricing

The current system of declining block rates penalizes the poor and other low energy consumers by making them pay for their economical ways. The more the household cuts its energy consumption, the higher the unit rate it pays. The household's energy bill is reduced, but not in proportion to the amount of energy conserved. Declining rates encourage greater and greater consumption among the affluent by rewarding them with reduced rates. A flat rate structure among residential users, with escalating peak-period charges for electricity, would relieve both the inequities of declining block rates and the unnecessary encouragement of consumption in this period of increasing energy shortages. Peak-period surcharges on electricity would discourage use of energy at such times and also reduce the amount of plant and equipment a utility would have to keep in reserve. Exemptions to equalizing rates could be made for existing users of electric space heat in an adjustment period.

Increasing rates for residential consumers without reducing the gap between low and high users (as has been the case in the past twenty years) can have a particularly serious impact on the poor. Electricity and natural gas already take over one-tenth of the income of the poor. Since the poor have already cut their consumption to the bone, rising prices cause real hardship.

Utility rates for all residential consumers could be cut if the trend toward equalizing price differentials between residential, commercial, and industrial users was accelerated. Utility rates could also be cut if regulatory commissions would require utilities to reduce their advertising and to pay for advertising out of profits instead of passing these costs directly on to consumers.[18]

Much more effort needs to be devoted to finding ways of conserving energy in the United States, but this is not the only issue: maldistribution and inequities must be addressed, as well as present and future shortages.

Chapter Six

People, Energy, and Pollution

William J. Kruvant

A great deal has been written about air pollution in and around American cities. "The air in Los Angeles is bad," or "Phoenix air is good" are common statements. It is true that some cities have generally higher quality air than others and that pollution in a given city varies on different days, but these statements obscure a very important dimension of the air pollution problem. Within any large metropolitan area air quality may vary tremendously, and some groups of people may be exposed to consistently poorer air than others. Considering the great size of our cities and the uneven way population, industry, commerce, and transportation are distributed within them, it would be surprising if air quality were uniform over the entire area. Thus it is important to know just which areas of a city have most or least air pollution and if some groups are disproportionately the victims of pollution. We should also know if antipollution policies are effective and where pollution is doing the most harm.

This chapter deals with the question of who are the most likely victims of pollution by examining pollution estimates for the major part of five metropolitan areas, and by a detailed study of the relationship between air pollution and the socioeconomic characteristics of people in the Washington, D.C. metropolitan area. Washington was chosen because it is about average for all six areas in size and climate and does not have any peculiarities such as the "punch bowl" geography that contributes so much to the smog problem of Los Angeles. The original research is related to findings by others about the health effects of pollutants and about the geographic distribution of these pollutants. Finally, it is based on the characteristics and determinants of air pollution.

The Washington data show that social and economic characteristics associated with disadvantage—poverty, occupations below management and professional level, low rent, and high concentrations of black residents—go hand in hand with poor quality air. The findings show also that these groups produce little of the polluted air. Instead, more affluent citizens who live somewhere else produce most of it. Furthermore, the findings show that antipollution policies have already helped disadvantaged groups, proving that well-enforced policies can be effective. The chapter concludes with policy alternatives.

THE POLLUTANTS

Pollution control is directed at five major air pollutants: carbon monoxide (CO), hydrocarbons (HC), oxides of nitrogen (NO_x), sulfur dioxide (SO_2), and particulates. A sixth pollutant, photochemical oxidants, is formed by the action of sunlight on NO_x and HC and does not come from sources on the ground.[1] Control of NO_x and HC would automatically lead to control of photochemical oxidants. As Table 6-1 shows, different sources cause widely differing proportions of the pollutants. Transportation, mostly automobiles, causes more than three-quarters of the CO emissions and more than half the HC and NO_x totals. Stationary fuel combustion, mostly in power plants generating electricity, produces SO_2. Eighty percent of the SO_2—an especially dangerous pollutant when combined with particulates—comes from such sources. Industry gives off about half of all particulate emissions.

The two pollutants caused chiefly by transportation—carbon monoxide and hydrocarbons—are reasonably well known: CO is a poisonous gas and HC is one of the primary ingredients of photochemical smog. These are mainly produced by the combustion of gasoline in auto engines. Sulfur dioxide comes from sulfur in a fuel being burned in the presence of oxygen. A typical power plant using coal containing 1 percent sulfur would produce 38 pounds of SO_2 per ton. Particulates are particles of various sizes produced along with SO_2 in the combustion of fossil fuels. Larger particles appear as soot or dirt. The same

Table 6-1.   Estimated Emissions of Air Pollutants, by Weight, Nationwide, 1971 (million tons per year)

Source	CO	Particu-lates	SO_2	HC	NO_x	Total
Total	100.2	27.0	32.6	26.6	22.0	208.4
Transportation	77.5	1.0	1.0	14.7	11.2	105.4
Fuel combustion in stationary sources (mostly power plants)	1.0	6.5	26.3	.3	10.2	44.3
Industrial processes	11.4	13.6	5.1	5.6	.2	35.9
Solid waste disposal	3.8	.7	.1	1.0	.2	5.8
Miscellaneous	6.5	5.2	.1	5.0	.2	17.0

Source: Environmental Protection Agency. Cited in Council on Environmental Quality, *Environmental Quality: The Fourth Annual Report of the Council on Environmental Quality*, Washington, D.C.: U.S. Government Printing Office, September 1973, p. 266.

power plant would produce particulates corresponding to the amount of ash in the coal.[2]

EFFECTS OF AIR POLLUTION

People are concerned about air pollution because it affects health and damages property. The potential damage to human beings is of primary concern. Some pollutants are more dangerous to humans than others. This study deals with four of the most dangerous and damaging; particulates, sulfur dioxide, carbon monoxide, and hydrocarbons. It excludes nitrogen oxides because NO_x sources are similar to HC. Of the four, particulates and SO_2 probably affect health the most, although CO and HC are also significant.[3] Discussing sulfur oxides and particulates, Dr. Ian Higgins of the University of Michigan School of Public Health, and Dr. Benjamin Ferris, Jr. of the Harvard School of Public Health say:[4]

> There is good evidence that exceptional episodes of pollution cause morbidity and mortality. There is also a good deal of evidence that sustained lower levels of pollution affect health adversely. While the major effects of pollution are on those who are already suffering from disease, particularly of the lungs or heart, evidence, especially studies of children, suggests that pollution can initiate disease as well as merely exacerbate it. Particulate and SO_2 pollution probably plays a considerable role in the development and progression of bronchitis and emphysema. On balance, the evidence suggests that it contributes to the toll of lung cancer.

Higgins and Ferris cite extremely serious diseases whose ill effects have been recorded at fairly low particulate levels. Particulate and SO_2 pollution are expressed in micrograms per cubic meter of air $(\mu g/m^3)$. Since the effects of the two pollutants are stronger when combined than when separate, the U.S. government has set air quality standards[a] accordingly.[5] These standards have been substantially exceeded in Washington, D.C.

[a]The federal standards are 75 $\mu g/m^3$ for particulates and 80 ug/m³ for sulfur dioxide, whereas all effects cited by Higgins and Ferris occur at 100 to 130 $\mu g/m^3$. The air quality standard for sulfur dioxide is an annual arithmetic mean; for particulates it is an annual geometric mean. These standards relate only to particulates by total weight. But there is more and more evidence being developed that the most dangerous component of particulate pollution is the "small particle" component. These particles, too small to be seen by the naked eye, apparently pass directly into the deepest part of the lung. SO_2 can irritate lung tissue directly, or, if certain trace minerals are present, can form sulfuric acid, which is more irritating still. There are no present standards for small particles.

For a complete discussion, see S. K. Friedlander, "Small Particles in Air Pose a Big Control Problem," *Environmental Science and Technology* 7 (12) (December 1973); and, "A Review of the Health Effects of Sulfur Oxides," submitted to the Office of Management and Budget (October 1973) at the request of the Director by D. P. Rall, Director, National Institute of Environmental Health Sciences, National Institutes of Health, Department of Health, Education, and Welfare.

Carbon monoxide reduces the amount of oxygen that blood can carry, and thus is hard on the heart. If a person has coronary artery disease, even low levels of CO can be harmful.[6] A study cited by the Environmental Protection Agency in drawing up the federal standard for CO noted that at a fairly low level "... there is evidence of physiologic stress in patients with heart disease."[7] Effects may be present at even lower levels. (see Tables 6-2 and 6-3). CO pollution is expressed in milligrams per cubic meter of air (mg/m^3) and the federal standard, at 10 mg/m^3, is lower than levels at which physiological effects may occur—at 35 mg/m^3 or even 23 mg/m^3.[8] The effects of SO_2, particulates, and CO, the levels of concentration where the effects take place, and the current federal standards are presented in Tables 6-2 and 6-3. As is readily apparent, the standards, especially for particulates and SO_2, were not set much lower than the thresholds of significant effects.

Hydrocarbons by themselves evidently do not threaten health.[9] But in the presence of sunlight they react with nitrogen dioxide to form ozone, a main ingredient of photochemical smog.[10] Ozone irritates the eyes, but beyond that its effects have not been established. However, some authorities cite dangers that could lead to ill health. For example, Dr. Oscar J. Balchum of the University of Southern California states:[11]

> It is apparent that ozone results in sensory irritation, inflammation of the airways and alveoli of the lungs, and reacts with cell membrane and lung tissue components .... morphological and cellular alterations ... could be the inception of chronic processes, resulting in persisting functional aberrations or even disease.

In any case, control of ozone means control of hydrocarbons, and the government has set standards.[12]

Professor Lyndon Babcock of the University of Illinois has estimated the relative damage from air pollutants. Since some air pollutants damage health more than others, there is little use in simply adding together the various amounts. So Professor Babcock has developed a way to measure air pollution's overall harm to health.[13] The method estimates roughly that effects of total suspended particulates (TSP) are three times the effects of their emissions (15 percent to 45 percent) and the effect of SO_2 is twice as large as its emission effect (15 percent to 30 percent). On the other hand, CO, which makes up nearly 50 percent of total pollution emissions, accounts for only 5 percent of total damage according to Babcock. HC makes up about 15 percent of emissions and causes around 5 percent of total effects.[14]

These and other effects of air pollution are expensive. Estimated costs for 1970 were $12.3 billion. Of that, damage to human health was $4.6 billion; reduced property values $5.8 billion; materials damage $1.7 billion; and

Table 6-2. Best Judgment[a] Exposure Thresholds for Adverse Effects Due to Sulfur Dioxide and Total Suspended Particulates (long term)

	Annual threshold ($\mu g/m^3$)	
Effect	*Sulfur Dioxide (SO_2)*	*Total Suspended Particulates*
Decreased lung function of children	200	100
Increased acute lower respiratory disease in families	90 to 100	80 to 100
Increased prevalence of chronic bronchitis	95	100
Present standard	80	75 (Geometric)

[a]Best judgment is within the range of expert technical evaluation.

Source: John F. Finklea, "Conceptual Basis for Establishing Standards" in National Academy of Sciences–National Research Council, *Proceedings of the Conference on Health Effects of Air Pollutants.* Prepared for the U.S. Congress, Senate, Committee on Public Works pursuant to S. Res. 135, 93rd Congress, 1st Session, Washington, D.C.: U.S. Government Printing Office, 1973, p. 661.

Table 6-3. Best Judgment[a] Exposure Thresholds for Adverse Effects Due to Carbon Monoxide (Short term, 8 hours)

	Threshold mg/m^3		
Effect	*Rest*	*Light Activity*	*Exercise*
Diminished exercise tolerance in heart disease patients	29	24	23
Decreased physical performance in normal adults	71	59	55
Interference with mental activity	50	41	39
Present standard (8 hours)	10 mg/m^3		

[a]Best judgment is within the range of expert technical evaluation.

Source: John F. Finklea, "Conceptual Basis for Establishing Standards" in National Academy of Sciences–National Research Council, *Proceedings of the Conference on Health Effects of Air Pollutants.* Prepared for the U.S. Congress, Senate, Committee on Public Works pursuant to S. Res. 135, 93rd Congress, 1st Session, Washingtion, D.C.: U.S. Government Printing Office, 1973, p. 661.

damage to crops $.2 billion.[15] Other costs, such as damage to animal health were not estimated, so the true total was higher.

POLLUTION AND WHERE PEOPLE LIVE

The question of where pollution is greatest and who suffers most from it is answered by determining who lives where. Using Washington, D.C. as the example, overlay mapping, together with statistics of income and pollution, gives us that answer. Mapping shows pollution and the kinds of people it affects, in the same reference frame and at a glance. It is visual and therefore more readily comprehended than are statistical tables.

The Washington maps show as completely as possible the relationship between air quality and the social and economic characteristics of those affected by it. Previous work has stressed one or two pollutants and one characteristic (usually income). This chapter considers the four major pollutants and five different socioeconomic characteristics for a recent period. Information on particulates compares data for two different years.

Step one in examining the incidence of air pollution by socioeconomic grouping was to map a group of characteristics by census tract for the most densely populated part of the metropolitan area.[b] This area includes all of the District of Columbia, Arlington County, Va., Alexandria, Va., and Falls Church, Va. It also includes large parts of Montgomery and Prince George's Counties in Maryland and of Fairfax County, Va. These places contain about two-thirds the population of the Washington, D.C. Standard Metropolitan Statistical Area. The social and economic characteristics used were two measures of income (poverty and a general income distribution); an index of rent levels; a measure of the proportion of professionals and managers in the labor force; and an indicator of racial concentration. Each of these characteristics was mapped on the identified area using 1970 census tract information.

The maps in Figure 6-1 show this more clearly. The first map (Fig. 6-1, part A) indicates areas where 15 percent or more of the households were poor[c] by the government's definition.[16] Part B indicates occupational status. It shows census tracts according to the percentage of professional and managerial workers in the labor force. The white areas are those where less than 25 percent of the labor force is professional and managerial, the grey areas are where 25 to 50 percent of the labor force is professional or managerial, and the dark areas have more than 50 percent. Part C divides the area according to rents

[b]Census tract information for Washington can be found in U.S. Bureau of the Census, Census of Population and Housing, *Census Tracts:* Final Report PHC (1)- 226, Washington, D.C.–Md.–Va. (Washington, D.C., U.S. Government Printing Office, 1972), Tables P-1, P-3, P-4, and H-1.

[c]Since in the Washington area only 8.3 percent of all households were poor, it is safe to say that sections where 15 percent or more were poor can be described as poverty areas by Washington standards.

Figure 6-1.   Four Socioeconomic Characteristics of People Living in the Washington, D.C. Metropolitan Area

Part A
Households in Poverty, 1969

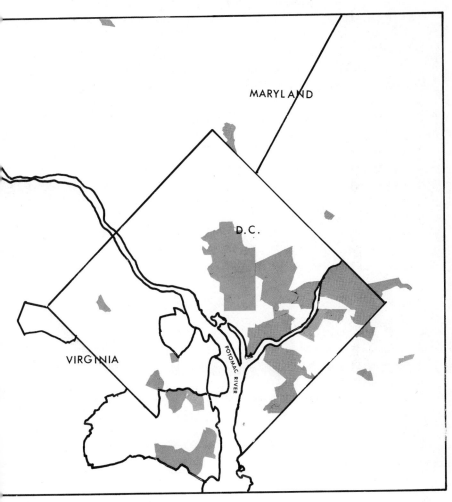

Y:
seholds in Poverty
less than 14.9% in poverty

15% or more in poverty

Prepared by the Washington Center for Metropolitan Studies from data in publications of the U.S. Bureau of the Census.

Figure 6-1.   Four Socioeconomic Characteristics of People Living in the Washington, D.C. Metropolitan Area (Continued)

Part B

Professional and Managerial Workers, 1970

KEY:

Professional or Managerial
            Workers

☐ less than 24.9%

▨ 25% – 49.9%

■ 50% or more

Prepared by the Washington Center for Metropolitan Studies from data in publications of the U.S. Bureau of the Census.

Figure 6-1.   Four Socioeconomic Characteristics of People Living in the Washington, D.C. Metropolitan Area (Continued)

Part C

Rent Levels, 1970

Y:
nt
low

middle

high

Prepared by the Washington Center for Metropolitan Studies from data in publications of
the U.S. Bureau of the Census.

Figure 6-1.   Four Socioeconomic Characteristics of People Living in the Washington, D.C. Metropolitan Area (Continued)

Part D
High Concentrations of Black Residents, 1970

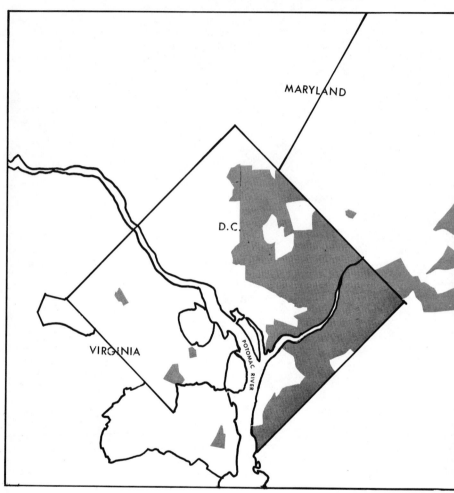

KEY:
Black Residents
☐ less than 74.9%

■ 75% or more

Prepared by the Washington Center for Metropolitan Studies from data in publications of the U.S. Bureau of the Census.

paid. In 1970, median rent was $135. Setting this equal to 100, an index was calculated. Tracts with median rents with an index between 0 and 75 are low rent areas (white on the map). Values between 75 and 125 were considered average. These areas appear in grey on the map. The darkest areas show the highest rents with an index of more than 125. Part D shows neighborhoods where 75 percent or more of the residents were black.

Maps of carbon monoxide and hydrocarbon concentrations are based on detailed analysis of traffic in one-kilometer squares.[d] A grid of one-kilometer squares was laid over the area, vehicle miles traveled in each square were counted, and average speed per vehicle was estimated. Miles traveled and speed are necessary quantities since CO and HC emissions rise with the number of vehicles on the road and decline as the speed of each vehicle increases.[17] The vehicle miles traveled in each grid in 1968 are for the eight hours from 11 A.M. to 7 P.M. when about 48 percent of vehicle miles are traveled.[18] The emissions data are then translated into pollutant concentrations using a mathematical model. This treatment, called diffusion modelling, attempts to take account of wind speed and direction, which greatly influences the concentrations.[19]

At this point a concentration value appears in each grid and it is possible to construct maps of a pollutant by linking concentrations that are equal. The resulting lines, technically called "isopleths," are lines of equal pollutant concentration. Since the results given by the diffusion model depend largely on wind speed and direction, an average wind speed of five meters per second, from the west, was assumed. A "worst case," with wind speed half that, was also mapped. Results are not shown, but they almost double the CO and HC concentrations at any given point.

For example in the isopleth for CO (Fig. 6-2, Part E) the innermost isopleth is equal to 10 mg/m^3. In other words, everything inside this isopleth is more than ten while everything outside it but inside the next isopleth is less than ten but more than five. Similarly, the area outside the 5 mg/m^3 isopleth is less than five but more than two. Thus, isopleths are like bullseyes: the closer to the center the higher the value. The same interpretation holds for the other pollutant isopleth maps (Fig. 6-2, parts F, G, and H).

A reasonable question might be, "Such numbers are well and good, but just how bad is the air?" In the case of CO the answer is straightforward. The National Ambient Air Quality Standard for CO is 10 mg/m^3 for an eight-hour period, and this level is not to be exceeded more than once per year.[20] The nominal CO isopleths (Fig. 6-2, part A) show that some areas in Washington

---

[d]The D.C. Department of Human Resources, the Environmental Protection Agency, TRW, Inc., and the Washington Metropolitan Council of Governments provided the Washington Center for Metropolitan Studies with data on pollution concentrations for the Washington SMSA.

Figure 6-2.   Isopleth Patterns of Four Air Pollutants in the Washington, D.C. Metropolitan Area

Part E
Carbon Monoxide

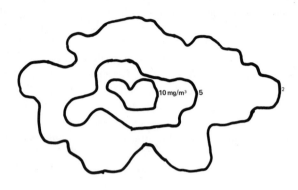

Part F
Hydrocarbons

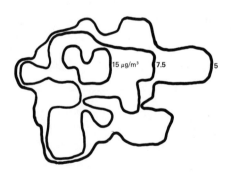

Prepared by the Washington Center for Metropolitan Studies from data supplied by TRW, Inc.

Figure 6-2. Isopleth Patterns of Four Air Pollutants in the Washington, D.C. Metropolitan Area (Continued)

Part G
Sulfur Dioxide

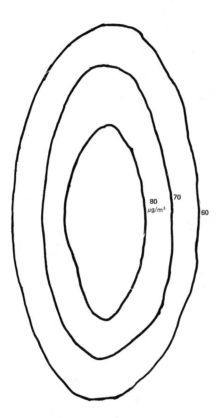

Prepared by the Washington Center for Metropolitan Studies from data in reports of the Dept. of Environmental Services, District of Columbia.

Figure 6-2.   Isopleth Patterns of Four Air Pollutants in the Washington, D.C. Metropolitan Area (Continued)

Part H
Particulates (in 1969)

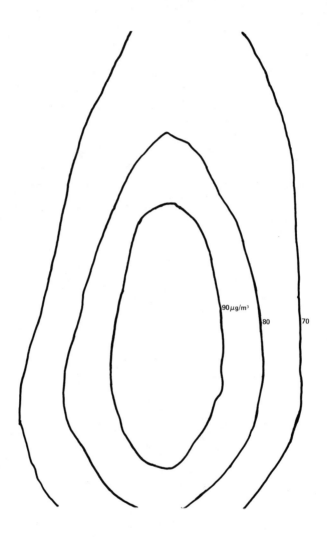

90 μg/m³   80   70

Prepared by the Washington Center for Metropolitan Studies from data in reports of the Dept. of Environmental Services, District of Columbia.

exceed the federal standard on a typical day and so are almost constantly exposed to very poor air. On stagnant days this area is much larger.

It is not possible to make as direct a comparison of the HC isopleths with federal standards because the federal standard uses different time periods and a slightly different chemical compound for measurement.[21] However, since hydrocarbons and carbon monoxide have essentially the same sources and enter the atmosphere in much the same way, the areas of high HC pollution are likely to be areas of low ambient air quality. Precise comparison with the federal standard is less important in the case of HC for another reason. We are examining people and pollution. The important task is to show variations in air quality, and HC isopleths do this.

Unlike the HC isopleths, the isopleths for particulates and sulfur dioxide[22] can be compared with the federal standards, since they are all based on an annual average.[e] Even though Washington lacks heavy industry, the city ranks about average in SO_2 level and only a little below average in particulate levels.[23] The federal particulate standard is 75 $\mu g/m^3$ and the SO_2 is 80 $\mu g/m^3$. Extensive areas in Washington are above these standards, so that we may safely conclude that people in these areas breathe chronically polluted air.

The last isopleth map, particulates for 1973, was developed from data supplied by the Metropolitan Washington Council of Governments. This map used data from 40 locations within the area of the study and was produced with the help of experts from the Health and Environmental Protection Department of the Council, who provided annual mean readings at each point. They show very marked reductions in pollution levels since 1969, indicating the effectiveness of air pollution control measures. The reason for this air quality improvement is discussed below.

THE TRANSPORTATION POLLUTANTS—
CARBON MONOXIDE AND HYDROCARBONS

As mentioned earlier, the isopleths for CO and HC result from traffic count data for 1968. Traffic volumes had not changed much by 1972. A survey of traffic counts in seven most heavily travelled avenues in the highest pollution area—roughly the 5 mg/m^3 CO and the 7.5$\mu g/m^3$ HC isopleths areas—show that traffic volume in 1968 and 1972 (the latest available year) was practically

---

[e]The main difference between the model used for generating particulate and SO_2 isopleths and CO and HC isopleths is that the former takes into account that particulate and SO_2 emissions come from specific points and are usually emitted through smokestacks of varying heights. For information on the importance of small particles, see footnote (a) above. Particulate isopleths are based on an annual geometric mean and sulfur dioxide on an annual arithmetic mean.

identical.[24] Since CO and HC are largely produced by transportation, the 1968 patterns still apply.[f]

The first set of maps (Figs. 6-3 to 6-6) relates variations in carbon monoxide to the four socioeconomic characteristics. Beginning with poverty and CO (Fig. 6-3), the most highly polluted areas (10 mg/m^3 and above, which is higher than the federal standard) are almost entirely in poverty areas. A few other vulnerable places include some affluent or middle income households on Capitol Hill and Embassy Row.

Figure 6-4, which matches CO concentration and occupations, shows that most of the highly polluted zones have low proportions of professional and managerial workers. Since low proportions in these categories is much more widespread than poverty, many such areas exist outside the isopleth pattern altogether. However, areas with a high proportion of professional and managerial workers are usually in low pollution zones.

Figure 6-5, which charts rent levels and CO, tells the same story. Here, most high rent zones are within the outermost isopleth and the area of highest CO pollution is almost entirely low rent. Figure 6-6 demonstrates it is highly probable that areas 75 percent or more black will have high CO pollution, although the correspondence here is not as close.

This introduces the idea of *probability* of living in a high pollution area—a very important concept to keep in mind with this and other sets of maps. Take the map of CO and poverty. It most emphatically does *not* mean that everyone who is poor lives in a high pollution zone and everyone who is well off lives in a low CO area. Many representatives and senators live on Capitol Hill, in the most polluted part of the city. They breathe the same air as the poor people who live there. Thus, areas reaching or exceeding federal pollution standards in Washington contain both rich and poor—and middle class, for that matter. The point is that, taking the entire population of rich and the entire population of poor, the probability is much greater that poor persons will live in a high pollution area. One need not be poor, or black, or live in a low rent apartment, or be low on the occupation ladder to call a polluted area home. However, if a person falls into one or more of those categories, the chance of living in such an area increases.

The second set of maps (Figs. 6-7 to 6-10) compare hydrocarbons and the same four socioeconomic characteristics and show the same basic relationships. This is not surprising since CO and HC come from the same sources in the same way at the same time. The HC-poverty map (Fig. 6-7) shows an even closer association between pollutant and characteristic than did the

---

[f]Installation of air pollution control devices in autos has not made an appreciable difference in the general level of CO in Washington's air between 1968 and 1972. (Health and Environmental Protection Technical Report No. 2, *Air Quality in the National Capital Air Quality Control Region—1972,* Metropolitan Washington Council of Governments, September 1973, graph no. 6).

Figure 6-3.   Incidence of Pollution Where People Live, Washington, D.C., Carbon
Monoxide and the Poor.

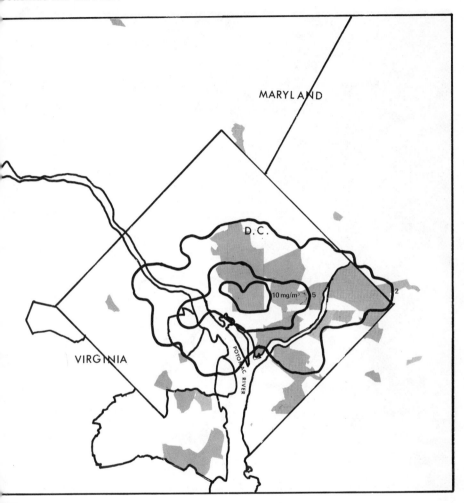

KEY:

Households in Poverty

less than 14.9% in poverty

15% or more in poverty

Source: Prepared by the Washington Center for Metropolitan Studies from data supplied
by TRW, Inc. and from data in publications of the U.S. Bureau of the Census. Carbon
monoxide data are for 1968, povery data for 1969.

Figure 6-4.   Incidence of Pollution Where People Live, Washington, D.C., Carbon Monoxide and Occupations.

KEY:

Professional or Managerial
         Workers

 less than 24.9%

[ ] 25% – 49.9%

[ ] 50% or more

Source: Prepared by the Washington Center for Metropolitan Studies from data supplied by TRW, Inc. and from data in publications of the U.S. Bureau of the Census. Carbon monoxide data are for 1968, occupational data for 1970.

Figure 6-5.   Incidence of Pollution Where People Live, Washington, D.C., Carbon Monoxide and Rent Levels.

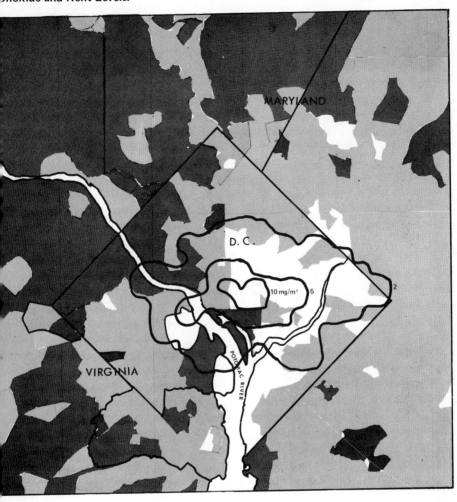

KEY:
Rent
☐ low
☐ middle
■ high

Source: Prepared by the Washington Center for Metropolitan Studies from data supplied by TRW, Inc. and from data in publications of the U.S. Bureau of the Census. Carbon monoxide data are for 1968, rent level data for 1970.

Figure 6-6.   Incidence of Pollution Where People Live, Washington, D.C., Carbon Monoxide and Predominantly Black Areas.

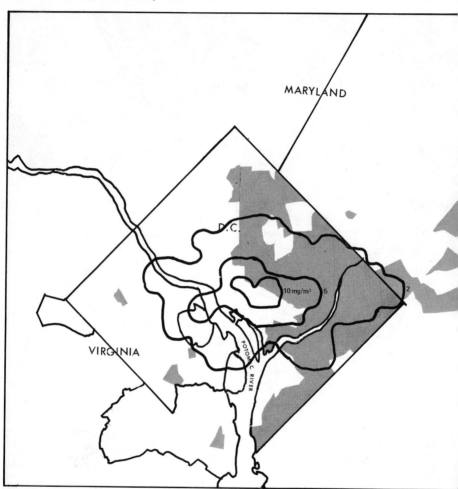

KEY:

Black Residents

☐ less than 74.9%

◼ 75% or more

Source: Prepared by the Washington Center for Metropolitan Studies from data supplied by TRW, Inc. and from data in publications of the U.S. Bureau of the Census. Carbon monoxide data is for 1968, racial data for 1970.

Figure 6-7.   Incidence of Pollution Where People Live, Washington, D.C., Hydro-carbons and the Poor.

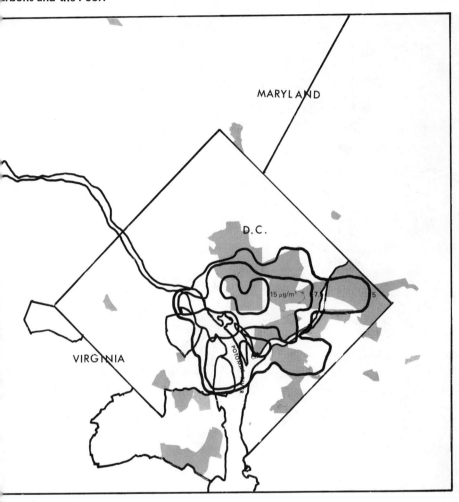

KEY:

Households in Poverty

☐ less than 14.9% in poverty

▨ 15% or more in poverty

Source: Prepared by the Washington Center for Metropolitan Studies from data supplied by TRW, Inc. and from data in publications of the U.S. Bureau of the Census. Hydrocarbon data are for 1968, poverty data for 1969.

Figure 6–8.   Incidence of Pollution Where People Live, Washington, D.C., Hydrocarbons and Occupations.

KEY:
Professional or Managerial
        Workers

☐ less than 24.9%

▨ 25% – 49.9%

■ 50% or more

Source: Prepared by the Washington Center for Metropolitan Studies from data supplied
by TRW, Inc. and from data in publications of the U.S. Bureau of the Census. Hydrocarbon data are for 1968, occupational data for 1970.

ﾟure 6-9. Incidence of Pollution Where People Live, Washington, D.C., Hydro-
ﾟbons and Rent Levels.

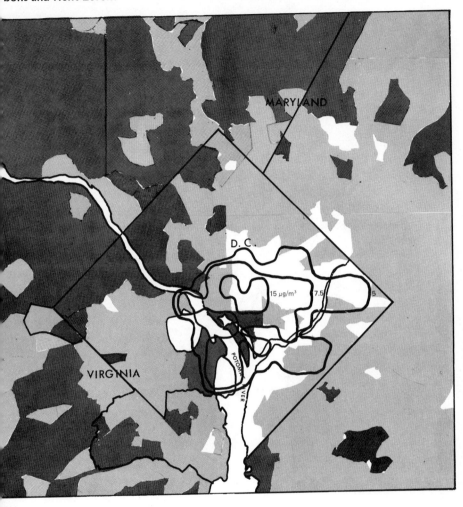

EY:
ﾟent
☐ low

☐ middle

■ high

ﾟurce: Prepared by the Washington Center for Metropolitan Studies from data supplied
ﾟ TRW, Inc. and from data in publications of the U.S. Bureau of the Census. Hydro-
ﾟrbon data are for 1968, rent level data are for 1970.

Figure 6-10.   Incidence of Pollution Where People Live, Washington, D.C., Hydrocarbons and Predominantly Black Areas.

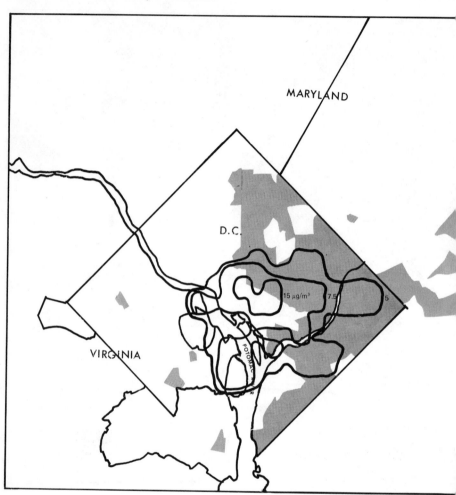

KEY:

Black Residents

☐ less than 74.9%

▨ 75% or more

Source: Prepared by the Washington Center for Metropolitan Studies from data supplied by TRW, Inc. and from data in publications of the U.S. Bureau of the Census. Hydrocarbon data are for 1968, racial data for 1970.

CO-poverty map. The same is true of the HC-occupation and HC-rent index maps (Figs. 6-8 and 6-9). In all three cases—especially poverty and low rent—a great percentage of the people with the characteristic live in highly polluted areas. The pattern is less clear in the case of Figure 6-10, which relates HC to black residents. Significant areas where high percentages of black people live completely escape the HC pattern. This reflects the movement of middle and upper income blacks away from the central city.[g]

A statistical summary of family income related to carbon monoxide concentration provides more background (Table 6-4). The four characteristics, after all, relate directly to income. Areas where over 15 percent of all households live in poverty will tend to have low median incomes. Also, since the professional-managerial group is the highest paid occupational category, a low proportion of them in an area would mean low median income.[25] The same is true of low rent levels. Finally, since a much larger proportion of black families are poor than nonblacks, high concentrations of blacks, other things being equal, tend to mean low median income.[26]

While around 90 percent of the $12,000 and over tracts fell in the lowest CO range, only 17 percent of the under $7,000 median family income census tracts did so. On the other hand, few of the over $12,000 median family income tracts were located in areas of 5 mg/m^3 CO or more, while 36 percent of the under $7,000 tracts were in such zones, indicating substantial pollution. The federal standard, it should be remembered, is 10 mg/m^3.

Preliminary mapping of poverty sections and CO levels for five other cities—New York, Chicago, Denver, Los Angeles, and San Francisco-Oakland—show similar results. High CO pollution areas and areas where more than 15 percent of the households are poor go hand in hand.

Jeffrey Zupan, in his book, *The Distribution of Air Quality in the New York Region,* cites similar evidence.[27] He found that in a 21-county region centered on New York City, high income people (defined as those filing tax returns reporting more than $10,000 per year in 1966) were exposed to significantly less CO and HC than were middle or low income people (less than $3,000 in 1966). Zupan also found approximately equal exposures for middle and low income people.[28] This result differs from our findings, but Zupan's methods of defining income and his way of calculating exposure were quite different, and the two results probably indicate highly technical differences in methods employed more than anything else.[29]

The strong negative correlation between CO and HC pollution and income in the Washington area, and the strong suggestion that the correlation also exists in other cities, is paralleled by research into stationary source pollutants.

[g]For a discussion of this movement see Eunice Grier, *Characteristics of Black Suburbanites,* (Washington, D.C.: The Washington Center for Metropolitan Studies, October 1973), pp. i–iii, 15–25.

Table 6-4.   Percent Distribution of Census Tracts, by Median Family Income and Carbon Monoxide (CO) Level (445 Census Tracts in the Washington SMSA: CO data for 1968, Income data for 1969)

Median family income per census tract[a]	All tracts	CO Level			
		Below federal standard			Above fed. standard
		Less than 2 mg/m^3	2-4.99 mg/m^3	5-9.99 mg/m^3	More than 10 mg/m^3
Total all tracts	100	76	16	7	2
Less than $7,000	100	17	47	23	13
$7,000 to $11,999	100	66	23	10	1
$12,000 to $15,999	100	92	3	4	1
$16,000 to $19,999	100	90	6	3	0
$20,000 and over	100	85	13	2	0

[a]Median income for the Washington SMSA was $12,933 in 1970.

Source: Derived by Washington Center for Metropolitan Studies using data from TRW, Inc. and U.S. Bureau of the Census, *1970 Census of Population and Housing, Census Tracts, Washington, D.C., Maryland, Virginia Standard Metropolitan Statistical Area* [PH C (1)–226], Washington, D.C.: U.S. Government Printing Office, May 1972, Table P–4.

POLLUTION FROM INDUSTRY, POWER, AND WASTE DISPOSAL—PARTICULATES AND SULFUR DIOXIDE

The first part of this section compares particulates and SO$_2$ pollution with four socioeconomic characteristics in 1969, summarizes the relationship between concentration of the two pollutants and family income in that year, and compares our findings with those of others. The second part looks at the decline of particulate levels in Washington between 1969 and 1973 and shows the reasons for it.

Figures 6-11 to 6-14 show sulfur dioxide and its relationships to the four characteristics. Figure 6-11 (SO$_2$ and poverty areas) shows that although there are nonpoverty pockets within the most polluted areas, poverty is disproportionately present. Most of the nonpoverty land on either side of the Potomac River within the highest isopleth is occupied by parks, highways, an airport and a military base. Thus, likelihood of a poor household living in a high SO$_2$ zone is greater than is immediately apparent. This innermost isopleth corresponds to the federal standard, although any place above 70 μg/m^3 should be considered highly polluted.

Figure 6-12 (SO$_2$ and occupations) tells a similar story. Although there are areas with 50 percent or more professional and managerial residents living in highly polluted places (SO$_2$ levels above 70 μg/m^3), there are very few

ʒure 6–11.   Incidence of Pollution Where People Live, Washington, D.C., Sulfur
ʒxide and the Poor.

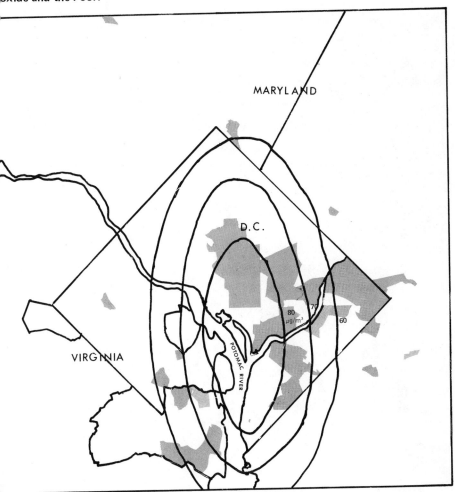

EY:

ouseholds in Poverty

☐ less than 14.9% in poverty

■ 15% or more in poverty

ʒource: Prepared by the Washington Center for Metropolitan Studies from data in reports
ʒf the Department of Environmental Services, District of Columbia, and the U.S. Bureau
ʒf the Census. Sulfur dioxide data are for 1969, poverty data for 1969.

Figure 6–12.   Incidence of Pollution Where People Live, Washington, D.C., Sulfur Dioxide and Occupations.

KEY:
Professional or Managerial
            Workers

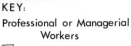

less than 24.9%

25% – 49.9%

50% or more

Source: Prepared by the Washington Center for Metropolitan Studies from data in report of the Department of Environmental Services, District of Columbia, and the U.S. Bureau of the Census. Sulfur dioxide data are for 1969, occupational data for 1970.

ıure 6-13.   Incidence of Pollution Where People Live, Washington, D.C., Sulfur
ıxide and Rent Levels.

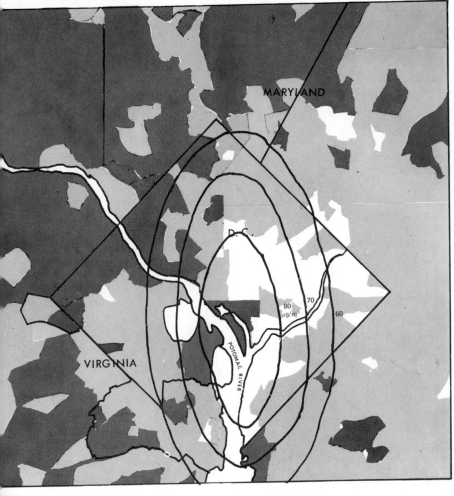

Y:

ınt

] low

] middle

▌ high

ıurce: Prepared by the Washington Center for Metropolitan Studies from data in reports
 the Department of Environmental Services, District of Columbia, and the U.S. Bureau
 the Census. Sulfur dioxide data are for 1969, rent level data for 1970.

Figure 6-14.   Incidence of Pollution Where People Live, Washington, D.C., Sulfur Dioxide and Predominantly Black Areas.

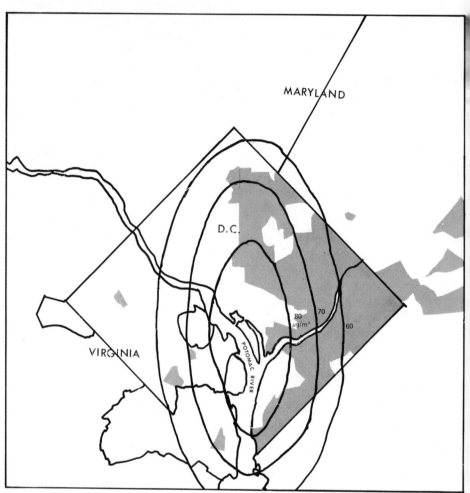

KEY:

Black Residents

☐ less than 74.9%

▨ 75% or more

Source: Prepared by the Washington Center for Metropolitan Studies from data in reports of the Department of Environmental Services, District of Columbia, and the U.S. Bureau of the Census. Sulfur dioxide data are for 1969, racial data for 1970.

Table 6-5. Percent Distribution of Census Tracts, by Median Family Income and Sulfur Dioxide (SO₂) Level (445 Census Tracts in the Washington SMSA: SO₂ and Income data for 1969)

Median family income per census tract[a]	All tracts	SO_2 Level			Above fed. standard
		Below federal standard			
		Less than 60 $\mu g/m^3$	60-69.9 $\mu g/m^3$	70-79.9 $\mu g/m^3$	More than 80 $\mu g/m^3$
Total all tracts	100	59	14	17	10
Less than $7,000	100	7	3	27	63
$7,000 to $11,999	100	44	18	31	7
$12,000 to $15,999	100	77	15	3	5
$16,000 to $19,999	100	79	6	6	8
$20,000 and over	100	76	9	13	2

[a]Median income for the Washington SMSA was $12,933 in 1969.

Source: Derived by Washington Center for Metropolitan Studies using data from D.C. Department of Human Resources for SO₂ and median family income figures in U.S. Bureau of the Census, *1970 Census of Population and Housing, Census Tracts, Washington, D.C., Maryland, Virginia Standard Metropolitan Statistical Area* [PH C (1)-226], Washington, D.C.: U.S. Government Printing Office, May 1972, Table P-4.

such areas. Likewise, the relationship between rent and SO₂, (Fig. 6-13) shows that most low rent areas are within the 70 $\mu g/m^3$ isopleth, but relatively few of the high rent areas are. Finally, Figure 6-14 shows that parts of the Washington region having 75 percent or more black residents are more likely to be highly polluted sections than are other areas. On the other hand, the movement away from the central core has put many nearly all-black neighborhoods outside high put many nearly all-black neighborhoods outside high pollution zones.

Table 6-5 compares sulfur dioxide levels with family income in the Washington area. As with CO, there is a strong negative correlation between income and pollution. Of the "less than $7,000" tracts, 90 percent were in areas of high pollution (annual mean of 70 $\mu g/m^3$ or above). The federal standard is 80 $\mu g/m^3$ and 63 percent of all the lowest income tracts were in areas above that level. In contrast, the standard was exceeded in fewer than 16 percent of tracts in each class with median family incomes over $12,000. The situation is reversed at low SO₂ levels. More than three-quarters of the high income tracts are in the lowest pollution (less than 60 $\mu g/m^3$) category compared to only 7 percent of the poorest tracts.

Works by A. Myrick Freeman, III, the Argonne National Laboratory, and Jeffrey Zupan agree that there is a decided tendency for low income neighborhoods to be more polluted by sulfur dioxide. Freeman found a very strong relationship in Kansas City, St. Louis, and Washington, D.C. in the

Table 6-6.   Percent Distribution of Census Tracts, by Median
Family Income and Particulate Level (445 Census Tracts in the
Washington SMSA: Particulate and Income data for 1969)

Median family income per census tract	All tracts	Less than 70 $\mu g/m^3$	70–79.9[a] $\mu g/m^3$	80–89.9 $\mu g/m^3$	More than 90 $\mu g/m^3$
			Particulate Level		
		Below federal standard	*Above federal standard (75 $\mu g/m^3$)*		
Total all tracts	100	32	25	21	21
Less than $7,000	100	3	3	13	80
$7,000 to $11,999	100	22	21	31	27
$12,000 to $15,999	100	38	36	20	6
$16,000 to $19,999	100	50	29	6	14
$20,000 and over	100	52	24	13	11

[a]Data do not relate directly to the federal standard. Thus, some of these tracts are slightly below and some slightly above the standard.

Source: Derived by Washington Center for Metropolitan Studies using data from D.C. Department of Human Resources for particulates (1969) and median family income figures in U.S. Bureau of the Census, *1970 Census of Population and Housing, Census Tracts, Washington, D.C., Maryland, Virginia Standard Metropolitan Statistical Area* [PH C (1)-2261], Washington, D.C.: U.S. Government Printing Office, May 1972, Table P-4.

1960s.[30] An Argonne National Laboratory computer simulation model[h] for the Chicago, Ill.–Gary, Ind. region also showed a decided relationship between poverty and high SO_2 concentrations.[31] In New York City, Zupan found a similar but less pronounced relationship perhaps because he limited his analysis to the city itself, rather than to the general New York area.[32]

Particulate Pollution

Washington area particulate data and maps for 1969 closely parallel the set for SO_2. Table 6-6 shows the general relationship between concentrations and income. Particulate concentration is markedly greater in nearly all the low-income tracts than it is in most of the high-income tracts. Particulate pollution was worse than SO_2 pollution. A much higher percentage of tracts were located in zones consistently above the federal standard for particulates than for SO_2. Figure 6-15, which shows poverty in relation to particulate concentrations, is very similar to the sulfur dioxide configurations set out earlier, except that larger areas were above federal standards. The three other 1969 particulate maps (6-16 to 6-18) repeat the pattern. Freeman, Argonne Na-

[h]The Argonne work takes the form of isopleth maps similar to the ones presented here. They show two pollutants (SO_2 and particulates) and one socioeconomic characteristic (poverty).

Figure 6-15. Incidence of Pollution Where People Live, Washington, D.C., Particulates and the Poor, 1969.

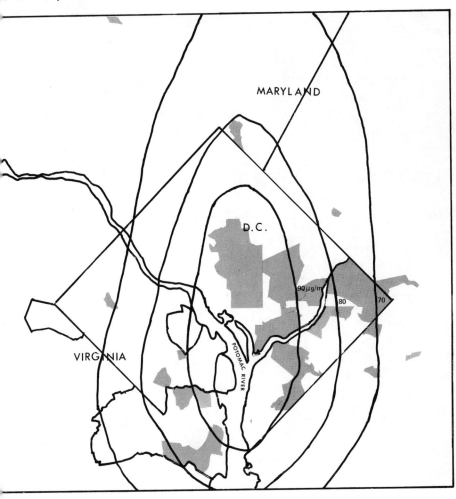

KEY:

Households in Poverty

less than 14.9% in poverty

15% or more in poverty

Source: Prepared by the Washington Center for Metropolitan Studies from data in reports of the Department of Environmental Services, District of Columbia, and the U.S. Bureau of the Census. Particulate data and poverty data for 1969.

Figure 6-16.   Incidence of Pollution Where People Live, Washington, D.C., Particulates and Occupations, 1969.

KEY:

Professional or Managerial
       Workers

☐   less than 24.9%

▨   25% — 49.9%

■   50% or more

Source: Prepared by the Washington Center for Metropolitan Studies from data in report of the Department of Environmental Services, District of Columbia, and the U.S. Bureau of the Census. Particulate data are for 1969, occupational data for 1970.

ure 6-17.   Incidence of Pollution Where People Live, Washington, D.C., Particulates
Rent Levels, 1969.

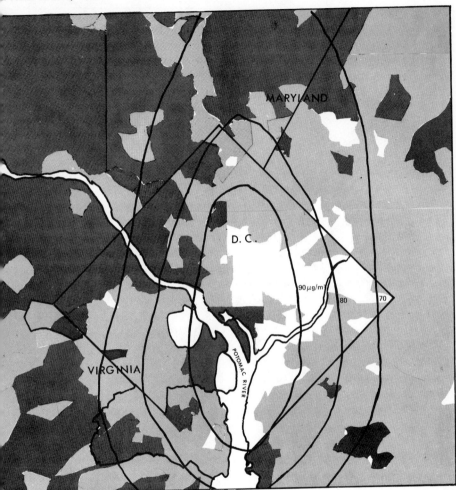

EY:
ent
☐ low

☐ middle

■ high

ource: Prepared by the Washington Center for Metropolitan Studies from data in reports
f the Department of Environmental Services, District of Columbia, and the U.S. Bureau
f the Census. Particulate data are for 1969, rent level data for 1970.

Figure 6-18.   Incidence of Population Where People Live, Washington, D.C., Particulat and Predominantly Black Areas, 1969.

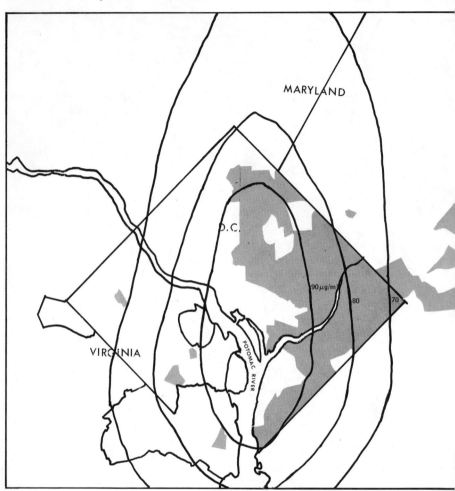

KEY:

Black Residents

☐ less than 74.9%

▨ 75% or more

Source: Prepared by the Washington Center for Metropolitan Studies from data in repo of the Department of Environmental Services, District of Columbia, and the U.S. Burea of the Census. Particulate data are for 1969, racial data for 1970.

Table 6-7. Percent Distribution of Census Tracts, by Median
Family Income and Particulate Level (445 Census Tracts in the
Washington SMSA: Particulate data for 1973, Income data for 1969)

		Particulate Level		
		Below federal standard	*Above federal standard*	*Percent increase in "less than 70 $\mu g/m^3$" category between 1969 and 1973*
Median family income per census tract	*All tracts*	*Less than 70 $\mu g/m^3$*	*70-79.9 $\mu g/m^{3a}$* *More than 80 $\mu g/m^{3b}$*	
Total all tracts	100	98	1 1	203
Less than $7,000	100	84	10 7	2400
$7,000 to $11,999	100	98	1 1	345
$12,000 to $15,999	100	100	0 0	163
$16,000 to $19,999	100	100	0 0	100
$20,000 and over	100	99	1 0	88

[a]Data do not relate directly to federal standard. Thus, some of these tracts are slightly below and some are slightly above the standard.

[b]No tracts above 90 $\mu g/m^3$.

Source: Derived by Washington Center for Metropolitan Studies using data on particulates from the Washington Metropolitan Council of Governments (1973) and median family income figures in U.S. Bureau of the Census, *1970 Census of Population and Housing, Census Tracts, Washington, D.C., Maryland, Virginia Standard Metropolitan Statistical Area* [PH C (1)-2261], Washington, D.C.: U.S. Government Printing Office, May 1972, Table P-4.

tional Laboratory, and Zupan also examined particulates in the same way as they did SO_2. Their results closely parallel these conclusions.[33]

Unlike CO and HC pollution, which have remained reasonably constant because of stable traffic patterns and densities, a major change has taken place in both the amount of particulates pollution and its pattern between 1969 and 1973. In 1970 the District of Columbia amended its health regulations to effectively prohibit incinerators, which were the main source of such pollution.[34] A large improvement occurred. Tables 6-6 and 6-7 illustrate this remarkable abatement, and Figures 6-15 to 6-22 provide a visual comparison. Table 6-7 shows no tracts at all in an over 90 $\mu g/m^3$ zone in 1973, whereas in 1969, 80 percent of the low income tracts were in one. More than four-fifths of the low income tracts were in the lowest pollution class in 1973, while only 3 percent were safely under the 75 $\mu g/m^3$ standard in 1969. This represents an increase of 2,400 percent!

Before 1970, about half or less of the wealthier tracts were in the lowest pollution zones; by 1973, virtually all those tracts were in areas that bettered federal standards. Figure 6-19 shows that the extremely large area above 70 $\mu g/m^3$ in 1969 shrank dramatically, to two very limited areas by 1973.

Figure 6–19.   Incidence of Pollution Where People Live, Washington, D.C., Particulates and the Poor, 1973.

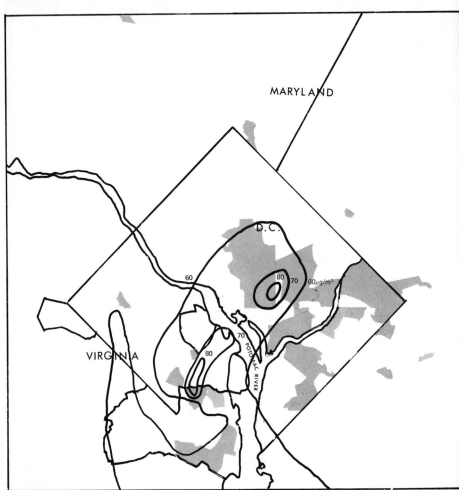

KEY:

Households in Poverty

☐ less than 14.9% in poverty

▨ 15% or more in poverty

Source: Prepared by the Washington Center for Metropolitan Studies from data in repor of the Washington Council of Governments and the U.S. Bureau of the Census. Particulate data are for 1973, poverty data for 1969.

Figure 6-20.   Incidence of Pollution Where People Live, Washington, D.C., Particulates and Occupations, 1973.

KEY:

Professional or Managerial
Workers

less than 24.9%

25% — 49.9%

50% or more

Source: Prepared by the Washington Center for Metropolitan Studies from data in reports of the Washington Council of Governments and the U.S. Bureau of the Census. Particulate data are for 1973, occupational data for 1970.

Figure 6-21. Incidence of Pollution Where People Live, Washington, D.C., Particulates and Rent Levels, 1973.

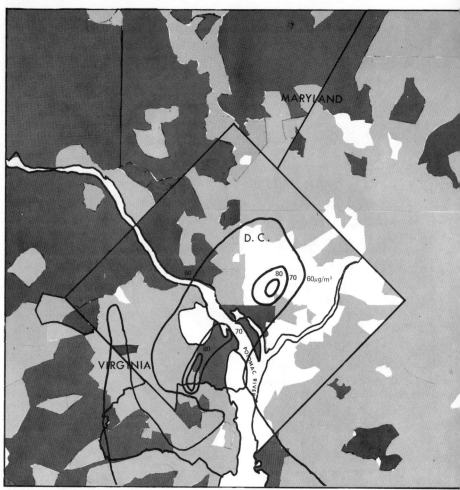

KEY:
Rent

☐ low

▨ middle

■ high

Source: Prepared by the Washington Center for Metropolitan Studies from data in repor of the Washington Council of Governments and the U.S. Bureau of the Census. Particulate data are for 1973, rent level data for 1970.

Figure 6-22. Incidence of Pollution Where People Live, Washington, D.C., Particulates
and Predominantly Black Areas, 1973.

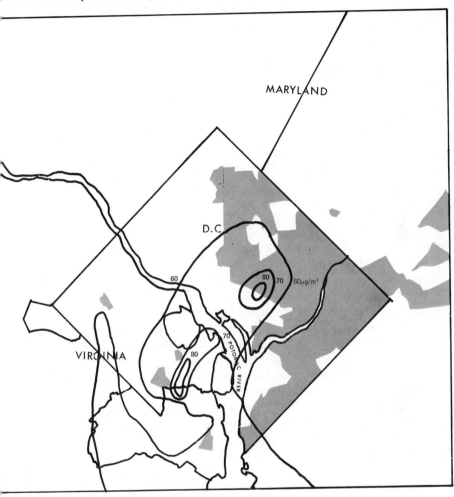

KEY:

Black Residents

less than 74.9%

75% or more

Source: Prepared by the Washington Center for Metropolitan Studies from data in reports
of the Washington Council of Governments and the U.S. Bureau of the Census. Particulate data are for 1973, racial data for 1970.

Figures 6-20 to 6-22 show the same change. While there was still more air pollution among less advantaged groups, the changes show how effective public policy decisions can be in improving air quality. Improvement in particulate pollution has been so dramatic that everyone's air has improved, and differences between groups have narrowed greatly.

WHO CAUSES POLLUTION?

Before proceeding further, one point should be made clear. The close parallel between poverty, low occupational status, low rents, segregation, and air pollution is not one of cause and effect. Disadvantaged people are not primarily responsible for air pollution. On the contrary, the richer a family is, the more it contributes to pollution because it uses more energy. Also, whites as a group use significantly more of all types of energy than do blacks. Previous chapters have shown that as incomes rise the consumption of electric power, gasoline and industrial products rises, and consumption of fuels, directly and indirectly, causes most air pollution.

The correlation between income, race, and direct fuel consumption by household is very high. In the case of electricity and natural gas, those in the $16,000 and over category consumed almost twice as much per household as the poor. In the case of gasoline, well-to-do households use more than five times as much. Whites, on the average, use 19 percent more electricity and natural gas and 113 percent more gasoline than do blacks.[35] In fact, disadvantaged people are largely victims of middle- and upper-class pollution because they usually live closest to the sources of pollution—power plants, industrial installations, and in central cities where vehicle traffic is heaviest. Usually they have no choice. Discrimination created the situation, and those with wealth and influence have the political power to keep polluting facilities away from their homes. Living in poverty areas is bad enough. High pollution makes it worse.

POLICY CHOICES AND EFFECTS

One general proposition is worth stating before discussing policies and their effects. Pollution becomes most damaging above a certain level, or threshold. The ecosystem, including human beings, can absorb varying amounts of pollutants with little harm. Above a threshold, however, effects become serious and worsen rapidly. This kind of thinking is involved in setting air quality standards. Because of this threshold phenomenon, general reduction in any air pollutant throughout a metropolitan area by say, 20 percent, should most benefit those people who live in areas above or near the federal standards. Having shown a positive correlation between air quality and income, the effects of a reduction in air pollution (other things remaining equal) should be progressive with respect to income. This has been shown in Table 6-7 where the greatest gains in air quality were registered in the lower income ranges.

Restrictions on private automobile operation are the measures most frequently suggested to reduce air pollution. Most proposals would increase the cost of owning or operating a car; those commonly mentioned are (1) parking taxes, (2) more elaborate emission controls, (3) increases in gasoline prices, and (4) taxes on cars according to engine size or gross weight. A step which would reduce costs is more carpooling. Increasing costs for buying and operating a car would obviously fall heavily on the poor. Although 47 percent of the poor own no car now and would not be immediately affected by increasing costs, increases would make it progressively harder for them to gain access to cars, which are still the most important mode of transportation to work.[36]

Industrial emission control—leading to higher prices for finished industrial goods—would probably mean benefits distributed somewhat progressively, while the costs, although regressive, would be partially offset by the smaller proportion of incomes spent by the poor for industrial products as opposed to food and shelter.

The effect of cleaning up one source of air pollution—electric utilities—is unknown. Rates would increase to cover higher costs, but since the poor consume only a small amount of electricity, raising the upper end of the rate structure would have a progressive effect, while proportional raises or raises concentrated on the lower end of the rate structure would be regressive. At present, poor people are discriminated against by electric utilities through the declining block rate pricing system. The fact that they are disproportionately victims of the utilities' pollution lends weight to proposals for flattening or inverting the rate structure.

Although there are reasonable grounds for supporting antipollution measures as strongly beneficial to poor and other disadvantaged people, an antipollution program will not solve their problems. It should not be promoted as a solution: there is no substitute for a direct attack on social problems. However, it is not true that the poor and other disadvantaged groups have no interest in pollution abatement. These people are saddled with the dirtiest air in the nation. It is wrong to suggest that clean air is only important to middle class lungs.

Chapter Seven

How Black Households Use Energy

Black Americans are the largest minority race in the United States. They are also the third largest identifiable ethnic group, surpassed only by the English-Scots-Welsh group and people of German descent. Blacks outnumber American Indians, Japanese, and Chinese by 25 times or more. They are four times as numerous as Mexican-Americans and fifteen times the Puerto Rican population on the mainland (Table 7-1).

The number and characteristics of this large and important part of the population—one in ten Americans—have been shown in every decennial census since 1790. A separate volume of the 1960 and 1970 Census Bureau publications gives detailed statistics about blacks. Since the mid 1960's the Census Bureau has published an annual report describing the social and economic situation of blacks in the United States.[1] Most federal agencies and many state and local agencies also collect and present statistics for blacks and others both regularly and in special studies. Data by race are now mandatory for assessing progress under civil rights statutes, so a wealth of information can be assembled about blacks.

Until now, however, no data have been available about household energy use by race—figures to show the way black households use energy compared to other households. The richest source of data for judging variations or likenesses in energy use can be derived by rough inference only. It exists in recent editions of the decennial Census of Housing, which show the housing characteristics of black and other households according to size and makeup, income class, and location. Aside from the occupants' demographic and economic characteristics the data cover such housing features as type and age of the structure, value or rent, number of rooms, plumbing facilities available, number of bathrooms, some details on home equipment, type of heating, and heating fuels used. However, this information does not compare household attributes with amount of energy used. The Washington Center's surveys fill this

Table 7-1.   Racial and Ethnic Population Distribution (1970 for
Race and 1972 for Ethnic Origin)

Racial or ethnic group	Number (in millions)	Percent
Race	203.2[a]	100.0
White	177.7	87.5
Black	22.6	11.1
American Indian	.8	.4
Japanese	.6	.3
Chinese	.4	.2
Filipino	.3	.2
All other	.7	.4
Ethnic group	204.8[a]	100.0
English, Scots, or Welsh	29.5	14.4
German	25.5	12.5
Irish	16.4	8.0
Spanish	9.2	4.5
Mexican-American	5.3	2.6
Puerto Rican	1.5	.7
Cuban	.6	.3
Central or South American	.6	.3
Spain and other	1.2	.5
Italian	8.8	4.3
French	5.4	2.6
Polish	5.1	2.5
Russian	2.2	1.1
Other or mixed[b]	85.1	41.6
Unknown or not reported	17.6	8.6

[a]Race data are for 1970 and ethnic origin data are for 1972, accounting for the difference in the total population.

[b]Includes Danish, Finnish, Swedish, and others not large enough to present separately as well as persons who reported they were of multiple origin.

Source: Prepared by Washington Center for Metropolitan Studies from data in U.S. Bureau of the Census, Census of Population, 1970, vol. I, Characteristics of the Population, Part I, U.S. Summary, Section 1, Table 48, p. 262; Current Population Reports, Population Characteristics, Characteristics of the Population by Ethnic Origin: March 1972 and 1971, Series P-20, No. 249, April 1973, p. 1, Table 1, p. 19; Series P-20, No. 238, March 1972, Table 1, p. 3.

gap. They compare black household characteristics with the amount, cost, and price of energy used, by source, with other households.

Analysis of energy use by race is significant for energy policy. On the one hand, blacks are a disadvantaged group in the American society and economy, so that energy availability and cost are critical influences on their level of living. On the other hand, black households have increasing importance in the consumer market for energy, because their level of living has improved over the past two decades, and because they make up a large percentage of the population in central cities of metropolitan areas.

Although these two views of the concern about energy use among black families differ, they also coincide in an important way. They differ by taking account both of low energy use among poor households and the much larger amount of energy the better-off black households use. They coincide because even well off black customers may be disadvantaged in the degree to which they can have the energy they can afford because of limited choice of housing and residential location.

The WCMS data show that poor or not, black households use less energy than others. Yet their energy consumption increases with rising income just as with other households. Differences between black households and others at every broad income level that could be measured[a] are less important than likenesses. When differences exist at similar income levels, the reason appears to be partly in the type, quality, and location of housing in which blacks live. Also, black households are at the lower end of each income class and have less wealth in each one than white households. Therefore, they have less buying power than those with whom they are being compared.[2]

Black *families* are 30 percent of poor families but 10 percent of all families.[3] Nearly half of black *households*[b] are poor, compared to 15 percent of other households (Table 7-2). About one-fifth had incomes over $12,000 in 1972 compared with two-fifths of all other households. Fewer than one in ten reported $16,000 or more (the well off in this study) compared with over twice that proportion among others (Table 7-2 and Figure 7-1).

On the other hand, the level of living among blacks has improved over the past twenty years, though not as much as for others. In 1951, three percent of all black families had $10,000 or more income (in 1971 dollars). This grew to 30 percent in 1971 (Table 7-3). With rising incomes blacks have become an important market for consumer goods. Business knows about this growing market. Market research about black households' buying habits has mushroomed in recent years.[4] Business used to watch the rest of the market almost exclusively—the part that showed an increase from 17 to 54 percent of all families in the $10,000 and over income bracket (Table 7-3).

The trend during the past decade toward attracting black consumers results partly from the increasing buying power of blacks. A good deal of the impetus, however, stems from the civil rights movement and the Civil Rights Acts of 1964 and 1968, which have emphasized equal access to all accommodations and services. Finally, there is the obviously expanding black trade in central cities of metropolitan areas, where almost 60 percent of the total black population fourteen years old and over lived in 1972.[5]

[a]For many, characteristics data on only the poor and nonpoor are available, but in some instances the lower middle among the nonpoor can be shown separately.

[b]Households include, besides families, single person households and other households in which unrelated persons live.

Table 7-2. Distribution of Households by Income and Race[a]
1972 (percent)

Income class	All households	Percent of all households		Percentage distribution	
		Black	Other[b]	Black	Other[b]
All households	100	9	90	100	100
Poor	100	23	76	46	15
Nonpoor	100	6	93	54	85
Under $12,000	100	8	91	37	43
$12,000–15,999	100	5	95	10	20
$16,000 and over	100	3	95	8	22

[a]For this and succeeding tables in Chapter 7, "Race" refers to black and all other races combined.

[b]Includes all races except black.

Source: Washington Center for Metropolitan Studies' Lifestyles and Energy Surveys.

Table 7-3. Income Distribution of Black and White Families, 1951, 1961, 1971 (Income in 1971 dollars) (percent)

Income class	1951		1961		1971	
	Black	White	Black	White	Black	White
All families	100	100	100	100	100	100
Under $3,000	47	17	35	13	19	7
$3,000–4,999	27	20	22	12	18	9
$5,000–6,999	15	26	17	15	15	11
$7,000–9,999	8	21	14	25	18	19
$10,000–11,999	2	7	5	12	9	13
$12,000–14,999	1	5	4	11	9	15
$15,000 and over	a	5	4	13	12	26

[a]Less than 0.5 percent.

Source: Derived by the Washington Center for Metropolitan Studies from U.S. Bureau of the Census, *Current Population Reports*, Series P-23, No. 46, The Social and Economic Status of the Black Population in the United States, 1972, July 1973, Table 9, p. 19.

TOTAL ENERGY USE

Black households used 1.5 trillion Btu's or 7 percent of the electricity, natural gas, and gasoline used by all private households in 1972–73. This was less than their proportionate share of the population (11 percent).

Blacks used 11 percent of natural gas but a much smaller proportion of electricity (6 percent) and of gasoline (5 percent) (Table 7-4). In line with other households in the poor and lower middle income groups, heating

Figure 7-1.   A Disproportionate Percentage of Blacks Are Poor (Their Proportion Among the Middle and Well Off Is Far Below that of Others)

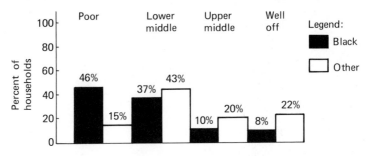

Source: Washington Center for Metropolitan Studies' Lifestyles and Energy Surveys.

Table 7-4.   Btu's of Electricity, Natural Gas, and Gasoline Used by Black Households Compared with All Households, 1972-1973 (percent)

| | | Black households | |
| | *All households (trillions Btu's)* | *Btu's (trillions)* | *Percent of all households* |
Energy source			
Three energy sources	20,295	1,458	7
Electricity	6,373	413	6
Natural gas	6,626	703	11
Gasoline	7,296	342	5

Source: Washington Center for Metropolitan Studies' Lifestyles and Energy Surveys.

and cooking fuel (natural gas) comes first. Whatever their broad income class, in fact, black households used less electricity and far less gasoline than others. Above the poverty level, however, blacks used *more* natural gas than other households. Why? Because blacks live chiefly in areas where natural gas is available and where most people use it—in large metropolitan areas and in the South (Table 7-5). About 70 percent of black households (compared to 60 percent of all others) use natural gas for heating (Table 7-6). Also, black households are much more likely than others to use natural gas for cooking—about 75 percent compared to about 50 percent. Besides, blacks are more likely to live in nonwinterized homes than are other households. All other things being equal, such homes use more natural gas (see Table 7-9).

Table 7–5. Residential Location, by Race, 1973 (percent of households)

Location	Black	Other
All households	100	100
Metro-nonmetro		
Inside metro area	72	69
Central city	55	31
Ring	17	39
Outside metro area	28	31
Size of metro area		
Large metro area	41	39
Other metro area	31	30
Region		
Northeast	15	25
North Central	23	30
South	49	30
West	13	16
Heating degree days		
< 3,500	51	30
3,500–5,499	27	37
5,500+	22	34
Cooling degree days		
< 1,000	24	46
1,000–1,499	38	31
1,500+	38	23

Source: Washington Center for Metropolitan Studies' Lifestyles and Energy Surveys.

Table 7–6. Energy Source for Heating, by Race, 1973 (percent of households)

Energy source	Black	Other
All households	100	100
Electricity	5	9
Natural gas	70	59
Oil	14	24
Bottled gas	6	5
Other	6	3

Source: Washington Center for Metropolitan Studies' Lifestyles and Energy Surveys.

The Average Black Household

The average black household used about 250 million Btu's of electricity, natural gas, and gasoline in 1972–73. This was about 25 percent less than other households. In the house itself (and therefore excluding gasoline for cars) blacks averaged 200 million Btu's of electricity and natural gas per

Table 7-7.   Average Btu's per Household, by Energy Source and
Race, 1972-1973

| Energy source | Average Btu's (millions) per household | | Ratio: Black to Other |
	Black	Other	
All households	254	350	.73
Electricity	64	96	.67
Natural gas	137	142	.96
Gasoline	53	112	.47

Source: Washington Center for Metropolitan Studies' Lifestyles and Energy Surveys.

dwelling compared to 238 million among others. Most of the difference was in the use of electricity (Table 7-7).

The explanation for the discrepancies in energy use within dwellings goes beyond the relative economic status of blacks, whose family income has been about 60 percent of white family income since 1967.[6] Limitations on home ownership influence the degree to which black households at every income level have less wealth than white households, since owning a home is the most important way of accumulating assets for most families, especially black families. Assets also influence the kind of house and equipment a family can afford. Assets depend on the alternatives available in housing choice. Both assets and housing choice influence the characteristics of homes and the amount and kinds of energy black households use.

A recent housing market study shows that restrictions in residential choice are largely responsible for the wide disparity in home ownership between otherwise identical kinds of black and white households, and for greater housing costs among blacks.[7]

The House Itself

The homes in which blacks live reflect in varying degrees lack of money or credit, and a restricted choice of the kinds or quality of dwellings, regardless of family income.

For instance, about 60 percent of black households are tenants, compared to 30 percent of all others. Even among black families in one-family houses, almost 40 percent are tenants, over twice as many (18 percent) as others (Table 7-8).

Tenants in general, whether they live in apartments or one-family houses, have less control over the amount, kind and quality of equipment and its maintenance than owners. For instance, although 80 percent of black households pay for their space heat, almost half (47 percent) have no thermostat or

Table 7-8. Home Ownership, by Type of Structure and Race, 1970 and 1973 (percent of households)

Tenure and type of structure	Black	Other
All households (1973)	100	100
Own	42	71
Rent	58	29
One-family homes (1970)	100	100
Own	62	82
Rent	38	18
Apartments (2 or more units) (1970)	100	100
Own	11	16
Rent	89	84

Source: Data for "All households" are from the Washington Center for Metropolitan Studies' Lifestyles and Energy Surveys and those for one-family homes and apartments are from U.S. Bureau of the Census, Census of Housing: 1970, *Detailed Housing Characteristics,* Final Report, HC (1)–B1, U.S. Summary, Table 22, p. 242 and Table 27, p. 268.

radiator valve to control it. In contrast, 86 percent of all other households pay for and can control their heat (Table 7-9).

The average black home is smaller than others' and built to require less heating and lighting energy. Almost 50 percent of black households live in attached one-family houses or apartments, compared to 25 percent of other households. There are fewer than ten windows in the average black family's house. The number of rooms and size of the living room tend to be small. Three-quarters of all black homes have no extra large windows, and very few have central air conditioning (6 percent compared to 16 percent). However, dwellings occupied by black households are less likely than others to have storm windows, storm doors, insulation, or a basement, so they need more energy to heat the small homes they have (Table 7-9).

Inside the House

By and large, the homes of black families have fewer appliances that provide extra comforts and conveniences than do others. Some dwellings black households live in reflect low levels of living according to American standards. About 10 percent had no indoor toilet or bathing facilities, no hot running water, and no central heating in 1973 (Table 7-10).

About 30 percent of black households live at a modest level that includes only the basics: a stove and manual defrost refrigerator, a clothes washer, and a black and white TV. One-third of the clothes washers blacks own are the wringer type (Table 7-11). The fact that these families had no more than this reflects lack of money to buy the extra comforts other major appliances provide.

Table 7-9. Dwelling Characteristics Affecting Energy Use, by Race, 1973 (percent of households)

Dwelling characteristics	Black	Other
All households	100	100
Structural characteristics		
One-family	68	80
Detached	54	70
Attached	14	6
Apartment	32	19
5 rooms or less	65	51
Fewer than 10 windows	61	31
No extra large windows	75	47
Size of living room		
Less than 150 sq. ft.	42	18
150 sq. ft. or more	58	82
No central air conditioning	94	84
Temperature control and responsibility		
No thermostat or radiator valve	47	16
Pay for space heat	80	86
Weather protection		
No storm windows	71	48
No insulation (one-family homes)	56	16
No basement (one-family homes)	68	48
No storm doors to outside[a]	69	43

[a]In dwellings with doors to outside.

Source: Washington Center for Metropolitan Studies' Lifestyles and Energy Surveys.

Table 7-10. House Characteristics That Reflect Levels of Living, by Race, 1973 (percent of households)

Characteristics	Black	Other
All households	100	100
Bathrooms		
Outside or shared	7	1
1	78	62
2 or more	15	36
Water heater		
With	78	92
Without	13	2
Not sure	10	6
Heating system		
Central	91	93
Not central	9	7
Necessary configuration of appliances: stove, refrigerator not frost-free, black and white TV	19	8
Add clothes washer	11	6

Source: Washington Center for Metropolitan Studies' Lifestyles and Energy Surveys.

Table 7-11. Appliance Index and Availability of Specific Appliances, by Race, 1973 (percent of households)

Appliance index and appliance availability	*Black*	*Other*
All households	100	100
Appliance index[a]		
Less than 40	61	30
40–59	21	30
60 and over	18	40
Appliances in the home		
Stove		
None	3	3
Gas	77	49
Electric	20	49
Refrigerator	99	100
Must defrost	58	47
Frost-free	41	52
Clothes washer	56	80
None	44	20
Wringer type	14	10
Automatic	42	73
Dryer (1 or more)	22	57
None	79	43
TV (any)	97	97
Black and white	84	62
Color	29	55
Dishwasher	4	27
Air conditioning		
None	73	50
Window–all	20	33
1 unit	17	22
2 or more	3	11
Central	6	16

[a]See Chapter 3 for description of the appliance index. Median appliance index for black households was 35, and it was 52 for "Other."

Source: Washington Center for Metropolitan Studies' Lifestyles and Energy Surveys.

On the other hand, many black households—mostly at the middle and upper end of the income scale—have additional amenities. About one-fifth of black households have an appliance index[c] of 60 or more, meaning that they are likely to have a dryer, an automatic clothes washer, a frost-free refrigerator, a color TV, perhaps a dishwasher, and either central air conditioning or several window units.

Some poor and lower middle black households also have the comforts and conveniences of major appliances. This appears to be true mostly

[c]For an explanation of the appliance index, see Chapter Three.

among older households, and the extras are most likely to be automatic clothes washers, frost-free refrigerators, and color TV. As discussed in Chapter Three, consumers in the retail market have little choice but to buy more energy using and expensive units: wringer machines and manual defrost refrigerators are virtually not for sale. Color TVs now predominate in the stores and few consumers understand their higher operating cost.

Black households have fewer major conveniences than others do in every income class. One explanation, aside from less wealth or actual income in each class, is that homeowners predominate among those who have each kind of appliance,[8] and blacks are not as often homeowners as whites.

Most major appliances run on electricity. Blacks, who are 11 percent of all households, used 6 percent of household electricity in 1972–73 (see Table 7-4). Aside from appliances, electricity supplies power for electric light (which is virtually universal), for cooking (in 20 percent of black households), and for electric heating (in 5 percent).

TRAVEL

Black households use much less gasoline than others—about half as much. Even among nonpoor blacks, gasoline consumption is only two-thirds what other nonpoor families use (Table 7-12).

This reflects the large proportion (45 percent) of black households with no car. Two-thirds of poor black households and one-quarter of nonpoor

Table 7-12.   Average Btu's per Household, by Income, Energy Source, and Race, 1972–1973

Income class and 3 energy sources	Average Btu's (millions) per household		Ratio Black to Other
	Black	Other	
Poor	172	218	79
Electricity	51	57	89
Natural gas	100	123	81
Gasoline	21	38	55
Lower middle	242	298	81
Electricity	60	82	73
Natural gas	139	128	109
Gasoline	43	88	49
Total nonpoor	311	371	84
Electricity	74	101	73
Natural gas	152	144	106
Gasoline	85	126	67

Source: Washington Center for Metropolitan Studies' Lifestyles and Energy Surveys.

black households had no car in 1973. These percentages are substantially higher than for other households at these income levels (Table 7-13).

Blacks had only about 15 percent more drivers than households; other races reported about 65 percent more. To a large degree this represents the extent to which the latter had more than one car. About 45 percent of nonblack homes (compared with 20 percent of all black households) had more than one car. Thus, the ratio of all cars to all households was less than one for blacks (.79), but close to one and one-half for others (1.43). The ratio of drivers to cars, similarly, indicates that 44 percent more blacks know how to drive than have cars, compared with only 16 percent more drivers than cars in other households.

These various relationships—cars to households, drivers to households, and drivers to cars—change substantially with income class, but blacks have less advantage in every one. Among the nonpoor as a whole, for instance, black households had about 20 percent more cars than households compared with over 50 percent more cars than households in other families. Blacks had 50 percent more drivers than households among the nonpoor compared with 80 percent more in other nonpoor households (Table 7-14).

Thus black households used substantially less gasoline and logged far fewer automobile miles than others. The median number of gallons of gasoline black households used in 1972 was about half the median for others—490 versus 910 (Table 7-15). Blacks drove a median of 9,000 miles while others drove 15,000. Less than one-fifth of black households drove 20,000 miles or more, compared to one-third of the others.

The amount of gasoline used depends on miles per gallon that cars get, as well as miles driven. Black households usually buy used cars, and their cars tend to be older, whether in single-car or multiple-car households (Table 7-16). Thus they report better mileage (Table 7-17). Older cars are lighter than new ones and tend to have fewer fuel using accessories. All those who bought used cars, in fact, report better mileage than those who bought their cars new. The weight of new cars is increasing, regardless of make or model—compact, standard, luxury, or van/pickup.

Among one-car black households, standard or full sized models predominate (75 percent), while 15 percent have a compact. Other one-car households tend to have more compacts. The newest car among multiple car households (mostly those with two cars rather than three or more) is less likely to be a standard model. The trend among blacks who can afford a second car is in two directions: toward a compact (26 percent compared to 15 percent in the one-car families) or toward a luxury car (14 percent compared to 6 percent in the one-car households). The standard model is still the black household's favorite even among those with two cars. Other households' second cars are overwhelmingly standard or compact models, but the number of vans or pickup trucks becomes relatively important (13 percent compared to 3 percent in the

Table 7-13. Cars and Drivers, by Race, 1973

	All households	
Cars and drivers	*Black*	*Other*
	Percent	
All households	100	100
Number of cars		
0	45	13
1	35	41
2 or more	20	46
Number of drivers		
0	26	11
1	42	27
2 or more	32	63
	Ratios	
Drivers to cars	1.44	1.16
Cars to households	.79	1.43
Drivers to households	1.14	1.67

Source: Washington Center for Metropolitan Studies' Lifestyles and Energy Surveys.

Table 7-14. Cars and Drivers, by Income and Race, 1972-1973

Cars and drivers	*Poor*		*All nonpoor*		*Lower middle*	
	Black	*Other*	*Black*	*Other*	*Black*	*Other*
	Percent					
All households	100	100	100	100	100	100
Number of cars						
0	66	40	25	8	30	15
1	30	40	40	40	50	53
2 or more	4	20	35	51	20	33
Number of drivers						
0	40	33	12	6	16	11
1	44	42	40	24	49	38
2 or more	16	25	48	70	35	51
	Ratios					
Drivers to cars	1.95	1.19	1.27	1.17	1.38	1.18
Cars to households	.40	.82	1.17	1.54	.93	1.25
Drivers to households	.78	.97	1.49	1.81	1.28	1.48

Source: Washington Center for Metropolitan Studies' Lifestyles and Energy Surveys.

Table 7-15. Miles Driven and Gasoline Used by Those Having Cars, by Race, 1972-1973

Miles driven and gasoline used	Black	Other
	Percent	
All households with cars[a]	100	100
Miles driven in year[a]		
Less than 10,000	61	30
10,000-19,999	22	39
20,000 or more	17	32
Gallons of gasoline in year[b]		
Less than 500	51	28
500-999	21	27
1,000 or more	29	45
	Medians[c]	
Miles driven in year[c]	9,000	15,000
Gallons of gasoline used[c]	490	910

[a]Cars owned for 12 months.
[b]Based only on data for households that reported gasoline consumption.
[c]For all households, regardless of whether they owned a car.
Source: Washington Center for Metropolitan Studies' Lifestyles and Energy Surveys.

Table 7-16. Type and Age of Car and Whether Bought New or Used, for One-Car and Multiple-Car Households, by Race, 1973 (percent of households)

Car characteristics	One-car households		Multicar households (newest car)	
	Black	Other	Black	Other
All households	100	100	100	100
Type of car				
Compact/subcompact	15	26	26	23
Standard	74	66	57	57
Luxury	6	5	14	7
Van or pickup	4	3	3	13
Age of car				
5 years old or over	60	48	34	23
2-4 years old	29	32	37	41
Less than 2 years old	11	20	29	37
Bought				
Used	66	46	62	39
New	34	54	38	61

Source: Washington Center for Metropolitan Studies' Lifestyles and Energy Surveys.

Table 7-17. Miles per Gallon Estimated for Local Driving, by Race, 1973 (percent of households with cars)

Miles per gallon[a]	Black	Other
	(percent)	
All households with cars	100	100
Less than 15 mi. per gal.	39	54
15–19	47	30
20 or more	15	16

[a]For all cars owned and for households reporting.
Source: Washington Center for Metropolitan Studies' Lifestyles and Energy Surveys.

one-car households) (see Table 7-16). This indicates increasing use of second vehicles for long weekends or vacations on the road.[9]

Only 30 percent of black household heads reported long auto trips (200 miles or more) in 1973 compared with twice that among others. This also contributes to blacks' low gasoline consumption. Indeed they were much less likely to take long trips by any means of transportation—railroad, bus, or airplane as well as by car (Table 7-18). Long trips are expensive. When black household heads take long trips they pay for them themselves. The long trips others take are more often work related.

Commuting

About eight in ten of the chief earners in black households get to work in a private automobile and seven in ten own one. Many black household heads ride with someone else—in fact the proportion is twice as large as for others. Among nonblacks, almost 90 percent commute in a private car, mostly by themselves.

Of the remaining black household heads who commute to a job, twice as large a proportion use some form of public transit—14 percent compared to 7 percent for others (Table 7-19). Black workers report the same reasons as everyone else for using a car to get to and from the job: no convenient public transportation. Black workers average about the same distance to work as others, but, mainly because a larger proportion use the more time consuming public transit, their trip takes a little longer. A number of studies document how public transportation fails to meet the needs of central city residents, and especially of black central city residents, many of whose jobs are in places where commuting by public transit would be very time consuming. Some studies go into both time lost in waiting and transfers on particular bus systems.[10]

A larger proportion of black men's wives than white men's wives work outside the home (45 percent compared to 35 percent). Wives seldom get

Table 7-18.   Major Trips by Household Head, by Transportation
Mode, by Race, 1972–1973 (percent of household heads)

Transportation	Black	Other
	(percent)	
All household heads	100	100
Percent making one or more[a] major trips		
None	58	31
Auto	29	63
Railroad or bus	11	6
Airplane	12	26
All major trips[b]		
0	58	31
1 or more	42	69
Auto[b]		
0	71	37
1 or more	29	63
Railroad or bus[b]		
0	89	94
1 or more	11	6
Airplane[c]		
0	88	74
1 or more	12	26

[a]Includes some who took more than one trip during the year.
[b]Going 100 miles or more each way.
[c]Any airplane trips of any distance.
Source: Washington Center for Metropolitan Studies' Lifestyles and Energy
Surveys.

to use the car for commuting in one-car families, regardless of race; the husband,
virtually always the chief breadwinner, takes it (Table 7-20). Since many black
households have no car at all, the black working wife is much more likely to ride
the bus than her nonblack counterpart. Also, she is less likely to carpool.

WHAT ENERGY COSTS

The average energy expenditures for blacks and other households show a
near classic case of the disadvantaged in the retail market. Blacks use less
electricity and natural gas per household, spend less money for it, but they pay
more per unit (Tables 7-21 and 7-22).

Gasoline prices are the same, whoever pulls up to the pump. Not so
for electricity and natural gas. Blacks have less choice than most people when it
comes to the energy sources they have at home. Segregation and limited
mobility still are so much a part of black life that when a family moves to
improve its living conditions, other factors besides energy are the important

Table 7-19. Transportation Mode, Miles, and Minutes to Work of Employed Household Heads by Race, 1973 (percent of employed household heads)

Mode, miles, and minutes to work	Black	Other
		(percent)
All employed household heads	100	100
Transportation mode[a]		
Car	80	89
Public transit	14	7
Walk, bicycle, other	8	5
Miles		
Less than 5	42	37
5–14	27	36
15 or more	31	27
Minutes		
Less than 16	39	50
16–30	44	32
Over 30	17	18

[a]May not add to 100 because more than one transportation mode was reported.
Source: Washington Center for Metropolitan Studies' Lifestyles and Energy Surveys.

Table 7-20. Chief Car User in Husband-Wife Households, by Number of Cars in Household and by Race, 1973 (percent of households)

Chief car user and number of cars	Black	Other
One-car households	100	100
Household head	78	70
Wife	7	18
Working wife	4	6
Other household member	11	6
Multiple-car households— newest car	100	100
Household head	38	41
Wife	32	34
Working wife	23	15
Other household member	7	10

Source: Washington Center for Metropolitan Studies' Lifestyles and Energy Surveys.

Table 7-21.   Amount, Cost, and Price of Energy, by Energy Source and Race, 1972-1973

Use, cost, and price	Black	Other
Btu's used per household	254	350
Electricity	64	96
Natural gas	137	142
Gasoline	53	112
Expenditures per household ($)	$465	$697
Electricity	147	198
Natural gas	161	167
Gasoline	157	332
Price per unit (millions Btu's)		
Electricity	$2.31	$2.07
Natural gas	1.18	1.18
Gasoline	2.96	2.96

Source: Price of gasoline at 37 cents per gallon from *1973 Platts Oil Price Handbook and Oilmanac*, New York: McGraw-Hill, 1974, p. 125. Consumption and other price data supplied by utilities for the Washington Center for Metropolitan Studies' Lifestyles and Energy Surveys.

Table 7-22.   Average Price per Unit for Electricity and Natural Gas, by Income and Race, 1972-1973[a]

Energy source	Black	Other
All households		
Electricity and natural gas	$1.75	$1.63
Electricity	2.31	2.07
Natural gas	1.18	1.18
Poor households		
Electricity and natural gas	1.87	1.79
Electricity	2.45	2.35
Natural gas	1.29	1.23
Nonpoor households		
Electricity and natural gas	1.69	1.61
Electricity	2.22	2.05
Natural gas	1.15	1.17
Lower middle[a]		
Electricity and natural gas	1.91	1.62
Electricity	2.54	2.05
Natural gas	1.28	1.19

[a]Data for upper middle and well off households are not reported by race because the number of interviews was too small for statistical stability.

Source: Washington Center for Metropolitan Studies' Lifestyles and Energy Surveys.

considerations. The household pays more per unit the less it uses (Table 7-22). Lack of choice of substitutes makes the home energy bill of special significance to black families.

DIRECTIONS FOR POLICY

Background

Energy policies that most affect blacks concern equity and relate especially to housing, community development, and land use. Energy policies should be designed to be equally advantageous to everyone. They should not reinforce the often subtle forms of discrimination in housing and housing related policies, or discourage homebuilding for those who need housing most.

When energy policy is primarily conservation oriented—lacking a broad view of community and regional needs—it may inadvertently emphasize high cost aspects of housing, land use, and construction that favor the well off. Such policies include low density land use, low growth, and reluctance to zone for low and moderate priced housing or for multiple family dwellings.[11] These practices limit housing within areas and close by. Blacks are especially victims, since many neighborhoods are already closed to them, either intentionally or in effect.[12]

According to the National Commission on Urban Problems:[13]

> . . . there are sometimes important nonfiscal policies behind certain types of exclusionary land-use decisions. "Undesirable" uses such as junkyards are not very attractive. "Undesirable" people—minority groups and the poor—would not "fit in."

Restrictions limit the kind of housing that can be built and how existing homes can be remodeled. These restrictions lead to inequities and through land use, zoning, or building code regulations often raise the cost and reduce the amount of housing available. Informal decisions about financing also effectively reduce the housing pool from which black families can choose.[14]

High housing cost and limited availability affect energy use. More costly homes are likely to be larger and more fully equipped and thus highly energy intensive per person living there. The less housing there is, the more limited the choice both of housing and energy using alternatives. These conditions affect blacks more than others, because fewer of them can afford high priced housing and they have a more limited choice of homes or neighborhoods regardless of what they can afford.

Well off white families already have good housing.[d] The main

[d]Only 7 percent of all white households, regardless of income, lived in substandard dwellings in 1970, compared to 23 percent of black households. (U.S. Bureau of the Census, *Current Population Reports, The Social and Economic Status of the Black Population in the United States 1973*, P-23, No. 48, Table 76, p. 108).

demand and need are elsewhere, both among blacks and whites. A breakthrough for "fair housing" would help to revive the homebuilding industry and overcome the critical housing shortage of the 1970s. New housing starts have been dropping sharply while vacancy rates remain very low. A large volume of homebuilding for those who need it most would give black families greater choice than before for buying or renting homes in which they have control of their energy sources and uses.

Recommendations

The situation described above leads to these recommendations. There are doubtless many others.

- Federal housing legislation should require communities receiving federal aid to provide tangible regional goals for open housing for minorities and low and moderate income families. Achievement should be reviewed annually and strong sanctions applied where patterns of discrimination persist. According to Babcock and Bosselman: "Open housing is an essential constitutional principle . . . , but it will remain only a generality unless translated into tangible goals."[15]
- The enforcement provisions of the Civil Rights Act of 1968, and, in this case, the housing provisions of Title Eight especially, should be strengthened to prevent covert as well as overt housing discrimination. The law should include funds for investigations to trace and document discriminatory patterns and actions by housing vendors or builders, land developers, and community officials.
- Home loan programs for low and moderate income households should be greatly expanded to encourage large scale building and rehabilitation of moderate and low priced housing with energy saving emphasis. The programs should include interest subsidies, low down payments, and long amortization periods for both new homes and rehabilitation of older homes.
- States that still do not have statewide building codes should have federal assistance to develop them. Such codes should include performance standards and bypass numerous local codes that permit individual judgment, case by case. Individual judgments often discriminate against low to moderate income housing and against minorities.

An open, expanded housing and real estate market would help black people choose energy saving dwellings and allow them (and others) to add features to their homes to save additional energy.

Chapter Eight

Energy Policies for People

PROLOGUE

The preceding chapters discuss national concern about energy resources and conservation in the context of household requirements. They show how much energy households of different kinds use, how they use it, and to what extent they can conserve it; and they outline some of the steps that might be considered to improve the efficiency of household energy use without reducing levels of living.

Levels of living vary widely from poor to rich as does the use of energy and the consequences of energy use in the form of pollution. Policies must take into account that poor and lower middle income groups use least energy, are able to conserve it least, and suffer the consequences of its production most. The affluent use most energy, have and can buy energy conserving features, and are the most likely to be protected from air pollution originating from such sources as electricity generation and the use of gasoline.

The House and Car

The study conclusions are unequivocal about contributions and obstacles to energy conservation both in homes and transportation. First, major energy use and savings are inherent in the basic features of the structure in which households live, and in their modes of transportation. In the home, energy requirements and savings stem chiefly from how well the structure is protected from the weather, how it is kept at comfort levels (winter and summer), and how much energy is used to heat water for cooking and washing.

A poorly constructed house that is not fitted with storm windows and insulation will use more energy per square foot than a tightly built house, all other things being equal. The same home and household that heats with electricity or has an electric hot water heater will use twice as much energy for space or water heating than if it uses natural gas, the most common heating fuel. The larger the home, the more energy it requires for heating, but apartments of the same size need less than a row house or a town house, and these need less than a semidetached house. The most energy consuming house is free standing—exposed to the weather on all sides. If it uses electric heat and central air conditioning and an electric water heater besides, and has no insulation or other winterizing features it is an energy glutton.

In transportation, energy conservation depends on the weight, number, and use made of the cars households own, if they own a car, and in the degree to which household members use local and intermetropolitan public transportation.

Choice

Another and perhaps as important a conclusion is the extraordinary degree to which households lack a choice in the most important energy using features of their homes or transportation. The only households with any substantial choice are affluent. Many of the others have little alternative but to live in areas where the air is the dirtiest, and the builder or landlord has already decided how the home is to be heated and what equipment for cooking and washing are available. But almost every household is locked into an energy system at home and in transportation from which it cannot easily escape. The home was there when bought or rented. It was not designed with an eye for energy savings. The majority of households haven't the money to change their structure. And to make matters worse, new housing is increasingly energy intensive.

The majority of households also live where public transportation is a long walk away, is time consuming, or otherwise inconvenient. Thus they use a car, especially to go to work. And the new cars as well as the new homes coming on the market are more and more energy consuming.

Recommendations

The proposals that follow reflect these findings. They are placed in the larger context of the major economic goal of full employment and economic growth and stability. They also allow for policy making procedures that are necessary for substantial modifications in household energy use or choice.

None of the proposals implies instant solution. But if plans begin now and steps are taken soon, many of the changes can come about in five years and perhaps most of them in a decade. A few that require technological development or depend on action at several levels of government may take longer. But nothing can happen without a beginning.

HOUSING

Background

Since most of the energy conservation that can be achieved in a household is in the house structure, the proposals begin with housing. They take into account the recession in the housing industry and its key position in the economy. A basic assumption is that policies to introduce energy conserving features into the existing housing stock and into new housing can contribute substantially to economic growth and stability.

It is urgent to begin now. Rehabilitating or retrofitting housing that is now standing and occupied comes first, because a year's construction of new housing, even in the best of times when housing volume is greatest, adds less than 4 percent to the total supply.[1] Also, the present housing stock includes about four million occupied dwellings that are substandard.[a] In addition, nine million homes that are in moderate to very cold climates[b] had no insulation in 1973, 12 million had no storm doors, over 20 million had one or more extra large windows, most of which were not double glazed and were not protected by storm sash.

Each year many households buy a new furnace or water heater. Many homeowners may want to switch to a less energy consuming kind or to one that is less expensive to run. Some homes just need weather stripping or caulking around windows. Others need replacements for windows or doors. Still others require major structural improvements, such as a sound roof, to prevent substantial leakage and permit the use of improved kinds of insulation.

The need for these important improvements in the existing stock, and for new housing that incorporates energy saving design features, comes at a time when the housing industry is in the doldrums and builders might gladly adjust to energy and conservation criteria. Housing starts in the first half of 1974 were at their lowest in seven years, and building permits, which precede new home building, had dropped even more than starts.

Expectations for the housing industry in 1974 were gloomy for many reasons. Among the most important were high and rising interest rates and construction costs and, therefore, increasing prices and rents. All except the well off were priced out of the housing market. The median price for new one-family homes was $34,700 in May 1974—the highest on record, and 25 percent above the median in 1972.[2]

Because the volume of new housing has plummeted and vacancy rates have been lower in the seventies than in the sixties, the supply of existing

[a]A total of 4.1 million dwelling units were substandard in 1970, according to the *United States Budget in Brief,* 1975, p. 37.
[b]Degree days of 3,500 or more. This includes places ranging from Nashville, Tenn. and Albuquerque, N.M. to Portland, Me. and Grand Forks, N.D.

housing lags far behind demand, especially with rapidly increasing numbers of marriages in recent years.[3] Therefore, prices and rents for existing housing have risen sharply also—rents by almost 10 percent from 1972 to 1974 (first half) and house prices by more than 10 percent—from a median of $26,700 in 1972 to over $30,000 in 1974.

Most of the need for energy saving features in housing, and most of the need for upgrading their housing (including moves to new dwellings) is among households that are middle income or below. These households represent a huge backlog of unmet housing need and demand. In fact, the American housing situation is reaching a crisis stage. What could be better timed than a substantially expanded national program to improve the housing stock and the housing supply, with special attention to energy conserving features?

Recommendations

1. *A substantially expanded FHA loan program should include incentives for rehabilitation and repair of moderate value and low value existing homes, with special emphasis on energy conservation.* The FHA rehabilitation loan program as of July 1974 places an upper limit of $5,000 for loans of no more than seven years at interest rates from 7.57 percent to 10.57 percent, depending on the loan size and term. The short term and the high interest rates, together with the low ceiling, make the present program too expensive and limited. A program that doubles the loan period and subsidizes the interest rate would provide strong incentives for both homeowners and landlords to improve their houses to include more and better insulation, space and water heating improvements, and other weatherproofing. A higher ceiling is required for major installations, for which costs are now well above $5,000. The proposed program as a whole would serve energy conservation needs and improve the total housing stock. With proper direction this program could substantially upgrade deteriorating neighborhoods and strengthen the economic situation of special trades contractors, their suppliers, and the industries that make the materials they use.

2. *A substantially expanded and low interest-long term FHA loan program should be introduced for builders of middle and lower income housing, to provide a mix of apartment and single family dwellings whose design takes energy conservation into account.* The present trend in housing subsidies by the Department of Housing and Urban Development is toward housing allowances for low income families. By itself even a modest program limited to housing allowances could exacerbate demand for a small supply, without commitment to provide new housing through the normal private market. Housing allowances are an improvement over the bewildering welter of subsidized programs, which were suspended on January 5, 1974.[4] (The remaining authorizations will take several years for housing to reach completion.)

However, the entire program is only for a small proportion of those who need housing assistance. In contrast, the suggested program would stimulate entrepreneurial know-how in the homebuilding industry by encouraging large scale homebuilding through normal channels.

A total of not quite $2.3 billion was allocated for housing assistance to low and moderate income families in fiscal year 1975.[5] In contrast, $6.7 billion in tax relief was allowed by the Treasury in the form of deductible mortgage interest and state and local property taxes paid by present homeowners.[6] Two-thirds of this tax relief went to households with taxable incomes of $15,000 or more.[7] The argument is not to remove such tax relief, but to provide at least the same amount of aid to stimulate housing production for those who are not so well off, who comprise the bulk of present housing demand.

Commitment to a graduated but sizable program of new housing would address energy, housing, social, and economic issues. For energy purposes, new housing would be authorized under the program only if it were designed with energy saving features. An expanded housing supply that reaches the majority also will introduce competition and choice into the housing market. This will benefit everyone, but especially those with least choice: the less than well off, and minority families. Finally, costs and prices would moderate, while business and employment would be helped. Homebuilding expansion has substantial effects in a widening circle on consumer and producer markets, and therefore on the total economy.[c]

3. A substantial support program should be planned and coordinated among involved federal agencies for improving building technology and design to conserve energy. Various technical programs are under way or soon to be started that will help architects, engineers, and builders improve both new and existing homes. These programs, at the National Bureau of Standards and elsewhere, require expansion and continuing support to ensure optimum results. The program should emphasize improvements in heating, ventilating and air conditioning design, with the goal of conserving energy without reducing comfort or increasing cost. Some of the research underway evaluates the residential application of heat pump systems and ways of best retrofitting a house to aid insulation and modify heating and cooling systems.

The results of these and related studies should be widely disseminated. Support would be required to provide a program of consumer, architect, and builder education, and of building code development to incorporate the findings. All such research addresses energy savings and cost. If

[c]For detailed rationale and quantification of a suggested similar program for an earlier year, which could be updated, see Dorothy K. Newman, "The Low-Cost Housing Market." *Monthly Labor Review* (December 1966), pp. 1362–1368.

implemented, therefore, the suggested housing expansion could trim the cost of new or rehabilitation work per square foot and add further to improving both the housing market and the economy.

     4. *The appropriate federal agencies should be given the power to enforce state and local observance of federal law and rulings about open housing and environmental protection, carrying strong sanctions. Enforcement must be based on thorough understanding and review of local situations.* Air quality and open and adequate community facilities are associated with housing quality and choice, and with neighborhood amenities. Practices that lead to exclusionary and discriminatory results for those seeking housing often stem from environmental concerns.[d] Environmental quality and housing choice need to be preserved for everyone. Review of local and state regulations and their administration for both these objectives are necessary for attaining and commanding compliance with the Constitution and federal law.

     A recent exhaustive analysis and review of the literature and of litigation on this subject by Randall W. Scott of the Urban Land Institute[8] documents the interrelationship of environmental concerns and housing discrimination. He concludes that:

> Philosophically, government appears unwilling to establish firm policy, guidance, and support relative to the equal opportunity/exclusion/discrimination issues in housing and land use, even though its potential arsenal for dealing with these problems is immense. . . .
>
> Since the first housing act of 1934, there has been evolving a thrust toward the development of a national housing policy . . . to provide adequate housing for all persons. Yet it has been shown time and again that exclusionary land use practices serve to frustrate the fulfillment of this national objective.

     Scott's list of community practices include many that affect minorities but relate primarily to growth: building moratoria, slow growth policies, and refusal to provide capacity or funding for municipal services, such as sewage and water systems. Among economic policies are large lot zoning, limitation on number of bedrooms, and prohibition against multifamily dwellings.[9]

     So far, significant investigations and litigation to remove obstacles to open housing have originated in local or national private groups with limited funds. Housing on equal terms for all citizens cannot be left entirely to local administration.

     In environmental matters also, attention to air quality standards and other concerns cannot be left to narrow interests. Environmental policies need forceful regional and national implementation on their own account.

[d]See Chapter Seven and Note 12 of Chapter Seven for documentation.

These are national concerns, requiring much more attention and enforcement than individual agencies such as the Department of Justice, HUD, the United States Civil Rights Commission, or the Environmental Protection Agency have used or possess. Additional and present legislation should give federal agencies monitoring and action power enough to improve the environment for all citizens and to remove housing and land use barriers that discriminate. Enough funds should be appropriated for investigation and regular review, and there should be stiff sanctions.

5. *Support vigorously the National Conference for Building Codes and Standards (a state oriented organization) in bringing about standard building codes, especially the suggested "Standard for Energy Conservation in Buildings."* More federal responsibility and involvement than has yet taken place must occur in helping states to put together statewide performance building codes. Many of such codes recently have preempted local codes with good results. Improved statewide codes protect consumers better than local codes and help builders to comply with specifications. State codes require that buildings meet certain standards of performance, whereas many local codes are so specific about materials and methods that they are confusing, expensive, or overlooked.

RECOMMENDATIONS TO IMPROVE
ENERGY EFFICIENCY AND EQUITY

1. *Require that state public utility commissions introduce a flat rate structure supplemented by a system of peak load pricing for electricity, as a matter of equity and national energy conservation.* The price consumers pay for household energy—all the bills from electric and gas companies—represent, chiefly, the economic costs of producing and distributing energy and of attacking the resulting pollution. These are legitimate costs and must be paid. The major issue for energy policy is whether the way the costs are paid is equitable and contributes to environmental improvement.

This book has shown that small users—usually poor and lower middle income households—pay more per unit than large users, and that the gap has been widening over the past two decades. Under these conditions, the poor and lower middle are probably using less energy than they might otherwise, and the rich are using more. A flat rate would cause electricity and natural gas to be sold like gasoline and most other products, at a constant price per unit. This serves the goal of equity as well as conservation by eliminating the reward of lower and lower prices to consumers who use more and more.

Peak load pricing would make electricity costlier at times of highest demand, preferably by the time of day or day of the week. Higher prices at peak demand would tend to reduce electricity requirements at peak hours, whatever the season. This would reduce the need for power plants. Costs would be held down and savings passed along to customers.

If the poor and low and middle income groups are able to afford more, and the well off would reduce their expanding rate of use, the total growth in household energy consumption could moderate. Revenues would not fall[e] while utilities could serve their customers more equitably with needed energy, and the environmental threat of more power plants would diminish. The end result would be economic as well as social improvement.

2. *Expand the consumer concerns of the Federal Power Commission and state utility commissions. These responsibilities should include rate reform as well as other consumer concerns.* Such a change in the scope of responsibility could improve substantially the energy consumers' economic situation and their environment. Some of the steps strongly recommended under an expanded mandate are as follows:

- *Prohibit promotional practices and other types of advertising by public utilities.* This would reduce cost induced price increases by eliminating artificial incentives to expand consumption, especially by the most well off. Slowing the growth in energy consumption will reduce the need for new capacity—a major reason for rate increases.

- *Make it obligatory to include consumer representatives—some of whom should be women and minorities—on utility regulatory commissions and the Federal Power Commission.* This is in line with civil rights legislation. It would bring better awareness of consumer needs and more equitable decisions that affect the community at large, as well as give a voice to those who now lack one. Restructured commissions also would be likely to curb practices that fall hard on particular consumers. Some special consumer concerns have to do with policies of turning off the gas or electricity because of nonpayment of bills, requiring advance deposits for installation, choosing the location of energy facilities, and moratoria that prevent utility lines from being extended to places where housing may be urgently needed. Consumers would be especially interested in the matter of how to save energy by having the gas furnace pilot light turned off in the summer. Much gas could be saved if this were done with no direct charge, so that everyone would do it. The service would be a legitimate cost in computing the price of natural gas.

- *Forbid persons in or from the energy industry or associated industries from membership on state regulatory commissions or from employment in the Federal Energy Administration.* Conflict of interest should be a key criterion in screening commission members or employees who may be in a position to affect energy policy.[f]

eThe problem of declining average revenues with increasing average costs as high use customers increase their consumption (revenue erosion) was discussed in Chapter Five.

fTwo conflict of interest cases reported by the General Accounting Office concern the Federal Energy Administration and are described in *The Washington Post,* "2d Conflict of Interest Seen by GAO in U.S. Energy Office," June 29, 1974, by Morton Mintz.

HELP CONSUMERS CHOOSE
AND USE APPLIANCES WISELY

Even though major appliances along with lighting account for only 15 percent of the average home's energy consumption in a year. the energy needed per appliance has been rising steadily. More households are buying major appliances, especially those that are not already a fixture in every home, such as clothes dryers, dishwashers and air conditioners. Replacement is a large market as well, especially for stoves and refrigerators. It is important, therefore that the voluntary steps taken already toward energy efficiency labeling on appliances be made mandatory. Consumers should also be instructed how to interpret the information when they shop.

The following recommendations would help consumers buy appliances more intelligently.

1. *A mandatory energy efficiency labeling program, now under consideration by Congress, should be passed and implemented in a way that consumers understand.* The labeling program should provide for attaching a chart that defines clearly what the energy efficiency rating of each appliance is, for easy comparison at the time of purchase.

2. *Federal support of research to improve the energy efficiency of appliances and establish performance ratings should be underwritten as necessary to administer the following suggested program.*

3 *The Federal Energy Administration should have the responsibility of using technical research results to discover and refer for prosecution manufacturers of major appliances that make products found to be below established limits of performance.*

HELP HOUSEHOLDS IMPROVE THE ENERGY
EFFICIENCY OF THEIR TRANSPORTATION

Almost half of the energy that households use directly is not consumed at home but in their cars. The steady rise in car weight, cost, and use, coupled with a declining trend in public transit use and increasing fares and deficits, spell crisis. The transportation crisis has many faces. One involves inexorably rising energy use and air pollution. Another involves falling public transit ridership, so that many systems still in use may soon wither away.

Just as in the case of housing, most people, and especially most of the work force, find they have no choice. A car is expensive, but public transportation does not take people where they have to go quickly enough or when they need to go, for the right price. The following recommendations are designed to reduce car weight, support alternatives to cars, and reduce automobile air pollution.

1. *Proposed "Truth in Energy" legislation should provide that buyers of all cars (used as well as new) be given information about car weight and miles per gallon of gasoline.* Since most cars are bought used, a labeling provision is especially important for them. This would have to be a local responsibility. Whether buying a new or used car, better consumer information could have an important effect on demand, and thus on eventual energy savings and reduced air pollution.

2. *A federal tax should be added to state license taxes (already on a weight basis) for all cars over 2,750 pounds, to go to a public transit trust fund.* (See recommendation (3) below for a description of the fund.)

3. *The federal gasoline tax should be amended to assess a higher gasoline tax on cars that weigh more than 2,750 pounds to go to the public transit trust fund.* Large cars would pull up to pumps set to include the higher tax in the metered reading. The FEA would provide car weight information annually to all registered gasoline dealers. The tax increase should be earmarked for a public transit fund. Revenues would go to states to assist public transportation systems according to a carefully developed formula. The formula should take into account commuting mileage and patterns, and population size and density. The U.S. Treasury should collect all the revenues and make sure that distribution occurs fairly.

    Consideration should be given to providing a greater proportional share to metropolitanwide, intercity, intermetropolitan, and cross-county systems. Some of the trust fund should be earmarked for innovation in flexible small vehicle group systems to serve sparsely populated areas. If successful, some of the systems could be spun off for private operation after testing.

    States and localities as well as the federal government can benefit from lower weight cars and better public transportation. This means less wear and tear on streets, roads, and highways, and reduced maintenance and repair. Air pollution could be reduced also, improving public health. Reduced air pollution would help communities and businesses that must use services to clean buildings affected by dirty air.

    These transportation alternatives address demand as well as supply. They ought to slow down rapidly increasing energy use, and improve air quality and daily transportation conditions at the same time. Federal support for urban transportation, excluding money for airports, was estimated at $2.2 billion for fiscal year 1975; space research and technology received $3.3 billion.[10] It is a present-day cliché to measure proposed expenditures for many things against how much the nation spends on space exploration; but comparing expenditures on earth with space travel is more apt than most. The discrepancy in allotment of funds could be the cause of confusion, problems, and hazards on the ground where everybody—even astronauts most of the time—live and work.

WHERE IS ALL THAT MONEY COMING FROM?

This book does not attempt to discuss national goals and priorities. Briefly, we assume that the people come first, and that the least powerful, even more than the most powerful, require a strong and growing economy with full employment. We suggest subsidizing human needs for the poor as well as for the well off.

A growing economy can accomplish everything that we have proposed. According to Henry C. Wallich,[11] economic growth *can* provide enough resources to equalize incomes and clean up the environment, if it diverts

> ... some of our growing output from its principal use, which is to raise consumption. But we would then have a clean environment, assured supplies for the future, liveable areas, and most of what environmentalists fear growth will destroy.... This will of course cost a lot of money. But if growth continues, that money will be available.

Appendix

Appendix A-1

Household Questionnaire: National Survey of Household Activities

NATIONAL SURVEY OF HOUSEHOLD ACTIVITIES

		TIME INTERVIEW
LOCATION #_____	HOUSING UNIT #_____	STARTED: _____

These first questions are about topics that some people are talking about today ...

1. Let's start with air and water pollution. In the United States today, do you think that air and water pollution is a major problem, a minor problem or not a problem at all?

```
                1  MAJOR PROBLEM
                2  MINOR PROBLEM
                3  NOT A PROBLEM AT ALL              121
                4  NO OPINION
```

2. How about shortage of fuels, such as natural gas, fuel oil, gasoline and electricity. In the United States today, do you think that shortages of fuel are a major problem, a minor problem, or not a problem at all?

```
                1  MAJOR PROBLEM
                2  MINOR PROBLEM
                3  NOT A PROBLEM AT ALL              122
                4  NO OPINION
```

3. In the United States <u>ten years from now</u>, which do you think will be the bigger problem -- air and water pollution, or shortages of fuels?

```
                1  AIR AND WATER POLLUTION
                2  SHORTAGES OF FUELS
                3  BOTH THE SAME                     123
                4  NEITHER
                5  NOT SURE
```

HAND RESPONDENT EXHIBIT A

4. Some parts of the U.S. had a fuel oil shortage this past winter. Which of these, if any, do you feel were mainly responsible for the fuel oil shortage?

```
                1  PRESIDENT NIXON
                2  CONGRESS
                3  NATIONAL OIL COMPANIES
                4  LOCAL OIL COMPANIES              124
                5  CONSUMERS
                6  ENVIRONMENTALISTS -- PEOPLE CONCERNED
                   WITH PRESERVING THE ENVIRONMENT
                7  ALL
                8  NONE
                9  OTHER (SPECIFY) _____
                0  DON'T KNOW
```

TAKE BACK EXHIBIT A

205

HAND RESPONDENT EXHIBIT B

5. If experts agreed there would be a shortage of electricity over the next 10 years or so, which of these ways of preventing a shortage of electricity would you favor?

        1 BUILD MORE POWER PLANTS
        2 INCREASE THE PRICE OF ELECTRICITY
        3 SLOW DOWN POPULATION GROWTH
        4 EVERYBODY BEING MORE THRIFTY AND   *125*
           CONSERVING ELECTRICITY
        5 OTHER (SPECIFY) _____

_____

        6 NO OPINION

TAKE BACK EXHIBIT B; HAND RESPONDENT EXHIBIT C

6. Some families use a lot of electricity and some use a little. This card shows three different ways that families who use different amounts of electricity in their homes might be charged. Suppose Family A uses twice as much electricity as Family B -- which way do you think Family A should be charged?

        1 TWICE AS MUCH (SAME RATE PER UNIT)
        2 LESS THAN TWICE AS MUCH (LOWER RATE PER UNIT)
        3 MORE THAN TWICE AS MUCH (HIGHER RATE PER UNIT)   *126*
        4 NO OPINION

TAKE BACK EXHIBIT C

These next questions are about your home.

7. First, I want to make the number of floors that you have here in your home. (INTER-VIEWER: DO NOT INCLUDE UNFINISHED BASEMENTS OR ATTICS.)

        1 ONE FLOOR
        2 1½ FLOORS
        3 2 FLOORS
        4 2½ FLOORS   *127*
        5 3 FLOORS
        6 OTHER (SPECIFY) _____

8. How many rooms are there in your home, excluding bathrooms? (INTERVIEWER: DO NOT IN-CLUDE UNFINISHED BASEMENTS OR ATTICS.)

        NUMBER OF ROOMS: _____   *128-129*

9. How many bathrooms do you have? (INTERVIEWER: COUNT ANY ROOM WITH A TOILET; THE ROOM NEED NOT HAVE A BATHTUB OR SHOWER IN IT.)

        NUMBER OF BATHROOMS: _____   *130*

0. In the winter, what is the usual temperature in your
home <u>during the day</u>?

        _____ DEGREES   *131-*

      X DON'T KNOW   *132*

1. In the winter, what is the usual temperature in your
home <u>during the night</u>, when people are asleep?

        _____ DEGREES   *133-*

      X DON'T KNOW   *134*

2. Are the usual temperatures in your home during the
winter the ones that you personally would like to
have?

   1 YES

   2 NO   *135*

   3 NOT SURE

IF "NO" ON Q. 12, ASK:

HAND RESPONDENT EXHIBIT D

13. Why is it that the temperature in your home is not the temperature you prefer?

      1 HEATING SYSTEM PROBLEM
      2 LANDLORD CONTROLS TEMPERATURE
      3 DIFFERENCE OF OPINION IN FAMILY   *136*
      4 FUEL SHORTAGE
      5 HIGH COST OF FUEL
      6 OTHER (SPECIFY) _____
      7 NOT SURE

TAKE BACK EXHIBIT D

14. In the winter, what temperature would you personally <u>like</u> to have your home <u>during the day</u>?

        _____ DEGREES   *137-*

      X DON'T KNOW   *138*

15. In the winter, what temperature would you personally <u>like</u> to have your home <u>during the night</u>?

        _____ DEGREES   *139-*

      X DON'T KNOW   *140*

16a. Do you have a thermostat or valve through which you
can control the temperature in your home?

   1 YES   *141*

   2 NO

IF "YES" ON Q. 16a, ASK:

16b. Which do you have -- a thermostat or a valve?

   1 THERMOSTAT   *142*

   2 VALVE

16c. How many?

   (NUMBER): _____ *143*

16d. On an average winter day, is the thermostat setting or valve usually left in
one place all day, or is it changed during the day?

      1 LEFT IN ONE PLACE   *144*
      2 CHANGED DURING THE DAY

17. In the winter, how often are one or more windows kept open during the night?

> 1 EVERY NIGHT, OR MOST NIGHTS
> 2 SOMETIMES
> 3 ALMOST NEVER
> 4 NEVER
> 5 NOT SURE

145

IF ANSWER TO Q. 17 IS CODE "1" OR "2," ASK:

18. When windows are kept open during the winter, are doors to those rooms usually shut, or usually not shut?

> 1 USUALLY SHUT
> 2 SOMETIMES SHUT, SOMETIMES NOT
> 3 USUALLY NOT SHUT

146

19. Which fuel is used most for heating your home -- gas, fuel oil, electricity, coal or something else?

> 1 GAS
> 2 FUEL OIL, KEROSENE, ETC.
> 3 ELECTRICITY
> 4 COAL
> 5 OTHER (SPECIFY) _____
> 6 NO FUEL USED

147

IF "GAS" ON Q. 19, ASK:

20. After the heating season, is the pilot light on your gas furnace turned off, or not?

> 1 YES, TURNED OFF
> 2 NOT TURNED OFF
> 3 NOT SURE

148

21. Do you (or someone in your household) pay for fuel used for heating your home, or is it included in your rent, or paid for in another way?

> 1 PAY FOR FUEL ⟶ | THIS ANSWER APPLIES IF COST OF FUEL IS INCLUDED IN GAS OR OTHER UTILITY BILL PAID BY THE HOUSEHOLD.
>
> 2 INCLUDED IN RENT
> 3 OTHER (SPECIFY) _____

149

IF "PAY FOR FUEL," ASK:

22. Do you have a special arrangement to pay the same amount each month during the heating season, or not?

> 1 YES
> 2 NO
> 3 NOT SURE

150

IF "FUEL OIL" ON Q. 19, ASK:

23. What is the approximate <u>total yearly cost</u> of fuel oil for heating your home?

> 1 UNDER $100
> 2 $100 - $149
> 3 $150 - $199
> 4 $200 - $249
> 5 $250 - $299
>
> 6 $300 - $399
> 7 $400 - $499
> 8 $500 - $599
> 9 $600 OR MORE
> X DON'T KNOW

151

24. In the winter, do you use any plug-in electric heaters, in addition to your main heating system, to help heat particular rooms? (INTERVIEWER: DO NOT INCLUDE ELECTRIC BLANKETS OR HEATLAMPS IN BATHROOMS.)

1 YES
2 NO   *152*
3 NOT SURE

IF YES: 24a. How many do you have? (NUMBER): _____   *153*

24b. Are they used frequently, occasionally or very little?

1 FREQUENTLY
2 OCCASIONALLY   *154*
3 VERY LITTLE

25. Do you have a humidifier in your house, either as part of the furnace or as a separate unit?

1 YES, PART OF FURNACE
2 YES, SEPARATE UNIT
3 NO   *155*
4 DON'T KNOW

HAND RESPONDENT EXHIBIT E

26. Which of these do you use in this household? Please read me the numbers.

1 AUTOMATIC WASHING MACHINE	7 SEPARATE FOOD FREEZER
2 WRINGER WASHING MACHINE	8 GAS CLOTHES DRYER
3 AUTOMATIC DISHWASHER	9 ELECTRIC CLOTHES DRYER
4 ELECTRIC REFRIGERATOR	10 GAS STOVE
5 GAS REFRIGERATOR	11 ELECTRIC STOVE
6 ICE BOX	12 BLACK AND WHITE TV
	13 COLOR TV

156-
157

TAKE BACK EXHIBIT E

IF "REFRIGERATOR" CIRCLED ON Q. 26, ASK:

27. Did you buy the refrigerator, did it come with your home, or was it a gift?

1 BOUGHT REFRIGERATOR
2 CAME WITH HOME
3 GIFT   *158*
4 OTHER (SPECIFY) _____
5 NOT SURE

28. Is your refrigerator frost-free, or does it have to be defrosted?

1 FROST-FREE
2 MUST DEFROST   *159*
3 NOT SURE

29. Does the freezer part of your refrigerator have a separate door -- that is, can you open the freezer part without opening the regular refrigerator part?

1 YES
2 NO   *160*
3 NOT SURE

30. How does this household usually wash clothes? Is the washing done here at home, is it done outside the home at a laundry, or at a laundromat, or is some of it done here at home and some at a laundry or laundromat?

        1 AT HOME
        2 LAUNDRY
          3 LAUNDROMAT   *161*
          4 SOME AT HOME, SOME AT LAUNDRY OR LAUNDROMAT

IF "AT HOME" OR "SOME AT HOME" ON Q. 30, ASK:

31. How many loads of wash per week are done here at home using hot or warm water?

        1 NONE
        2 ONE TO THREE
          3 FOUR TO SIX
          4 SEVEN TO TEN   *162*
            5 ELEVEN OR MORE
            6 NOT SURE

32. Which way are your clothes usually dried -- by hanging to dry, or in a dryer at home, or in a dryer at a laundry or laundromat?

        1 HANG DRY
        2 DRYER AT HOME   *163*
          3 DRIED AT LAUNDRY
          4 DRIED AT LAUNDROMAT

33. Other than appliances that you now own, are there any additional appliances that you feel you should own?

        1 YES
        2 NO   *164*
          3 NOT SURE

IF "YES" ON Q. 33, ASK:

34. What appliances do you feel you should own? (DO NOT READ LIST.)

        1 AIR CONDITIONER
        2 CLOTHES DRYER
          3 COLOR TELEVISION
          4 DISHWASHER   *165*
            5 WASHING MACHINE
            6 OTHER (SPECIFY) _____

                _____

35. What type of water heater do you have in your home -- electric, gas, oil or something else?

        1 ELECTRIC
        2 GAS
          3 OIL   *166*
          4 OTHER (SPECIFY) _____
            5 NONE
            6 NOT SURE

6. Do you have air conditioning here in your home -- either window or central air conditioning?

                    1 YES   *167*
                    2 NO -- SKIP TO Q. 44

IF "YES" ON Q. 36, ASK:

37. Is it window or central air conditioning?   1 WINDOW   *168*
                                                     2 CENTRAL AIR CONDITIONING

     IF "WINDOW" ON Q. 37, ASK:

     38. How many window air conditioners?   (NUMBER): _____   *169*

     IF "CENTRAL" ON Q. 37, ASK:

     39. Is your air conditioning gas or   1 GAS   *170*
          electric?   2 ELECTRIC
                                                     3 NOT SURE

     ASK RESPONDENTS WHO LIVE IN CENTRALLY AIR-CONDITIONED APARTMENTS:

     40. Can you control whether or not your   1 CAN CONTROL
          air conditioning is on?   2 CANNOT CONTROL   *171*
                                                     3 NOT SURE

41. What temperature do you like to keep
     your home during the summer?   _____ DEGREES   *172-*
                                                   X DON'T KNOW   *173*

42. Did you buy the air conditioning or did it come with your home?

                    1 BOUGHT IT
                    2 CAME WITH HOME   *174*
                    3 OTHER (SPECIFY) _____
                    4 NOT SURE

43. How many rooms do you cool here in your home?

                    NUMBER OF ROOMS: _____   *175*
                    Y ENTIRE HOUSE OR APARTMENT

ASK EVERYONE

HAND RESPONDENT EXHIBIT F

44. This exhibit shows costs for two different models of air conditioners. They look the
     same and work the same, but B costs $50 more to buy and $20 less per year to operate.
     Suppose you decided to buy an air conditioner and had two to choose from -- which one
     would you buy?

                    1 WOULD BUY A
                    2 WOULD BUY B   *176*
                    3 DON'T KNOW

TAKE BACK EXHIBIT F

45. This question may require a little thought. How many windows are there in your home? Please include basement and attic windows only if those areas are heated.

    1 LESS THAN 5   5 20-24
    2 5-9   6 25-29
    3 10-14   7 30 OR MORE   *211*
    4 15-19   8 DON'T KNOW

46. How many of the windows have storm windows or insulating glass? (SINGLE PANE WINDOWS MADE OF THERMOPANE AND OTHER KINDS OF INSULATING GLASS ARE THE SAME AS STORM WINDOWS.)

    1 ALL WINDOWS HAVE STORM WINDOWS OR INSULATING GLASS

    2 SOME WINDOWS DO (RECORD NUMBER BELOW)   *212*

       NUMBER WITH STORM WINDOWS OR INSULATING GLASS: _____   *213*

    3 NO STORM WINDOWS OR INSULATING GLASS -- SKIP TO Q. 48

IF "1" OR "2" ON Q. 46, ASK:

47. Did you buy the storm windows or did they   1 BOUGHT THEM
    come with your home?   2 CAME WITH HOME   *214*
                                                    3 OTHER (SPECIFY) _____

                                                    _____

IF "3" ON Q. 46, ASK:

48. Do you have weatherstripping on your   1 YES
    windows?   2 NO   *215*
                                                    3 DON'T KNOW

HAND RESPONDENT EXHIBIT G

49. This exhibit shows diagrams of three different types of windows. Which type do you mostly have in your home?

    1 TYPE A -- DOUBLE-HUNG
    2 TYPE B -- CASEMENT
    3 TYPE C -- SLIDING   *216*
    4 OTHER (DESCRIBE) _____

TAKE BACK EXHIBIT G

50a. Are any of the windows in your home extra large?   1 YES
                                                          2 NO   *217*

     IF YES: 50b. How many?   (NUMBER): _____   *218*

51. INTERVIEWER: PLEASE RECORD THE APPROXIMATE   LARGEST WINDOW:
    DIMENSIONS (IN FEET) OF THE LARGEST WINDOW
    IN THE MAIN ROOM OF THE HOUSE.   HEIGHT: _____ FEET   *219*

                                                        WIDTH: _____ FEET   *220*

2. Do you have insulation in your home, either in the ceiling or the walls? (INTER-
VIEWER: INSULATION DOES NOT INCLUDE AIR POCKET OR SPACE BETWEEN OUTSIDE AND INSIDE
WALL.)

       1 YES, CEILING INSULATION
       2 YES, WALL INSULATION
       3 YES, CEILING AND WALL INSULATION   221
       4 NO INSULATION
       5 DON'T KNOW

3. How many doors do you have that go outside or to an <u>unheated</u> area? (INTERVIEWER:
INCLUDE DOORS THAT GO TO AN UNHEATED PORCH OR GARAGE; <u>DO NOT INCLUDE</u> DOORS TO A
<u>HEATED</u> HALLWAY IN AN APARTMENT BUILDING.)

       NUMBER OF DOORS OPENING OUTSIDE: _____   222

ASK IN HOMES WITH OUTSIDE DOORS ONLY:

HAND RESPONDENT EXHIBIT H

54. In an average 24-hour period during the winter, about how many times are doors
opened that lead directly to the outside from your home? Try to think of all
the times the door might be opened because you, other members of your family,
friends or pets came in and went out -- just the approximate number of times.
Please read me the letter from the exhibit.

       A LESS THAN 5   F 25 TO 29
       B 5 TO 9   G 30 TO 39
       C 10 TO 14   H 40 TO 49   223
       D 15 TO 19   I 50 TO 59
       E 20 TO 24   J 60 OR MORE

TAKE BACK EXHIBIT H

55. Do your doors to the outside have storm   1 YES
doors?   2 NO   224
                                                 3 SOME DO, SOME DO NOT

    IF NO: 56. Do you have weatherstripping   1 YES
            on your doors to the outside?   2 NO   225
                                                 3 DON'T KNOW

IF RESPONDENT LIVES IN AN APARTMENT BUILDING, SKIP TO Q. 58.

HAND RESPONDENT EXHIBIT I

57. Which of these do you have here in your home? Just give me the numbers.

       1 BASEMENT
       2 CRAWL SPACE BELOW THE HOUSE
       3 ATTACHED UNHEATED GARAGE
       4 ATTACHED HEATED GARAGE   226
       5 UNFINISHED ATTIC OR CRAWL AREA ABOVE
          THE LIVING AREA
       6 NONE OF THESE

TAKE BACK EXHIBIT I

58. Do you happen to know how many square feet of living space you have here in your home (not including unfinished areas in an attic or basement)?

        1 YES   *227*
        2 NO

    IF YES: 59. How many square feet (just approximately)? _____ SQ. FT.

    IF NO: 60. What would be your best guess about the number of square feet? _____ SQ. FT.
                                               228
                       X HAVE NO IDEA   *229*

61. How about the main room (living or family room) of your house -- what is your estimate of the length and width in feet?

    INTERVIEWER: PUT RESPONDENT'S ESTIMATES IN BOXES IN SKETCH AT RIGHT.

                   IF RESPONDENT IS UNABLE TO MAKE ESTIMATE, PUT IN YOUR OWN BEST ESTIMATES.

              No. of feet   *230*
                                            232
              No. of feet

    CIRCLE TO SHOW SOURCE OF ESTIMATE: 1 ESTIMATES MADE BY RESPONDENT
                                            2 ESTIMATES MADE BY INTERVIEWER   *233*

These next questions are about some of the ways you and your family use electricity and fuel.

62. What wattage light bulbs do you usually buy -- 75 watts or less, or 100 watts or more?

        1 75 WATTS OR LESS
        2 100 WATTS OR MORE (INCLUDING 3-WAY BULBS)
        3 SAME AMOUNT OF EACH   *234*
        4 NOT SURE

63. How many rooms in your home, if any, usually have lights on continuously during the evening before everyone goes to sleep?

    NUMBER OF ROOMS: _____   *235*

64. Do you or your family keep any electric lights on all night outside or inside your home?

        1 YES
        2 NO   *236*
        3 NOT SURE

IF "YES" ON Q. 64, ASK:

65. Are the lights kept on in order to see better or because it keeps the household safer?

        1 TO SEE BETTER
        2 KEEPS HOUSEHOLD SAFER   *237*
        3 BOTH
        4 OTHER ANSWER (SPECIFY) _____ _____
        5 DON'T KNOW

6. Now I have some questions about the people who live here. Please tell me who they are, just in relation to the head of household, and their ages.

INTERVIEWER:

LIST EVERYONE, INCLUDING CHILDREN AND INFANTS, WHO IS NOW A MEMBER OF THE HOUSEHOLD.

INCLUDE PERSONS WHO ARE UNRELATED TO THE MAIN FAMILY IF THEY SHARE THIS HOUSING UNIT.

PERSONS WHO ARE NORMALLY MEMBERS OF THE HOUSEHOLD, BUT WHO ARE NOW LIVING AWAY FROM HOME (E.G., COLLEGE STUDENTS OR MEMBERS OF THE ARMED FORCES) SHOULD NOT BE LISTED.

CIRCLE NUMBER OF HOUSEHOLD MEMBER WHO IS RESPONDENT

NUMBERS WILL BE USED TO REFER TO HOUSEHOLD MEMBERS IN SOME QUESTIONS ON THE FOLLOW-ING PAGES

238

HOUSEHOLD MEMBER #	RELATION TO HEAD	AGE	SEX (CIRCLE ONE)
1			1 MALE 2 FEMALE
2			1 MALE 2 FEMALE
3			1 MALE 2 FEMALE
4			1 MALE 2 FEMALE
5			1 MALE 2 FEMALE
6			1 MALE 2 FEMALE
7			1 MALE 2 FEMALE
8			1 MALE 2 FEMALE
9			1 MALE 2 FEMALE
10			1 MALE 2 FEMALE

FROM HOUSEHOLD COMPOSITION TABLE ABOVE, YOU WILL PROBABLY KNOW WHETHER RESPONDENT IS MARRIED.

CIRCLE CODE FOR APPROPRIATE ANSWER BELOW. ASK IF NECESSARY.

67. Are you single, married, widowed, divorced or separated?

    1 SINGLE
    2 MARRIED
    3 WIDOWED
    4 DIVORCED OR SEPARATED

68. Does another family share your home here with you?

    1 YES
    2 NO

INTERVIEWER:

IF ANOTHER FAMILY SHARES THE SAME HOUSING UNIT, MEMBERS SHOULD BE LISTED IN HOUSEHOLD COMPOSITION TABLE ON PRECEDING PAGE.

IF ANOTHER FAMILY HAS A SEPARATE APARTMENT THAT IS DEFINED BY OUR RULES AS A SEPARATE HOUSING UNIT, THE ADDITIONAL HOUSING UNIT SHOULD BE LISTED ON YOUR HOUSING UNIT LISTING SHEET AND A SEPARATE INTERVIEW COMPLETED WITH THAT FAMILY.

69. Thinking of all meals eaten here, about how many times a week does your family have frozen meals that have to be heated in the oven?

    312-
    313

_____ TIMES PER WEEK THAT FROZEN MEALS ARE SERVED

70. About how many times a week is any type of meat, poultry or fish served at a meal here in your home? Count any meal at which meat, poultry or fish is a main item, including use in sandwiches, bacon with breakfast, and so on.

_____ TIMES PER WEEK THAT MEAT, POULTRY OR FISH
IS SERVED

    314-
    315

1. This question is about meals that you and other members of your household buy away from home. I have two numbers to write down (HAND RESPONDENT EXHIBIT J) --

      -- the first is the number of meals in <u>restaurants or cafeterias</u>

      -- the second is the number of meals in <u>quick-service places or carry-out shops</u>

Let's take the last seven days, starting with yourself. How many meals have you had in a --

      -- restaurant or cafeteria

      -- quick-service or carry-out shop

ASK FOR EACH HOUSEHOLD MEMBER LISTED ON PINK PAGE.

IF "NONE," PUT "0" IN PROPER BOX.

316

HOUSEHOLD MEMBER #	NUMBER OF MEALS IN PAST 7 DAYS	
	RESTAURANT OR CAFETERIA	QUICK-SERVICE OR CARRY-OUT
1		
2		
3		
4		
5		
6		
7		
8		
9		
10		

335

<u>TAKE BACK EXHIBIT J</u>

Now let's talk about automobiles ...

72. Do you, or anyone else in your family living here, own or have the regular use of an automobile? (INCLUDE PICK-UPS, TRUCKS, CAMPERS, ETC.)

    1 YES
    2 NO -- SKIP TO Q. 85   *336*

IF "YES" ON Q. 72, ASK:

73. How many cars do you own or have the use of?

    1 ONE
    2 TWO   *337*
    3 THREE
    4 FOUR OR MORE

74. Please tell me the make and model year (of each one).

	FIRST AUTO	SECOND AUTO	THIRD AUTO
MAKE			
MODEL YEAR			

Now I have some questions about your (first/second/third) car.

		FIRST AUTO	SECOND AUTO	THIRD AUTO
75. Is it owned by somebody living here?	YES / NO / NOT SURE	1 / 2 / 3	2 / 3	1 / 2 / 3
76. Was it new or used when you got it?	NEW / USED / NOT SURE	1 / 2 / 3	1 / 2 / 3	1 / 2 / 3
IF USED: 77. In what year did you get it?				
78. Is it a standard size car, or would you call it a compact, or subcompact, or what?	STANDARD / COMPACT / SUBCOMPACT / LUXURY / VAN OR PICKUP	1 / 2 / 3 / 4 / 5	1 / 2 / 3 / 4 / 5	1 / 2 / 3 / 4 / 5
79. How many miles per gallon does it get in local driving, just approximately?	MILES PER GALLON			
80. How many miles per gallon does it get in long-distance driving?	MILES PER GALLON / NOT USED FOR LONG-DISTANCE DRIVING	Y	Y	Y
81. How many thousand miles was it driven during the past 12 months, just approximately?	MILES / HAD AUTO LESS THAN 12 MONTHS	Y	Y	Y

338-348   *349-359*   *360-370*

IF "YES" ON Q. 72 (CONTINUED)

		FIRST AUTO	SECOND AUTO	THIRD AUTO
82. Which member of the household drives this car most?	RECORD HOUSEHOLD MEMBER # FROM PINK PAGE			
83. How many more years do you think you will keep this car?	YEARS DON'T KNOW	X	X	X
84. What is the car used most frequently for -- work, shopping, school, recreation, or something else?	WORK SHOPPING SCHOOL RECREATION/SOCIAL OTHER (SPECIFY)	1 2 3 4 5	1 2 3 4 5	1 2 3 4 5
		371-373	*374-376*	*377-379*

85. Which members of the household can drive a car? (RECORD BELOW)

86. Which members of the household are employed? (RECORD BELOW) (INTERVIEWER: COUNT ANY EMPLOYMENT FOR PAY, OR IN A FAMILY BUSINESS OR FAMILY FARM.)

	HOUSEHOLD MEMBER #	Q. 85 DRIVE CAR	Q. 86 EMPLOYED	Q. 87 HOURS PER WEEK	Q. 88 DAYS PER WEEK
	1	1 YES 2 NO	1 YES 2 NO	HOURS	DAYS
	2	1 YES 2 NO	1 YES 2 NO	HOURS	DAYS
USE	3	1 YES 2 NO	1 YES 2 NO	HOURS	DAYS
HOUSEHOLD	4	1 YES 2 NO	1 YES 2 NO	HOURS	DAYS
MEMBER	5	1 YES 2 NO	1 YES 2 NO	HOURS	DAYS
NUMBERS	6	1 YES 2 NO	1 YES 2 NO	HOURS	DAYS
FROM	7	1 YES 2 NO	1 YES 2 NO	HOURS	DAYS
PINK	8	1 YES 2 NO	1 YES 2 NO	HOURS	DAYS
PAGE	9	1 YES 2 NO	1 YES 2 NO	HOURS	DAYS
	10	1 YES 2 NO	1 YES 2 NO	HOURS	DAYS
		411-420	*421-430*	*431-450*	*451-460*

ASK FOR EACH EMPLOYED PERSON:

87. How many hours per week (do you/does he or she) usually work? (RECORD ABOVE)

88. How many days per week (do you/does he or she) usually work? (RECORD ABOVE)

NOTE: IF EMPLOYED PERSON WORKS AT MORE THAN ONE JOB, ANSWERS TO Q. 87 AND Q. 88 SHOULD BE TOTAL HOURS AND DAYS FOR ALL JOBS.

	89a. For what kind of company or business do you work? (What do they make or do?)	
IF RESPONDENT IS EMPLOYED, ASK INDUSTRY AND OCCUPATION	INDUSTRY: _____	*461*
	89b. What is your particular job and job title? (What are your duties?)	
(ASK ABOUT MAIN JOB IF RESPONDENT HAS MORE THAN ONE JOB)	OCCUPATION: _____	*462*

	89c. PLEASE CIRCLE: 1 OWNS BUSINESS: HIRES OTHERS
	                             2 SELF-EMPLOYED: HIRES NOBODY
	                             3 WORKS FOR SOMEONE ELSE
	                             4 OTHER: _____
	
	                                _____
		463

IF RESPONDENT
IS NOT EMPLOYED
 	
MARK ANSWER
THAT FITS BEST
(ASK IF NECESSARY)
	1 UNEMPLOYED, LOOKING FOR WORK
	2 STUDENT
	  3 HOUSEWIFE
	  4 RETIRED
	    5 OTHER (SPECIFY) _____
		464

IF RESPONDENT IS MARRIED,
COMPLETE APPROPRIATE QUESTIONS BELOW FOR HUSBAND OR WIFE:

	90a. For what kind of company or business does he/she work? (What do they make or do?)	
IF SPOUSE IS EMPLOYED, ASK INDUSTRY AND OCCUPATION	INDUSTRY: _____	*465*
	90b. What is his/her particular job and job title? (What are his/her duties?)	
(ASK ABOUT MAIN JOB IF SPOUSE HAS MORE THAN ONE JOB)	OCCUPATION: _____	*466*

	90c. PLEASE CIRCLE: 1 OWNS BUSINESS: HIRES OTHERS
	                             2 SELF-EMPLOYED: HIRES NOBODY
	                             3 WORKS FOR SOMEONE ELSE
	                             4 OTHER: _____
	
	                                _____
		467

IF SPOUSE
IS NOT EMPLOYED
 	
MARK ANSWER
THAT FITS BEST
(ASK IF NECESSARY)
	1 UNEMPLOYED, LOOKING FOR WORK
	2 STUDENT
	  3 HOUSEWIFE
	  4 RETIRED
	    5 OTHER (SPECIFY) _____
		468

QUESTIONS ON THE NEXT THREE PAGES APPLY TO: • RESPONDENT -- IF HE/SHE IS EMPLOYED

• SPOUSE -- IF HE/SHE IS EMPLOYED

	RESPONDENT	SPOUSE
RECORD HOUSEHOLD MEMBER NUMBER FROM PINK PAGE	_____	_____

ASK ABOUT RESPONDENT FIRST, THEN SPOUSE

91. (Do you/Does your husband or wife) now have any of the following benefits on (your/his or her) job?

	RESPONDENT	SPOUSE
a. Health insurance	1 YES 2 NO	1 YES 2 NO
b. Life insurance	1 YES 2 NO	1 YES 2 NO
c. Pension plan	1 YES 2 NO	1 YES 2 NO

92. How long (have you/has your husband or wife) been with (your/his or her) present employer?

	RESPONDENT	SPOUSE
YEARS	_____	_____

93. How many miles is it from home to the place where (you work/your husband or wife works)? (IF LESS THAN 1/2 MILE (5 BLOCKS) WRITE ZERO. IF RESPONDENT OR SPOUSE HAS NO FIXED PLACE OF WORK, CIRCLE "NO FIXED PLACE.")

	RESPONDENT	SPOUSE
MILES	_____	_____
NO FIXED PLACE	X	X

94. How (do you/does your husband or wife) usually get to work?

	RESPONDENT	SPOUSE
BUS OR STREETCAR	1	1
SUBWAY, ELEVATED	2	2
COMMUTER TRAIN	3	3
TAXI	4	4
AUTOMOBILE OTHER THAN TAXI	5	5
TRUCK	6	6
MOTORCYCLE	7	7
WALK OR BICYCLE	8	8

IF "AUTOMOBILE OTHER THAN TAXI" ON Q. 94, ASK:

95. (Do you/Does your husband or wife) usually ride alone or with other people?

	RESPONDENT	SPOUSE
ALONE	1	1
WITH OTHERS	2	2

IF WITH OTHERS:

96. How many other people?

	RESPONDENT	SPOUSE
NUMBER	_____	_____

	RESPONDENT	SPOUSE

97. How much time is usually required for (you/your husband or wife) to get to work -- from time left home until arrived at work? MINUTES FOR TRIP, ONE WAY

	_____	_____

98. About how much does it cost (you/your husband or wife) <u>per day</u> to go to work and to come back home? (Just your best guess for the <u>round trip</u>.) (IF BY CAR, INCLUDE RESPONDENT'S ESTIMATE OF COST FOR MILES DRIVEN, PARKING, TOLLS, ETC.) TOTAL COST FOR ROUND TRIP

	$_____	$_____

IF PUBLIC TRANSPORTATION IS USED (CODE 1, 2, 3) ON Q. 94, ASK:

99. About how long would it take per day to go to work if (you/your husband or wife) went by car? MINUTES FOR TRIP, ONE WAY

	_____	_____

100. What is the main reason (you/your husband or wife) use(s) public transportation to get to work?

	RESPONDENT	SPOUSE
NO DRIVER'S LICENSE	1	1
NO CAR AVAILABLE	2	2
NO CAR POOL AVAILABLE	3	3
NO PARKING PROBLEMS	4	4
PUBLIC TRANSPORTATION CHEAPER THAN AUTO	5	5
PUBLIC TRANSPORTATION SAFER THAN AUTO	6	6
PUBLIC TRANSPORTATION FASTER	7	7
DON'T LIKE TO DRIVE	8	8
OTHER (SPECIFY)	9	9
	_____	_____
	_____	_____
DON'T KNOW	0	0
	531-537	*538-544*

SKIP TO Q. 105

IF PUBLIC TRANSPORTATION IS NOT USED (CODES 4, 5, 6, 7) ON Q. 94, ASK:

	RESPONDENT	SPOUSE
101. How far is it to the nearest public transportation that could be used for (you/your husband or wife) to get to work?		
LESS THAN 1/2 MILE (5 BLOCKS OR LESS)	1	1
1/2 MILE - 1 MILE	2	2
OVER 1 MILE	3	3
NONE AVAILABLE	4	4

IF ANSWER TO Q. 101 IS CODE 1, 2 OR 3, ASK:

	RESPONDENT	SPOUSE
102. About how long would it take (you/your husband or wife) per day to go to work if some form of public transportation were used? MINUTES FOR TRIP, ONE WAY	_____	_____
103. About how much would it cost (you/your husband or wife) per day to get to work and back if (you/he or she) used some form of public transportation, such as a bus or subway? TOTAL COST FOR ROUND TRIP	$_____	$_____

104. What is the main reason (you do not use/your husband or wife does not use) public transportation to go to work?	RESPONDENT	SPOUSE
NOT CONVENIENT TO HOME	1	1
NOT CONVENIENT TO PLACE OF WORK	2	2
TOO MANY TRANSFERS	3	3
PUBLIC TRANSPORTATION COSTS ALMOST AS MUCH OR MORE THAN MY PRESENT TRANSPORTATION	4	4
TOO CROWDED OR UNCOMFORTABLE	5	5
TAKES TOO LONG	6	6
NEED AUTO FOR WORK	7	7
AFRAID WAITING AT BUS STOP AND WALKING	8	8
OTHER (SPECIFY)	9	9
	_____	_____
	_____	_____
DON'T KNOW	X	X
	545-550	*551-556*

ASK QUESTIONS 105-108 ABOUT RESPONDENT; ASK ABOUT SPOUSE ALSO IF RESPONDENT IS MARRIED

105. In the past 12 months, how many trips (have you/has your husband or wife) taken by airplane of 500 miles or more one way? (RECORD BELOW)

106. In the past 12 months, how many trips (have you/has your husband or wife) taken by airplane of less than 500 miles one way? (RECORD BELOW)

107. In the past 12 months, about how many trips (have you/has your husband or wife) taken by railroad or bus of 100 miles or more, one way? (RECORD BELOW)

108. In the past 12 months, about how many trips of 100 miles or more one way (have you/ has your husband or wife) taken by car? (RECORD BELOW)

NOTE: BOTH DIRECTIONS (GOING AWAY AND RETURNING) COUNT AS A SINGLE TRIP, BUT THE DIS-TANCES IN THE QUESTION ARE ONE-WAY DISTANCES.

IF RESPONDENT/SPOUSE IS EMPLOYED, ASK:

109. How many of the _____ trips were for (your work/your husband's or wife's work)? (RECORD BELOW)

IF NONE, PUT "0" IN PROPER SPACES IN TABLE		Respondent		Spouse	
		Total Trips	Work-Related Trips	Total Trips	Work-Related Trips
Q 105	AIRPLANE TRIPS OF 500 MILES OR MORE, ONE WAY				
Q 106	AIRPLANE TRIPS OF LESS THAN 500 MILES, ONE WAY				
Q 107	RAILROAD OR BUS TRIPS OF 100 MILES OR MORE, ONE WAY				
Q 108	AUTOMOBILE TRIPS OF 100 MILES OR MORE, ONE WAY				
		557-560	*561-564*	*565-568*	*569-572*

AND RESPONDENT EXHIBIT K

0. In the past month, did you or other members of your household use public transportation locally for any of the things on this exhibit? (CIRCLE ALL THAT APPLY)

    1 GROCERY SHOPPING
    2 SHOPPING FOR CLOTHES
    3 SHOPPING FOR THINGS FOR THE HOME
    4 VISITING THE DOCTOR OR DENTIST
    5 VISITING FRIENDS
    6 VISITING RELATIVES   *611*
    7 GOING TO A RELIGIOUS SERVICE
    8 GOING TO ANY SOCIAL ACTIVITY
    9 GOING TO SCHOOL

    0 NO, NONE OF THEM

TAKE BACK EXHIBIT K, HAND RESPONDENT EXHIBIT L

1. Sometimes people are unable to do a particular thing because they do not have transportation. In the past year, would that be true for you or other members of your household for any of the things listed on the exhibit? (CIRCLE ALL THAT APPLY)

    1 UNABLE TO GO TO A MEDICAL DOCTOR OR DENTIST
    2 UNABLE TO APPLY FOR A PARTICULAR JOB
    3 UNABLE TO TAKE A PARTICULAR JOB
    4 UNABLE TO SHOP AT LESS EXPENSIVE STORES   *612*
    5 UNABLE TO VISIT FRIENDS AND RELATIVES
    6 UNABLE TO ATTEND A RELIGIOUS SERVICE

    0 NO, NONE OF THESE APPLY

TAKE BACK EXHIBIT L

2. Some people have suggested that the price of gasoline be increased by ten cents a gallon. The government would collect the extra money and use all of it to help clean up our air, water and the country around us.

Do you think this extra ten cents a gallon on the price of gasoline would be a good idea or a poor idea?

    1 GOOD IDEA
    2 POOR IDEA   *613*
    3 QUALIFIED ANSWER -- RECORD COMMENT:

These next questions are different ...

113. If you won $1,000 in a contest and had to spend the money within a month, how would you be likely to spend it? (INTERVIEWER: DO <u>NOT</u> READ LIST OF POSSIBLE RESPONSES.)

        1 TRAVEL, VACATION
        2 PAY BILLS
         3 HOME IMPROVEMENTS (NEW ROOF, FIX UP HOUSE, ETC.)
         4 BUY CAR
          5 BUY HOUSEHOLD ITEMS (APPLIANCES, TV, FURNITURE, ETC.)
          6 BUY PERSONAL THINGS (CLOTHES, CAMERA, ETC.)
         7 INVEST IN BUSINESS OR FARM
         8 BUY STOCKS OR BONDS
         9 GIFTS FOR FAMILY OR FRIENDS

        0 OTHER (SPECIFY) _____

        X DON'T KNOW

61

114. If there were an emergency and you needed $1,000 more than you had, who would you be most likely to ask -- a relative, a friend, an employer, a bank, a loan company or a credit union?

        1 RELATIVE
        2 FRIEND
        3 EMPLOYER
         4 BANK OR SAVINGS & LOAN
         5 FINANCE COMPANY
         6 CREDIT UNION
         7 NONE OF THESE

61

<u>HAND RESPONDENT EXHIBIT M</u>

115. Does anyone in this household own any of the items listed on this exhibit?

    IF YES: Which ones?

        1 BICYCLE FOR CHILDREN
        2 BICYCLE FOR ADULTS
         3 MOTORCYCLE OR MOTOR SCOOTER
         4 SNOWMOBILE
          5 SAILBOAT
          6 BOAT WITH MOTOR
         7 AIRPLANE
         8 SEWING MACHINE
         9 STEREO OR HI-FI

        0 NONE OF THE ABOVE

61

<u>TAKE BACK EXHIBIT M</u>

Now some questions for background purposes only ...

116. Are you buying your home here, or do you rent?

    1 BUYING (OWN)
    2 RENTING   *617*

IF "BUYING" OR "OWN" ON Q. 116, ASK:

117a. Do you own any other property as well?

    1 YES
    2 NO
    3 NOT SURE   *618*

IF YES: 117b. Do you have a second home?

    1 YES
    2 NO   *619*

IF "RENTING" ON Q. 116, ASK:

118a. Do you own any property?

    1 YES
    2 NO
    3 NOT SURE   *620*

IF YES: 118b. Do you have a home elsewhere?

    1 YES
    2 NO   *621*

119. How long have you and your family been living at this address?

    _____ YEARS   *622*

IF LESS THAN ONE YEAR, ASK: 120. How many months?

    _____ MONTHS   *623*

121. About what percentage of the traffic on this street or road is caused by trucks, buses and cars of persons not living on this street?

    1 LESS THAN 10%   5 40% - 49%
    2 10% - 19%   6 50% - 59%   *624*
    3 20% - 29%   7 60% OR MORE
    4 30% - 39%   8 DON'T KNOW

122. What is the highest grade that you completed in school?

    1 GRADE SCHOOL OR LESS
    2 SOME HIGH SCHOOL
    3 GRADUATED HIGH SCHOOL   *625*
    4 SOME COLLEGE
    5 GRADUATED COLLEGE
    6 SOME POST GRADUATE

IF RESPONDENT IS MARRIED, ASK:

123. What is the highest grade that your husband/ wife completed in school?

    1 GRADE SCHOOL OR LESS
    2 SOME HIGH SCHOOL
    3 GRADUATED HIGH SCHOOL   *626*
    4 SOME COLLEGE
    5 GRADUATED COLLEGE
    6 SOME POST GRADUATE

HAND RESPONDENT EXHIBIT **N**

124. During 1972, in which of these ways did you and other members of your family living here have money coming in as part of your family income? Just read me the numbers.

        1 INCOME FROM A JOB OR BUSINESS OR FARM
        2 INTEREST ON SAVINGS
        3 DIVIDENDS OR INTEREST ON STOCKS OR BONDS
        4 GIFTS OR INHERITANCE   *627*
        5 RENTALS OR OTHER INCOME FROM PROPERTY
        6 SOCIAL SECURITY OR RETIREMENT INCOME
        7 VETERANS BENEFITS
        8 OTHER (SPECIFY) _____

TAKE BACK EXHIBIT N, HAND RESPONDENT EXHIBIT O

125. Now let's look at this list of income groups. Please tell me which group number best describes the total combined income in 1972 of all members of your <u>family</u> from all sources -- wages, rentals, dividends, social security, and so forth -- before taxes and deductions. (THE FAMILY INCLUDES ALL RELATED PERSONS LIVING IN THE HOUSE-HOLD.)

                        1 UNDER $1,500
                        2 $1,500 - $2,999
                        3 $3,000 - $4,999
        TOTAL   4 $5,000 - $6,999
        FAMILY   5 $7,000 - $8,999   *628*
        INCOME   6 $9,000 - $11,999
                        7 $12,000 - $15,999
                        8 $16,000 - $24,999
                        9 $25,000 AND OVER

                        0 REFUSED
                        X DON'T KNOW   INTERVIEWER ESTIMATE: _____

IF HOUSEHOLD HEAD IS MALE <u>AND</u> WIFE WAS EMPLOYED IN 1972, ASK ABOUT WIFE'S INCOME:

126. Now looking at the list of income groups again, please tell me which group number best describes (your/your wife's) income from working in 1972.

                        1 UNDER $1,500
                        2 $1,500 - $2,999
        WIFE'S   3 $3,000 - $4,999
        INCOME   4 $5,000 - $6,999   *629*
                        5 $7,000 - $8,999
                        6 $9,000 - $11,999
                        7 $12,000 - $15,999
                        8 $16,000 - $24,999
                        9 $25,000 AND OVER

TAKE BACK EXHIBIT O

127a. Does part of your household income go to help support   1 YES
      anyone who does not live in this household?   2 NO
                                                                     3 NOT SURE   *630*

      IF YES: 127b. How many people <u>outside your household</u>
                     do you support?   NUMBER: _____ *631*

               127c. Who (is that/are they)? (CIRCLE ALL THAT APPLY)

                        1 CHILD(REN) IN COLLEGE
                        2 OTHER ADULT CHILD(REN)
                        3 RESPONDENT'S PARENT(S)   *632*
                        4 WIFE'S/HUSBAND'S PARENT(S)
                        5 OTHER (SPECIFY) _____

128. Who usually keeps track of the money and bills in your household?

1 RESPONDENT
2 RESPONDENT'S HUSBAND OR WIFE
3 SOMEONE ELSE -- Who?

633

129. We may have covered some of these points before, but just to be sure, which of these do you use here in your home?

	Q. 129		Q. 130			
	USED BY HOUSEHOLD YES	NO	PAID FOR BY HOUSEHOLD	INCLUDED IN RENT	PAID SOME OTHER WAY	
a. Electricity?	1	2	1	2	3 SPECIFY:	*634-635*
b. Gas? (bottled or piped in)	1	2	1	2	3 SPECIFY:	*636-637*
c. Fuel oil? (for heating or hot water)	1	2	1	2	3 SPECIFY:	*638-639*

FOR EACH FUEL USED BY HOUSEHOLD, ASK:

130. Do you (or someone in this household) pay for _____, or is it included in your rent, or paid for in some other way? (RECORD ANSWERS ABOVE.)

IF GAS IS USED BY HOUSEHOLD, ASK:

131. Is the gas piped-in, or bottled gas?

1 PIPED IN
2 BOTTLED
3 NOT SURE

640

IF FUEL OIL IS USED AND PAID FOR BY HOUSEHOLD, ASK:

132. May I have the name of the fuel oil company that supplies your household?

NAME OF FUEL OIL COMPANY: _____

641

IF HOUSEHOLD PAYS FOR ELECTRIC AND/OR GAS

133. We are interested in the amounts that people pay for electricity and gas in different parts of the United States, and it would be very helpful to us to have some additional information about the amounts of your (electric/gas/electric and gas) bills for the past year.

I have a form that would authorize your (electric/gas) company to provide that information to the Washington Center for Metropolitan Studies.

INTERVIEWER: REMOVE PERFORATED PAGES AND HAND APPROPRIATE ELECTRIC AND/OR GAS FORMS TO RESPONDENT. EITHER YOU OR RESPONDENT SHOULD FILL IN THE NAME OF COMPANY.

1 ELECTRIC AUTHORIZATION FORM COMPLETED
2 GAS AUTHORIZATION FORM COMPLETED
3 FORMS NOT COMPLETED: EXPLAIN:

642

TURN TO INSIDE BACK COVER TO COMPLETE INTERVIEW

ELECTRIC COMPANY AUTHORIZATION

Please
print name of
electric co.

I hereby give my permission to my electric company,

_____,

to give to the Washington Center for Metropolitan Studies/Ford
Foundation-sponsored study on family energy use, the following
information on my electric bills for the past twelve months:

1) the total amount of electricity consumed in each
   month, and

2) the total price charged for electricity for each
   of those months.

A photocopy of this authorization may be accepted with the same
authority as the original.

Signed: _____

PLEASE PRINT

Name: _____

Address: _____

Apt. No.: _____

City: _____

Date: _____

REMOVE FORM CAREFULLY AT PERFORATION

GAS COMPANY AUTHORIZATION

Please
print name of
gas company

I hereby give my permission to my gas company,

_____,

to give to the Washington Center for Metropolitan Studies/Ford
Foundation-sponsored study on family energy use, the following
information on my gas bills for the past twelve months:

1) the total amount of gas consumed in each month,
   and

2) the total price charged for gas for each of
   those months.

A photocopy of this authorization may be accepted with the same
authority as the original.

Signed: _____

PLEASE PRINT

Name: _____

Address: _____

Apt. No.: _____

City: _____

Date: _____

REMOVE FORM CAREFULLY AT PERFORATION

134. For interview verification purposes, may I have your name and phone number, please?

RESPONDENT'S NAME: _____

PHONE NUMBER: (AREA CODE: _____) _____

Thank you very much for your help.

> COMPLETE QUESTIONS BELOW AFTER LEAVING HOUSEHOLD

INTERVIEWER OBSERVATION:

135. Is there a gas light burning outside the home?   1 YES
                                                         2 NO   *643*

136. What type of structure is this?

    1 MOBILE HOME OR TRAILER   *644*

    2 SINGLE-FAMILY HOME DETACHED ──→ IS IT: 1 ONE FLOOR (RANCH STYLE)
       FROM ANY OTHER BUILDING   2 TWO-STORY   *645*
                                                 3 THREE-STORY
    3 SINGLE-FAMILY HOME   4 SPLIT LEVEL
       ATTACHED ON ONE SIDE

    4 SINGLE-FAMILY HOME
       ATTACHED ON TWO SIDES

    5 2-4 HOUSEHOLDS IN
       SAME BUILDING

    6 5-8 HOUSEHOLDS IN
       SAME BUILDING

                                                                                 646
    7 APARTMENT BUILDING   ──→ IS IT: 1 GARDEN-TYPE (3 STORIES OR LESS)
       WITH MORE THAN   2 HIGH-RISE (4 STORIES OR MORE)
       8 HOUSEHOLDS
                                   DOES IT HAVE AN ELEVATOR: 1 YES
                                                             2 NO   *647*

137. Sex of respondent: 1 MALE
                             2 FEMALE   *648*

138. Race of respondent: 1 WHITE
                             2 BLACK OR NEGRO
                             3 CHICANO, PUERTO RICAN OR OTHER LATIN AMERICAN   *649*
                             4 ORIENTAL
                             5 OTHER: _____

TIME INTERVIEW COMPLETED: _____   LENGTH OF INTERVIEW: _____ MINUTES   *650-*
                                                                                     651

INTERVIEWER'S SIGNATURE: _____   DATE: _____

How We Did The Study

NATIONAL HOUSEHOLD SURVEY—SUMMARY

The basis of the Lifestyles and Energy Household Survey is information obtained from a probability sample of households in the United States. Interviews were completed in 1,455 households in May and June 1973, by members of the national interviewing staff of Response Analysis Corporation of Princeton, New Jersey. The questionnaire used in the survey was drawn up after extensive consultation with physicists, engineers, sociologists, consumer economists, statisticians, and environmentalists.

The respondent for the interview was the head of household, (either spouse was eligible in the case of households headed by husband and wife). Since much of the interview was concerned with factual information about the housing unit and members of the households, interviewers were instructed to accept answers to factual questions from either the respondent or spouse. Interviews ranged from about 30 to 90 minutes in length, with a median length of 50 minutes.

Drafts of the survey questionnaire were reviewed and revised on a number of occasions. To test for clarity of questions, ability of respondents to answer in meaningful terms and length of interview, 35 pretest interviews were conducted. Test interviews were completed in ten different locations throughout the United States.

Sampling Method

Multistage area probability sampling procedures were used to select households for the survey. Households were selected at 177 different locations—including metropolitan areas, smaller urban places, and rural areas—in all parts of the United States. A sample location was usually a block or group of blocks in an urban area, or a geographic segment well defined by roads, streams, or other landmarks in a rural area.

In some locations, addresses were selected at the central survey office from listings previously compiled by interviewers. In other locations, interviewers listed addresses and selected specific households during the same visit to the sample location, following explicit instructions for both the listing and the selection processes. Once households were selected, no replacements or substitutions were permitted.

Oversampling the Poor. Locations in the lowest socioeconomic quartile (identified either on the basis of percent of families below the poverty level in 1969, or average value of housing units in the area) were selected with higher probability than were other locations. The purpose of the oversampling was to include in the sample a larger number of poor households than would have been included in a proportionate sample of the total household population. In the analysis of survey data, weights were used to compensate for differences in probability of selection.

Response Rates

Altogether, 2,224 households (occupied housing units) were included in the survey sample. Interviewers normally made up to four visits to sample households, as necessary, to complete the interview. Interviews were completed for 1,455 households, or 65 percent of those assigned. Interview completion rates were highest in nonmetropolitan areas and lowest in central cities of metropolitan areas.

Weighting Procedures

Weights were calculated for each sample household to (1) compensate for differences in probabilities of selection by socioeconomic quartile, (2) adjust for differences in interview completion experience in different sampling locations, and (3) expand data for sample households to estimates for the total universe (all households in the United States as of that time).

Survey Reliability

All survey data are, of course, subject to random sampling variability. Sampling error figures are estimates of the differences that might be expected between the survey results and results of a complete enumeration using the same survey procedures. Sampling error may have a substantial effect on survey figures, particularly when results are reported for small subgroups of the total sample.

Results are also subject to response and nonreporting errors. Weighting procedures were used to adjust for variations in interview completion experience in different interviewing locations, but no additional corrections were introduced for nonresponse patterns. Estimates based on the sample, however, are generally close to independent estimates of household characteristics based on the Current Population Survey of the U.S. Bureau of the Census. Details of the procedures of the national household survey are given later in this Appendix.

SURVEY OF SAMPLE HOUSEHOLDS' ELECTRIC AND GAS COMPANIES

The Survey

Other survey research organizations made clear to us that consumers are far from universally aware of their total fuel consumption and costs, and often do not keep receipts or records. For this reason the Washington Center initiated a separate survey of the electric and gas companies serving sample households that were billed directly.

The first step was to ask the sample households who paid directly for their electricity and natural gas to sign an authorization giving the names of their utilities, and allowing them to provide the Center with information about the amount and cost of the fuel the households used during the previous twelve months (See Appendix A1, pp. 231 and 233). A large percentage of the households signed the authorization—85 percent for electricity and 87 percent for natural gas (Table A2-1).

The next step was to write personally to the president of each of the 142 companies from which this large percentage of households received utility service. In some instances a single utility served a household, providing both gas and electricity; in most cases, however, two letters were required for each household—one to an electric company and one to a gas company. Each letter was accompanied by a form developed at the Center to make the recording task as simple as possible for the companies and to permit easy handling for statistical purposes. The letter and the forms are Figures A2-1 to A2-3.

Response Rates

The response from utilities was very high, chiefly because of the guidance and personal support the Center received from Reid Thompson, President of the Potomac Electric Power Company, and Paul E. Reichardt, President of the Washington Gas Light Company. Both officials took a keen interest in the survey, both as members of the Washington Center for Metropolitan Studies' Board, and as active associates in the affairs of utilities nationally. As a result, almost 90 percent of the companies provided the data requested (Table A2-2). A detailed analysis of the household response rate is shown in Table A2-1. Table A2-3 segregates the origin of the small refusal rate, whether by households or by companies.

Time Schedule

The survey of electric and natural gas companies extended from June 28 to September 7, 1973. Almost all the companies supplied data for the

Table A2-1.   Household Responses, by Type of Fuel Used and
Paid For

Household response	Electricity		Natural gas	
	Number	Percent	Number	Percent
All households	1,455	100	1,455	100
Use the fuel	1,452	100	929	64
Do not use the fuel	3	a	526	36
All households using each fuel	1,452	100	929	100
Pay	1,349	93	817	87
Do not pay	103	7	112	12
All households paying	1,349	100	817	100
Gave authorization	1,149	85	709	88
Refused	200	15	108	13
Fuel data requested	1,149	100	709	100
Received and useable[b]	947	82	622	88
Not received[c]	202	18	87	12

[a]Less than 0.5 percent.

[b]This includes all households for which data were available for six months or more. For almost all the households, the data were for a full year ± 35 days (95 percent in the case of electricity; 96 percent in the case of natural gas). Before the analysis, the consumption figures for each household were adjusted to a 365-day year, using the household's average daily consumption for the reported period.

[c]Besides those households for whom the company refused to provide data, this group includes a small number of households for whom data were shown for less than six months.

Source: Washington Center for Metropolitan Studies' Lifestyles and Energy Surveys.

Table A2-2.   Utility Company Responses, by Type of Company

Type of company	Sent	Received[a]	
	Number	Number	Percent
Total	142	124	87
Gas only	47	43	91
Gas and electricity	18	17	94
Electricity only	77	64	83
Gas–total companies	65	60	92
Electricity–total companies	95	81	85

[a]Data from an additional electric company (involving twelve households) were received too late to be included in the analysis.

Source: Washington Center for Metropolitan Studies' Lifestyles and Energy Surveys.

Figure A2-1. Letter to Utility Companies

The Washington Center for Metropolitan Studies

1717 Massachusetts Avenue, NW Washington DC 20036   462-4868

June 28, 1973

Mr. _____, President
_____ Gas Company or Electric Power Company
Post Office Box _____
_____ Street
City, State Zip code

Dear: _____

     Enclosed are authorizations which permit us to ask you for the cost of fuel and the amount used during each of the most recent 12 months for which you have the data readily available, for the households listed on the attached forms.

     I am requesting these data for use in a nationwide study of how households use energy. The study, "Lifestyles and Energy," is being conducted by the Washington Center for Metropolitan Studies under a grant from the Ford Foundation and its Energy Policy Project.

     Mr. Reid Thompson, President of the Potomac Electric Power Company of Washington, D.C. and Mr. Paul E. Reichardt, President of the Washington Gas Light Company, Washington, D.C., are on the Board of Trustees of the Washington Center. They have agreed to provide data from their files and have authorized me to indicate their interest in the project and their support. They emphasize the importance of the results for national policy planning and the many uses of the information to them and to all other utilities.

     The individual data we receive will be kept strictly confidential and will not be identified by household or company. They will be summarized within large groupings for statistical purposes.

     A self-addressed stamped envelope is enclosed for your reply.

     We will place your firm on the mailing list to receive an advance copy of our reports as soon as they are printed, probably in the winter of 1973-74.

     We would be most grateful for your cooperation.

           Sincerely,

           Dorothy K. Newman
           Senior Associate

Figure A2-2

The Washington Center for Metropolitan Studies

1717 Massachusetts Avenue, N.W. Washington, D.C. 20036

_____

Questionnaire Number

Please refer questions to:
Dawn Day
(202) 462-4868

ELECTRICITY USE BY HOUSEHOLDS
(for most recent 12 months available)

Household: Name _____

Street: _____   Apt. # _____

City and State: _____

Number of Period	Date of Period From	To	Amount (kwhr)	Amount is: A-Actual or E-Estimated	Bill[a]
	Billing Period		Quantity used		
				(circle one)	
1	____	____	____	A E	____
2	____	____	____	A E	____
3	____	____	____	A E	____
4	____	____	____	A E	____
5	____	____	____	A E	____
6	____	____	____	A E	____
7	____	____	____	A E	____
8	____	____	____	A E	____
9	____	____	____	A E	____
10	____	____	____	A E	____
11	____	____	____	A E	____
12	____	____	____	A E	____

[a]Please _include_ taxes but _exclude_ merchandise and service charges. If the household is on a budget plan, simply provide the billed amounts.

Form completed by _____

(Name)

Figure A2-3

The Washington Center for Metropolitan Studies

1717 Massachusetts Avenue, N.W. Washington, D.C. 20036

_____
Questionnaire Number

Please refer questions to:
Dawn Day
(202) 462-4868

GAS USE BY HOUSEHOLDS
(for most recent 12 months available)

Household: Name _____

Street: _____ Apt. # _____

City and State: _____

	Billing Period		Quantity used		Bill[b]
	Date of Period		Amount[a]	Amount is:	
Number of Period	From	To		A-Actual E-Estimated	
				(circle one)	
1	_____	_____	_____	A E	_____
2	_____	_____	_____	A E	_____
3	_____	_____	_____	A E	_____
4	_____	_____	_____	A E	_____
5	_____	_____	_____	A E	_____
6	_____	_____	_____	A E	_____
7	_____	_____	_____	A E	_____
8	_____	_____	_____	A E	_____
9	_____	_____	_____	A E	_____
10	_____	_____	_____	A E	_____
11	_____	_____	_____	A E	_____
12	_____	_____	_____	A E	_____

[a]The quantity used is expressed in terms of: (check one)
_____ THERMS
_____ CUBIC FEET

[b]Please *include* taxes but *exclude* merchandise and service charges. If the household is on a budget plan, simply provide the billed amount.

Form completed by _____
(Name)

Table A2-3.   Response Rate by Households and Utility Companies, by Fuel Type

Data availability from households and companies	Electricity		Natural gas	
	Number	Percent	Number	Percent
All households[a]	1,349	100	817	100
Data available	947	70	622	76
Data not available	402	30	195	24
Respondent refused	200	15	108	13
Company refused[b]	202	15	87	11

[a]Only households that paid directly for fuel.
[b]This group includes, besides those households for whom the company refused to provide data, a small number of households for whom data were shown for less than six months.
Source: Washington Center for Metropolitan Studies' Lifestyles and Energy Surveys.

Table A2-4.   Electricity and Natural Gas Data, by Last Month and Number of Months of Reporting Period

Last month of report	Percent	Data provided for (Number)		
	Total	Total	12 months	6 to 11 months
All households	100	1,588	1,515	73
Sept.–Dec. 1972	a	7	7	0
Jan.–April 1973	1	20	20	0
May 1973	22	355	336	19
June 1973	54	864	827	37
July 1973	19	298	282	16
August 1973	3	44	43	1

[a]Less than 0.5 percent.
Source: Washington Center for Metropolitan Studies' Lifestyles and Energy Surveys.

year ending May to July 1973 (Table A2-4). The fuel using year depended on each company's available records and date of response. Processing the responses for the computer took several weeks.

Data from the utilities were matched with data from the households according to predesigned tabulation plans, and to some specifications that were developed in progress, as results revealed important omissions or significant directions for investigation.

Preliminary household data not including fuel usage were available in the fall of 1973. Most of the tabulations were completed during the winter of 1973–74. Table A2-5 lists participating utility companies.

Table A2-5.   Participating Utility Companies

Adams Electric Co-op Gettysburg, Pennsylvania	Cincinnati Gas & Electric Co. Cincinnati, Ohio	Equitable Gas Co. Pittsburgh, Pennsylvania
Alabama Gas Corp. Birmingham, Alabama	Clairborne Electric Co-Op, Inc. Homer, Louisiana	Fayetteville Public Works Commission Fayetteville, North Carolina
Alabama Power Co. Birmingham, Alabama	Coffey Co. Rural Electric Co-op Assn., Inc. Burlington, Kansas	First Electric Co-Op Corp. Jacksonville Arkansas
Appalachian Power Co. Roanoke, Virginia	Columbia Gas of Ohio, Inc. Columbus, Ohio	Garland Electric Dept. Garland, Texas
Arkansas Louisiana Gas Co. Shreveport, Louisiana	Columbia Gas Distribution Companies Columbus, Ohio	Gas Service Co. Kansas City, Missouri
Arkansas Power & Light Co. Little Rock, Arkansas	Columbia Gas of West Virginia, Inc.	Georgia Power Co. Atlanta, Georgia
Atlanta Gas Light Co. Atlanta, Georgia	Charleston, West Virginia	Harper Heights Gas Co. Eccles, West Virginia
Atlantic City Electric Co. Atlantic City, New Jersey	Columbus & Southern Ohio Electric Co. Columbus, Ohio	Harriman Utility Board Harriman, Tennessee
Baltimore Gas & Electric Co. Baltimore, Maryland	Commonwealth Edison Co. Chicago, Illinois	Houston Natural Gas Corp. Houston, Texas
Black Diamond Power Co. Charleston, West Virginia	Community Public Service Co. Fort Worth, Texas	Illinois Power Co. Decatur, Illinois
Blue Ridge Electric Membership Corp. Lenoir, North Carolina	Connecticut Light & Power Co. Hartford, Connecticut	Indiana & Michigan Electric Co. Fort Wayne, Indiana
Boston Edison Co. Boston, Massachusetts	Consolidated Edison Co. of New York New York, New York	Iroquois Gas Corp. Buffalo, New York
Boston Gas Co. Boston, Massachusetts	Consolidated Natural Gas Co. Cleveland, Ohio	Jacksonville Electric Authority Jacksonville, Florida
Bountiful Electric Dept. Bountiful, Utah	Consumers Power Co. Jackson, Michigan	Kansas City Power & Light Co. Topeka, Kansas
Brooklyn Union Gas Co. Brooklyn, New York	Crescent Electric Member- ship Corp.	Kansas Power & Light Co. Topeka, Kansas
Burlington Electric Light Dept. Burlington, Vermont	Statesville, North Carolina	Laclede Gas Co. St. Louis, Missouri
Carolina Power & Light Co. Raleigh, North Carolina	Cumberland Electric Member- ship Corp. Shelbyville, Tennessee	Le Sueur Municipal Utilities Le Sueur, Minnesota
Central Indiana Gas Co., Inc. Muncie, Indiana	The Dayton Power & Light Co. Dayton, Ohio	Lone Star Gas Co. Dallas, Texas
Central Power & Light Co. Corpus Christi, Texas	Delta Electric Power Assn. Greenwood, Mississippi	Long Island Lighting Co. Mineola, New York
Chattanooga Electric Power Board Chattanooga, Tennessee	The Detroit Edison Co. Detroit, Michigan	Los Angeles Dept. of Water & Power Los Angeles, California
Chattanooga Gas Co. Chattanooga, Tennessee	Duke Power Co. Charlotte, North Carolina	Loudon, City Utilities of Loudon, Tennessee
Chicopee Electric Light Dept. Chicopee, Massachusetts	Duquesne Light Co. Pittsburgh, Pennsylvania	

(continued)

Table A2-5 continued

Louisiana Gas Service
Harvey, Louisiana

Magic Valley Electric
Co-op, Inc.
Mercedes, Texas

New England Power
Service Co.
Westboro, Massachusetts

Metropolitan Edison Co.
Reading, Pennsylvania

Michigan Consolidated Gas Co.
Detroit, Michigan

Minneapolis Gas Co.
Minneapolis, Minnesota

Minnesota Natural Gas Co.
Minneapolis, Minnesota

Mississippi Valley Gas Co.
Jackson, Mississippi

Mountain Fuel Supply Co.
Salt Lake City, Utah

Nashville Electric Service
Nashville, Tennessee

Nashville Gas Co.
Nashville, Tennessee

New York State Electric
& Gas Corp.
Ithaca, New York

Niagara Mohawk Power Corp.
West Syracuse, New York

North Georgia Electric
Membership Corp.
Dalton, Georgia

Northern Illinois Gas Co.
Aurora, Illinois

Northern Indiana Public
Service Co.
Hammond, Indiana

Northern States Power Co.
Minneapolis, Minnesota

Northwest Natural Gas Co.
Portland, Oregon

Ohio Edison Co.
Akron, Ohio

Ohio Power Co.
Southwest Canton, Ohio

Pacific Gas & Electric Co.
San Francisco, California

Pasadena Water & Power Dept.
Pasadena, California

Pennsylvania Electric Co.
Johnstown, Pennsylvania

Pennsylvania Gas Co.
Warren, Pennsylvania

Peoples Gas Co.
Chicago, Illinois

Peoples Natural Gas Co.
Greensburg, Pennsylvania

Philadelphia Gas & Electric Co.
Philadelphia, Pennsylvania

Philadelphia Gas Works
Division of UGI Corp.
Philadelphia, Pennsylvania

Portland General Electric Co.
Portland, Oregon

Potomac Electric Power Co.
Washington, D.C.

Public Service Co. of
Colorado
Denver, Colorado

Public Service Electric &
Gas Co.
Newark, New Jersey

Puget Sound Power &
Light Co.
Bellevue, Washington

Rio Grande Valley Gas Co.
Brownsville, Texas

Rock Hill Lighting Dept.
Rock Hill, South Carolina

Sacramento Municipal
Utility District
Sacramento, California

San Diego Gas & Electric Co.
San Diego, California

Santa Clara Electric Dept.
Santa Clara, California

Shelby Electric Co-op.
Shelbyville, Illinois

South Carolina Electric
& Gas, Inc.
Columbia, South Carolina

Southern California Edison Co.
Rosemead, California

Southern California Gas Co.
Los Angeles, California

Southwest Electric Co-op
Boliver, Missouri

Springfield, City Utilities of
Springfield, Missouri

Springfield Gas Light Co.
Boston, Massachusetts

Tacoma City Public Utilities
Tacoma, Washington

Tampa Electric Co.
Tampa, Florida

Texas Power & Light Co.
Dallas, Texas

Union Electric Co.
St. Louis, Missouri

United Gas Distribution Co.
Houston, Texas

Utah Power & Light Co.
Salt Lake City, Utah

Vermont Gas System, Inc.
South Burlington, Vermont

Virginia Electric Co-op.
Bowling Green, Virginia

Virginia Electric Power Co.
Richmond, Virginia

Washington Gas Light Co.
Washington, D.C.

Washington Natural Gas Co.
Seattle, Washington

Water and Electric Dept.
Glouster, Ohio

West Ohio Gas Co.
Lima, Ohio

West Penn Power Co.
Greensburg, Pennsylvania

Western Massachusetts
Electric Co.
West Springfield, Massachusetts

York County Natural Gas
Authority
Rock Hill, South Carolina

Village of Yellow Springs
Electric Co.
Yellow Springs, Ohio

ESTIMATING NATIONAL FUEL USE

Based on the households for which data were available, national estimates of fuel consumption were made for each fuel. The estimates were made by taking the average fuel use per household for all households for which fuel consumption data were available and multiplying that figure by the total number of households reported using the particular fuel. The formula used was as follows: $(b) [(a)/(c)]$ where

> a = the total energy used by all households with consumption reports on the fuel
> b = the total number of households using the particular fuel
> c = the total number of households with consumption reports on the particular fuel.

These estimates were made separately for each household characteristic for which national fuel consumption estimates were given.

Gasoline Estimates

Estimates of gasoline consumption are based on survey respondent estimates of car mileage for the previous twelve months, and gasoline mileage (miles per gallon) in local driving. Only households for which complete information was available on both these items for all cars were used in the estimates.[a] For cars owned six months or more, estimates of annual mileage were made on the basis of mileage reported. For the few households (3 percent) with four or more cars, the gasoline consumption estimates were based on three of the cars. Respondents' estimates of local rather than long distance gasoline mileage were used, since most car usage is local.[b]

The WCMS estimates of average gallons consumed per vehicle are probably low as a result of these unavoidable adjustments and assumptions. However as Table A2-6 indicates, even if we had used only the reports of thousands of miles traveled (instead of converting to gasoline), the outcome of the analysis would have been much the same.

DEFINING POVERTY

The definition of poverty used in the Lifestyles and Energy Study is based on the U.S. government's definition of the poor and near poor in 1972. The near poor are those with incomes of 125 percent of the low income or poverty threshold or lower, and are included in tables of the U.S. Bureau of the Census publications about the low income population.

[a]Gasoline estimates were made on the basis of data provided by 58 percent of the households with cars.

[b]Only 17 percent of all vehicle miles in 1970 comprised trips of 100 miles or more one way; 63 percent of all vehicle miles involved trips of 30 miles or less one way.[1]

Table A2-6.   Estimated Miles Driven and Gasoline Used for All Households with Cars, by Income, 1972-1973

Miles driven and gasoline used	*All households*	*Poor*	*Lower middle*	*Upper middle*	*Well off*
All households with cars	100	100	100	100	100
Estimated miles driven in past year[a]					
Less than 15,000	52	80	65	33	28
15,000 or more	48	20	35	67	72
Estimated gallons of gasoline used in past year[a]					
Less than 1,000[b]	56	83	69	35	32
1,000 or more	44	17	31	65	68

[a]Excludes unknowns.

[b]One thousand gallons of gasoline is approximately 125 million Btu's.

Source: Washington Center for Metropolitan Studies' Lifestyles and Energy Surveys.

The 125 percent cutoff for 1972 was chosen because the official U.S. poverty level has been adjusted only for changes in prices and not for changes in the level of living since the poverty definition was first established in the 1960s. We felt that the higher cutoff more accurately reflected the incidence of poverty.

People are sometimes reluctant to say exactly what their family income is. To get as large a response rate as possible to the income question and to improve its accuracy, the Lifestyles and Energy Household Survey followed the common practice in private surveys of asking respondents to indicate their total family income within certain ranges. The poverty thresholds (poor plus near poor) derived from these ranges are similar to the 1972 results shown by the U.S. Bureau of the Census, including adjustments for family size (Table A2-7).

Using this definition of poverty, U.S. households were divided into the poor and nonpoor, with the nonpoor subdivided into three groups: lower middle, upper middle, and well off. The poor, upper middle, and well off groups each include about one-fifth of all households. The remaining two-fifths of all households fall in the lower-middle group (Table A2-8).

A poverty definition that takes account of family size as well as income leads to varying proportions of income groups being classified as poor. All those with family incomes under $3,000 were poor according to our figures; 30 percent of those with incomes between $3,000 and $4,999; 9 percent of those with incomes between $5,000 and $6,999; and only 3 percent of those with incomes between $7,000 and $8,999 (Table A2-9).

Table A2-7.   Poverty Thresholds, by Family Size—Census Compared to Lifestyles and Energy Study, 1972

Family size	Census Poor	125 percent of poor	Lifestyles and energy poverty line
1	$2,101	$2,626	$3,000
2	2,703	3,379	3,000
3	3,319	4,149	5,000
4	4,247	5,309	5,000
5	5,011	6,264	7,000
6	5,633	7,041	7,000
7 or more	6,917	8,646	9,000

Source: Derived from U.S. Bureau of the Census, *Current Population Reports*, P60–91, "Characteristics of the Low-Income Population, 1972," Washington, D.C.: U.S. Government Printing Office, 1973, Table A–2, p. 143, and the Washington Center for Metropolitan Studies' Lifestyles and Energy Surveys.

Table A2-8.   Income Groups in the Lifestyles Study, 1972 (percent of households)

All households	100
Poor	18
Nonpoor	82
Lower middle (Under $12,000)	42
Upper middle ($12,000–15,999)	19
Well off ($16,000 and over)	20

Source: Washington Center for Metropolitan Studies' Lifestyles and Energy Surveys.

The poor, using the Center's definition and sample, were 13.5 percent of all families—the same as the Census estimate for the percent of poor and near poor families in 1972.[2]

The Lifestyles and Energy Surveys data are not directly comparable with the 1972 Census report on the low income population because the Lifestyles tables relate to households while the Census reports are about families and unrelated individuals.[c] The Energy study focused on households because energy is used by all those who live in the dwelling—including roomers or several families. The characteristics of poor and nonpoor households in the Lifestyles and Energy Surveys are given in Table A2-10.

[c]A family is defined as any group of two or more related persons living in the same house or apartment. A household includes all persons living together whether related or not. In this study only 2 percent of households contained persons unrelated to head. In the few households that included unrelated persons, the unrelated persons and their incomes were not included in determining whether or not the household was poor.

Table A2-9. Poverty Status, by Family Income, 1972

	Family income					
Poverty status	All house-holds	Under $3,000	$3,000-4,999	$5,000-6,999	$7,000-8,999	$9,000 & over
	Number (millions)					
All households	68.6	9.1	6.3	6.5	7.5	36.0
	Percent of households					
All households	100	100	100	100	100	100
Poor	17	100	30	9	3	0
Nonpoor	78	0	70	91	97	100
Unknown	5	—	—	—	—	—
	Percent of income class					
All households						
Poor	100	77	16	5	2	0
Nonpoor	100	0	8	11	14	67

Source: Washington Center for Metropolitan Studies' Lifestyles and Energy Surveys.

TECHNICAL TERMS AND THEIR USE

British thermal unit (Btu)—An energy unit defined as the amount of heat required to raise the temperature of one pound of water one degree Fahrenheit.

British thermal unit conversion
  1 cubic foot of natural gas = 1,032 Btu's[d]
  1 gallon of gasoline = 125,000 Btu's
  1 kwh = 10,910 Btu's[e]
  1 therm = 100,000 Btu's

Cooling degree days—The number of degrees the daily average temperature is above 65 degrees Fahrenheit. Normally cooling is not required in a building when the outdoor average daily temperature is below 65 degrees. Cooling degree days are determined by subtracting the base of 65 from the daily average temperature. For example, a day with an average temperature of 85

[d]The conversion factor used in the Lifestyles and Energy work is 124,952 Btu's per gallon derived from (5,248,000 Btu's per barrel) (1 barrel = 42 gallons).
[e]This conversion factor takes into account both the energy used to create electricity in the power plant and transport it, as well as the electricity consumed in the home.[3]If the concern was only with energy consumed in the home, the conversion factor would be 1 kwhr = 3,412 Btu's.
For heat rates (Btu/kwhr) over the years in the electric utility industry, see the *Statistical Yearbook of the Electric Utility Industry for 1972* (New York: Edison Electric Institute, November 1973), Table 41S, p. 49.

Table A2-10.   Characteristics of Poor and Nonpoor Households, 1973 (percent of households)

Characteristics	Total	Poor	Nonpoor
All households	100	100	100
Race			
Black	9	23	6
Other	90	76	93
Household structure			
Husband-Wife	71	41	78
Other	29	59	22
Tenure			
Own	68	47	72
Rent	32	53	28
Life cycle			
Head less than 45	42	32	45
With children	32	25	34
Without children	10	7	11
Head 45 and over	55	64	52
Head 65 and over	20	43	15
Education of head			
High school or less	68	87	63
College	31	12	36
Number of earners			
0	22	56	14
1	45	33	48
2 and over	33	11	38
Employment of head			
Not employed	28	64	19
Employed	72	36	81
Occupation of employed heads of households[a]			
Prof., mgr.	31	7	34
Clerical, sales	15	8	16
Fore., crafts, oper.	34	26	34
Other	20	59	16
Employment status of wife (hus./wife households)			
Not employed	64	78	62
Employed	36	22	38

[a]Unknowns excluded.

Source: Washington Center for Metropolitan Studies' Lifestyles and Energy Surveys.

degrees has 20 cooling degree days $(85 - 65 = 20)$ while one with an average temperature of 65 degrees or lower has none.[4] In the Lifestyles and Energy Surveys, the cooling degree days used were those for the summer of 1972.[f]

[f]Approximately 300 stations in the United States issue climatological data. Estimating the appropriate heating and cooling degree days for survey households involved matching survey sampling points with the appropriate weather station for which degree day information was available. This called for study of various maps. Elevation lines (indicative of temperature) as well as longitude were considered. Once the household was assigned to a

Cubic foot of gas—The most common unit of measurement of gas volume. It is the amount of gas required to fill a volume of one cubic foot under stated conditions of temperature, pressure and water vapor.[5]

Heating degree days—Heating degree days are the number of degrees the daily average temperature is below 65 degrees Fahrenheit. Normally heating is not required in a building when the outdoor average daily temperature is above 65 degrees. Heating degree days are determined by subtracting the average daily temperature below 65 degrees from the base 65. For example, a day with an average temperature of 50 degrees has fifteen heating degree days (65 – 50 = 15), while one with an average temperature of 65 or higher has none.[6] In the Lifestyles and Energy Surveys, the heating degree days used were the most recently published 30-year average (1931-60). Heating degree days for the heating year 1972-73 were not yet available.

Kilowatt hour (kwhr)—A unit of heat value, used to measure electricity. A kilowatt is a unit of power equal to 1,000 watts.

Therm—A unit of heat value, used to measure natural gas.[7]

HOUSEHOLD SURVEY PROCEDURES
BY
REUBEN COHEN[g]

Sampling Procedures
This section describes the area probability sampling methods used for the Lifestyles and Energy Household Survey. The procedure was roughly equivalent to dividing the United States into small geographic units—each consisting of a cluster of about fourteen housing units—and making a systematic random selection of 177 such clusters for the survey.

A number of steps were carried out in the selection:

- The approximately 3,000 counties and independent cities in the United States were grouped into 1,140 primary sampling units.
- The 1,140 primary sampling units were next divided into 103 groups or strata; each stratum consisted of primary sampling units as much alike as possible in terms of geographic region, community type and socioeconomic characteristics.

---

particular weather station, the relevant degree day information was taken from the appropriate report from the series *Local Climatological Data, Annual Summary with Comparative Data*, U.S. Department of Commerce, National Oceanic and Atmosphere Administration, Environmental Data Service.

[g]Response Analysis Corporation, Princeton, New Jersey.

- One primary sampling unit was selected from each of the 103 strata; these selected primary sampling units were the primary areas for the survey.
- Within primary areas, specific segments were selected and assigned to interviewers; at this stage of selection, segments in the lowest socioeconomic quartile in the United States were oversampled (that is, selected at higher rates than other segments); this procedure was used to provide an oversampling of the poor in the United States.

Probability methods were used at each stage of sample selection. Interviewers had no choice in the selection of households for the survey.

Primary Sampling Units

The national sample is comprised of 103 primary areas. To select the primary areas, the entire area of the coterminous United States was first divided into approximately 1,140 primary sampling units (PSUs). Each PSU is a well defined geographic unit, usually a county or a group of counties. For administrative reasons, both upper and lower limits of population size were established for primary sampling units. The range is from a minimum population of 50,000 (in 1970), to a maximum population of 3.3 million persons. PSUs are of two general types: (1) metropolitan areas, or parts of metropolitan areas; and (2) nonmetropolitan areas.

Metropolitan areas. In most cases, PSUs that are metropolitan areas are the same as Standard Metropolitan Statistical Areas (SMSAs) defined by the Bureau of the Census. In the Census definition, each SMSA is a county or group of contiguous counties that contains at least one city of 50,000 inhabitants or more, or "twin cities" with a combined population of at least 50,000. In addition to the county or counties containing a central city or cities, contiguous counties are included in an SMSA if, according to certain criteria, they are essentially metropolitan in character and are socially and economically integrated with the central city.

In the sample, exceptions to the SMSA definitions were of three general types:

1. In New England, SMSAs consist of towns and cities, rather than counties. In the sample, we retained counties and equivalent units as the basic jurisdictions for formation of PSUs. Thus, our PSUs in New England may include all or parts of two or more SMSAs.
2. Some SMSAs include counties in two Census geographic divisions (e.g., the Cincinnati SMSA consists of counties in Ohio and Indiana in the East North Central Division, and in Kentucky in the East South Central Division). In order to maintain a strict stratification for primary sampling units on a geographic division basis, these SMSAs were divided into two parts, corresponding to the geographic divisional classifications.

3. Seven very large metropolitan areas (New York, Boston, Philadelphia, Chicago, Detroit, Los Angeles, and San Francisco) were subdivided into two or more PSUs. Altogether the seven SMSAs comprise 20 PSUs. The reason for these subdivisions was to create smaller areas that are more efficient field administration units.

Nonmetropolitan Areas. PSUs that are not metropolitan areas consist of a county or a group of contiguous counties, and include a minimum population of 50,000 (in 1970). The minimum size condition was intended to create PSUs of sufficient population size to serve diverse survey needs, including sampling of special populations, over a long period of time. A number of criteria were used in combining counties to form PSUs to meet the minimum size requirement:

1. Whenever possible, a city or large town was the central point for the PSU.
2. Convenience of travel to different parts of the PSU from the central point was considered.
3. Heterogeneity of population characteristics was a further criterion—e.g., whenever possible, entirely rural counties were added to other counties that were partly urban.

Stratification and Selection of Primary Sampling Units. Because of their large population size, 38 large PSUs were placed in strata by themselves and were thus automatically included as primary areas in the national sample. These PSUs range (in 1970 population size) from 1.1 million to 3.3 million. Altogether, these 38 primary sampling units make up the 25 largest SMSAs in the United States.

All other primary sampling units (a total of 1,102) were grouped into 65 strata, with an average stratum population of approximately two million persons in 1970. Within a stratum, primary sampling units are as much alike as possible in terms of geography, metropolitan or nonmetropolitan areas, population density, and other characteristics. Actual criteria used in the stratification, and the priority assigned to them were:

- Geographic division (within a stratum, all PSUs are in the same Census geographic division).
- Metropolitan or nonmetropolitan (with the exception of a few counties, strata consist entirely of SMSAs or entirely of other counties). The few exceptions occurred when an SMSA was partly in each of two geographic divisions, and one of the parts was not large enough to meet the size criterion for a PSU.
- For SMSAs, stratification criteria were: size of the SMSA, population

density, percent black (in the South only), percent employed in manufacturing, and population growth between 1960–1970.

- For other than SMSAs, stratification criteria were: percent black (in the South only), population density, percent employed in manufacturing, and percent of land in farms.

One PSU was selected with probability proportionate to size (preliminary 1970 population count) from each of the 65 strata that included two or more PSUs. The selected PSUs are primary areas in the national sample. Together with the 38 large PSUs that were automatically included, the Response Analysis Corporation sample includes a total of 103 primary areas.

Interviewing Locations

Secondary sampling units (SSUs) in the sample are areas of approximately 2,500 population (in 1970). An SSU may be as small geographically as a block or two in a densely populated portion of a city or it may be an entire county or even larger in a sparsely populated rural area. They usually consist of a number of administrative units used in the Census—either enumeration districts or block groups. For the total national sample, 600 secondary sampling units were selected with probability proportional to population.

Census block statistics and field counts by interviewers were used to divide the secondary sampling units into survey assignment units, or segments, of relatively small numbers of households. A segment may be a small land area with clear boundaries such as roads, streams, or other distinct landmarks; or it may be a part of a block with a specific address as a starting point and another specific address as a stopping point.

Oversampling of low income locations. A total of 177 specific sample locations was selected for the Lifestyles and Energy Household Survey. These steps were followed in the selection:

1. Systematic random procedures were used to select 300 secondary sampling units (one-half of the total of 600 available in the national sample). This selection retained the region and community type of stratification in the total sample.
2. Within this subset of 300 secondary sampling units, the 75 locations in the lowest socioeconomic quartile were identified thus:
   - In metropolitan areas for which census tract statistics were available, the socioeconomic definition was based on the percent of all families below the poverty level, using the poverty index adopted by a federal interagency committee in 1969; and

- In nonmetropolitan areas, the socioeconomic definition was based on the estimated average value of housing units (data from Census enumeration districts and block groups were used for this purpose).

3. The 177 locations selected for the Lifestyles and Energy Household Survey included:

   - All the 75 locations (one-fourth of the 300 secondary sampling units) in the lowest socioeconomic quartile; and

   - 102 locations selected as the result of a further systematic random subsampling of the upper three socioeconomic quartiles (five-elevenths of 225 locations).

The purpose of the identification of the lowest socioeconomic quartile and the oversampling of the group of locations was to provide a larger sample of poor households, as defined for the Lifestyles and Household Energy Survey, than would have been available in a cross-section sample selected to represent all types of households proportionately. In a proportionate sample, approximately 350 household interviews would have been completed in the low socioeconomic quartile of locations. This number was increased to approximately 600 by the oversampling of low socioeconomic locations.

In the analysis of survey data, the definition of the poor was based on family income and number of persons in the family, and thus was independent of the characteristics of locations from which survey households were selected. Some households from the upper three socioeconomic quartiles were defined as poor. Conversely, many households selected from the lowest socioeconomic quartile were defined as nonpoor.

Sample Households

Interviewer assignments averaged approximately fourteen housing units per location. Two procedures were used:

1. In 46 of the 177 locations, address listings were available from earlier studies. In these locations housing units were randomly selected in the survey office from the prelistings and assigned to interviewers by specific addresses, usually in the form of three clusters of about five housing units each.

2. In locations for which prelistings were not used, the interviewer received a detailed map or sketch of the sample segment (and address starting and stopping points, if applicable). Specific housing units that were part of the assignment were indicated by numbered lines on a housing unit listing sheet provided for that sample location.

Altogether, 2,409 housing units were assigned for the survey. Of these, 185 were reported to be vacant, leaving a total of 2,224 occupied units eligible for the survey. Interviews were completed at 1,455 households, or 65 percent of the eligible assigned units. Additional information on interview completion experience is contained in the section on field results.

As shown in Table A2-11, about one-third of all respondents were men and about two-thirds were women. In husband/wife households, about two-fifths of respondents were men and three-fifths were women. The larger number of female respondents is not surprising in view of the larger proportion of wives than of husbands who are not employed outside the home.

Field Results

About 65 percent of those eligible for the survey were interviewed (Table A2-12). An eligible respondent could not be found at home, even after repeated attempts, in 13 percent of households, and 20 percent refused. In a few additional cases, interviewers were either unable to contact a sample household, or did not report a reason for being unable to complete the interview.

Completion experience in different geographic regions and in different types of communities is summarized in Table A2-13. Interview

Table A2-11. Sex of Respondent by Household Type, 1973

Sex of respondent	All households		Husband/wife households		Other households	
	Number	Percent	Number	Percent	Number	Percent
Total	1,455	100	1,027	100	428	100
Male	507	35	399	39	108	25
Female	948	65	628	61	320	75

Source: Washington Center for Metropolitan Studies' Lifestyles and Energy Surveys.

Table A2-12. Interview Completion Experience and Reasons for Incomplete Interviews, 1973

Interview completion experience	All households	
	Number	Percent
Total	2,224	100
Interviews completed	1,455	65
Interviews not completed		
Eligible respondent not at home	296	13
Refused	445	20
Not contacted, or unknown reason	28	1

Source: Washington Center for Metropolitan Studies' Lifestyles and Energy Surveys.

Table A2-13. Interview Completion Experience by Geographic Region and Community Type, 1973

Region and community type	All households		Interviews completed		Interviews not completed	
	Number	Percent	Number	Percent	Number	Percent
Total	2,224	100	1,455	65	769	35
Geographic region						
Northeast	488	100	304	62	184	38
North Central	634	100	395	62	239	38
South	750	100	549	73	201	27
West	352	100	207	59	145	41
Community type						
Metropolitan—central cities	833	100	505	61	328	39
Metropolitan ring	776	100	503	65	273	35
Nonmetropolitan	615	100	447	73	168	27

Source: Washington Center for Metropolitan Studies' Lifestyles and Energy Surveys.

completion experience was higher in the South (73 percent) than in other regions. Completion rates also varied by type of community, with the highest rates observed in nonmetropolitan areas (73 percent) and the lowest in central cities of metropolitan areas (61 percent). These patterns are similar to those observed in other surveys. Weighting adjustments to compensate for differences in interview completion rates are described in the section on weighting procedures.

A letter announcing the survey was mailed in advance of the interviewer's visit to those households whose addresses were selected in the central survey office. For all other households, the letter was hand carried by the interviewers and used as an introduction at the discretion of the interviewer. Persistent efforts were made throughout the field phase of the study, both to find designated respondents at home and to urge cooperation from those who were reluctant to participate. Interviewers were instructed to make an original visit and up to three callbacks, if necessary, in an effort to complete the interview at each sample household. Callbacks were required at different times of the day and evening, and on different days of the week. In a number of sample locations, additional callbacks, beyond the four contact attempts originally planned for the study, were assigned in an effort to increase completion.

Approximately 175 interviewers partipated in the field phase of the study. A systematic sample of about 12 percent of all the interviews was verified by telephone or mail. Verification contacts included a brief series of questions designed primarily to determine whether the interview was, in fact, completed with the intended respondent, and that it covered the range of interview subject matter. In the verification sample, there was no evidence of questionable interviewing.

Weighting Procedures

Weight factors were computed to project the survey sample to the total universe of households, and were made part of the computer tape record for each completed interview. In general weights were inversely proportionate to the probability of inclusion of each household in the sample.

Overall weights for households were based on a combination of three factors:

1. *Differences in probability of selection used for socioeconomic quartiles.* As described in the section on sampling procedures, sample locations and households in the lowest socioeconomic quartile were given a higher probability of selection than those in the upper three socioeconomic quartiles. The weights assigned to households in the two groups of locations were inversely proportionate to the probability of selection.

2. *Interview completion rate in specific locations.* Within a given socioeconomic stratum, each sample location represented an equal unit of the household population of the United States. Differences in interview completion experience among sample locations were corrected by weighting interviews inversely proportionate to the number of interviews completed in the location. Locations in which no interviews were completed, or in which very small numbers of interviews were completed, were grouped with other locations of similar characteristics at this step. In general, this factor in the weighting procedure adjusted the total sample for composition by region and type of community.

3. *A constant factor used to expand results to the total universe of households.* The number of private households in the United States in May–June 1973 was estimated to be approximately 68.6 million.

The weight for each household in the sample was computed as follows:

$$W_i = Fs_i m_i$$

where F is the constant factor used to expand results to the survey universe, s_i is the weight for the socioeconomic stratum, and m_i is inversely proportionate to the number of interviews completed in the sample location.

Comparison of Household Survey Sample
Characteristics with Census Estimates

Survey estimates of household characteristics from the Lifestyles and Energy Household Survey are generally close to independent estimates based on *Current Population Reports* of the U.S. Bureau of the Census. As described in the preceding section, weights were used to adjust for differences in interview completion experience in different sample locations.

The result of this weighting procedure would be expected to produce reasonably close agreement between the sample and independent population estimates for geographic region and community type. For other characteristics, however, sample estimates might be expected to differ somewhat from Census estimates as a result of nonresponse patterns or differences in survey procedures or definitions, or as a result of sampling error in either set of estimates. Some differences can be expected also because of the base period to which the estimates apply.

Comparisons in Table A2-14, however, show few noteworthy differences between the two sets of estimates. Socioeconomic characteristics, such as family income and occupation of head of household, are particularly close in agreement. Similarly, sex of head and age of head of household agree closely in the two sets of data.

Survey estimates differ from Census estimates by three or four percentage points for home ownership and for number of small households. On the other hand, survey households and Census estimates were very close for presence of children related to the household's head. Among survey households, 43.6 percent owned two or more motor vehicles, compared with the Census estimate of 39.7 percent for one year earlier.

The three to four percentage point differences between survey and Census estimates are at the outer range of the size of differences that might be observed as a result of random sampling error alone. The differences in size of household, in particular, may be affected by nonresponse patterns, since interviewers would ordinarily have greater difficulty finding members of small households at home and available for interview.

Sampling Error

All survey results are subject to some error due to random sampling variation. The tables in this section provide a general guide to the amount of possible variation between the sample result and the result that would have been obtained had the same survey procedures been used to study the entire household population.

A principal factor affecting sampling variation is the size of the sample: the larger the sample, the smaller the range of sampling error. The range of sampling error around survey percentages is also dependent on the size of the survey percentages: results near 50 percent are subject to wider percentage point

Characteristics	Survey estimate	Census estimate
Total households	100.0	100.0
Region		
Northeast	23.9	23.9
North Central	28.9	27.5
South	31.7	30.7
West	15.5	17.9
Community type		
Metropolitan areas, 1,000,000 or larger	39.5	39.5
Central cities	15.4	18.2
Ring	24.1	21.3
Metropolitan areas, under 1,000,000	30.1	30.1
Central cities	17.6	15.2
Ring	12.5	14.9
Nonmetropolitan	30.4	30.4
Race		
White	89.2	88.8
Black	9.5	10.0
Other	.4	1.2
Unknown	.9	—
Own or rent home		
Own	67.9	64.4
Rent, other	32.1	35.6
Ownership of motor vehicles		
Own none	16.2	18.9
Own one	40.1	41.4
Own two	34.2	31.3
Own three or more	9.4	8.4
Size of household		
One person	16.2	18.5
Two persons	28.0	30.2
Three persons	17.9	17.3
Four persons	18.2	15.7
Five persons	10.1	9.4
Six persons	4.4	4.8
Seven or more persons	5.1	4.1
Presence of children related to head		
None under 18	54.7	55.0
One or more under 18	45.3	45.0
None under 6	77.5	78.6
One or more under 6	22.5	21.4
Family income in 1972		
Under $1,500	3.8	4.5
$1,500–$2,999	9.5	9.2
$3,000–$4,999	9.2	11.2
$5,000–$6,999	9.5	10.6
$7,000–$8,999	11.0	10.7
$9,000–$11,999	14.5	15.6

(continued)

Characteristics	Survey estimate	Census estimate
$12,000–$24,999	32.1	32.0
$12,000–$15,999	18.4	a
$16,000–$24,999	13.7	a
$25,000 and over	5.9	6.2
Unknown	4.5	—
Sex of head		
Male	78.1	77.4
Female	21.9	22.6
Age of head		
14–24	7.1	8.0
25–34	19.4	19.9
35–44	15.7	17.2
45–54	19.2	18.8
55–64	14.9	16.4
65 and over	20.5	19.7
Unknown	3.2	—
Education of head		
Grade school or less	20.9	24.5
Some high school	18.3	16.1
High school graduate	28.4	32.6
Some college	15.3	12.4
College graduate or postgraduate	16.0	14.3
Unknown	1.0	—
Occupation of head		
Professional	12.5	10.8
Managerial	9.7	10.2
Clerical	6.5	6.9
Sales	4.4	4.4
Craftsmen	12.2	13.8
Operatives	11.7	12.3
Service workers	7.5	6.5
Laborers	3.9	3.2
Farmers	2.8	2.9
In Armed Forces	b	1.3
Not employed	27.5	27.7
Unknown	1.4	—

[a]Not available.

[b]Not specified separately.

Sources: Census estimates are from U.S. Bureau of the Census, *Current Population Reports,* as follows:

Characteristics	Report and Data
Region Community type	Series P-20, No. 246, Feb. 1973; "Household and Family Characteristics, March 1972"
Race, size of household, presence of children related to head, sex of head, age of head, education of head, occupation of head, family income	Series P-60, No. 89, July 1973; "Household Money Income in 1972 and Selected Social and Economic Characteristics of Households"
Ownership of motor vehicle, own or rent home	Series P-65, No. 44, Feb. 1973; "Household Ownership of Cars and Light Trucks, July 1972"

Table A2-15. Approximate Standard Errors and Sampling Tolerances for Survey Percentages, by Size of Sample or Group

Survey percentages near	*Size of sample or group*					
	1,455	*1,000*	*750*	*500*	*250*	*100*
Standard error: 68 chances out of 100						
50	2	2	2	3	4	6
40 or 60	2	2	2	3	4	6
30 or 70	2	2	2	3	4	6
20 or 80	1	2	2	2	3	5
10 or 90	1	1	1	2	2	4
Sampling tolerance: 95 chances out of 100[a]						
50	3	4	4	5	8	12
40 or 60	3	4	4	5	8	12
30 or 70	3	4	4	5	7	11
20 or 80	3	3	4	4	6	10
10 or 90	2	2	3	3	5	7

[a]Sampling tolerances are approximately equal to two standard errors.

variations than are results near the ends of the percentage distribution (for example, near 10 percent or near 90 percent).

A third factor affecting sampling error is the sample design: for example, the stratification and clustering procedure used for this national sample. This third factor affects different survey results in different ways, even when the size of the sample and other factors are the same. Thus the guides presented in this section are generally appropriate to the sample used for the Lifestyles and Energy Household Survey. They may be overestimates for some results and underestimates for others.[h]

Approximate standard errors and sampling tolerances of survey percentages are summarized in Table A2-15.

- The chances are 68 out of 100 that an estimate from the sample would differ from a complete census by less than the standard error.
- The chances are 95 out of 100 that an estimate from the sample would differ from a complete census by less than the sampling tolerance (two standard errors).

To illustrate, the survey estimate of households using public transportation for one or more specific purposes during the past month is 23 percent.

[h]Sampling error figures presented in the tables are based on estimates of *sampling variances* that are 1.5 times the sampling variances for a simple random sample; the WCMS Lifestyles and Energy Household Survey is based on a stratified, multistage area probability sample.

- There are about 68 chances in 100 that this figure differs by one percentage point or less from the result of a complete census, using the same survey procedures.
- There are about 95 chances in 100 that the survey figure differs by three percentage points or less from the result of a complete census.

The approximate sampling variability figures presented in Table A2-15 may also be used to obtain measures of sampling error of population estimates as well as percentages. For example, the estimated number of households using public transportation for specified purposes in the past month is 15.4 million (corresponding to the 23 percent cited above). The sampling tolerance for this figure is 2.1 million (3 percent of the estimated total of 68.6 million households in the United States at the time of data collection for this survey).

Approximate measures of sampling variability for survey estimates of household energy consumption are summarized in Table A2-16. These measures are for per-household averages presented in terms of millions of Btu's for each of three fuels separately, and also for an index of fuel consumption computed for subgroups of households.

- As an example, the average annual electricity consumption for single family structures was estimated by the survey as 101.5 million Btu's. There are 1,151 households in the sample in this group. The average of 101.5 million Btu's has a standard error of approximately three million Btu's. Thus there are approximately 68 chances in 100 that the survey average Btu estimate for consumption of electricity would differ by no more than about three

Table A2-16. Approximate Standard Errors and Sampling Tolerances for Average Energy Use per Household (millions of Btu's), and for Index of Energy Consumption, by Size of Sample or Group[a]

Measure of sampling variability	Size of sample or group					
	1,455	*1,000*	*750*	*500*	*250*	*100*
Standard error (68 chances out of 100)	3	3	4	5	6	10
Sampling tolerance (95 chances out of 100)[b]	5	6	7	9	13	20

[a]Figures in the table apply approximately to averages (millions of Btu's) for each of three specific fuels—electricity, natural gas, and gasoline—and also to the index of household usage for each of the three fuels. See text for examples.

[b]Sampling tolerances are approximately equal to two standard errors.

million Btu's (101.5 million plus or minus three million) from an estimate based on a complete census.

• Similarly, the index of electricity consumption for single family households is 109 (all households = 100). The standard error for this index is approximately three index points.

All survey results are also subject to errors of response and nonreporting. In particular, errors of response may have large effects on survey responses that are based on memory (e.g., trips taken in past twelve months). Errors due to nonreporting may have occurred at various points in the development of estimates of household energy consumption (e.g., interview not completed, authorization to obtain information from utility companies not signed, information not obtained from utility company). Possible errors resulting from these nonreporting patterns are not reflected in sampling error estimates.

Notes

Notes to Introduction

1. We hope that the work of Lansing, Kish, Morgan and others could expand into this area to test their findings about the significance of family life cycle as an independent variable. See, for instance, James E. Morgan, and others, *Five Thousand American Families—Patterns of Economic Progress* (Survey Research Center, Institute for Social Research, Ann Arbor: University of Michigan, 1974). John B. Lansing and Leslie Kish, "Family Life Cycle as an Independent Variable," *American Sociological Review* 22 (5) (October 1957), pp. 512–519. Keizo Nagatani, "Life Cycle Savings: Theory and Fact," *American Economic Review* 62 (3) (June 1972), pp. 344–353. Robert Ferber, "Consumer Economics, a Survey," *Journal of Economic Literature* 11 (4) (December 1973), pp. 1306–1309; 1333–1342.

2. Milton Friedman, *Theory of the Consumption Function* (Princeton: National Bureau of Economic Research, 1957).

3. See also, Milton Friedman, "Windfalls, the 'Horizon,' and Related Concepts in the Permanent-Income Hypothesis," in Carl F. Christ et al., *Measurement in Economics; Studies in Mathematical Economics and Econometrics in Memory of Yehuda Grunfeld* (Stanford, Calif.: Stanford University Press, 1963), pp. 3–28; F. Modigliani, "The Life Cycle Hypothesis of Saving, the Demand for Wealth and the Supply of Capital," *Social Research* (Summer 1966), pp. 160–217; Julian L. Simon and Carl B. Barnes, "The Middle-Class U.S. Consumption Function: A Hypothetical Question Study of Expected Consumption Behaviour," *Oxford Institute of Economics and Statistics Bulletin* (February 1971), pp. 73–80; Lester Thurow, "The Optimum Lifetime Distribution of Consumption Expenditures," *American Economic Review* (June 1969), pp. 324–330; Jacob Mincer, "The Distribution of Labor Incomes: A Survey with Special Reference to the Human Capital Approach," *Journal of Economic Literature* (December 1973), pp. 1306–1342 and 3138; and Prem S. Laumas and Khan A. Mohabbat, "The Permanent Income Hypothesis: Evidence from Time-Series Data," *American Economic Review* (September 1972), pp. 730–734.

4. Edited by Alexander Szalai and published in The Hague and in Paris by Mouton in 1972. see p. 213ff for Susan Ferge's study.

5. *Ibid,* p. 213.

Notes to Chapter One

1. For a social history about the discovery and use of energy sources, see David J. Boorstin, *The Americans–The Democratic Experience* (New York: Random House, 1973), p. 717. See also U.S. Department of Labor, *How American Buying Habits Change* (Washington, D.C., 1959, Chapters 1, 2 and 8). Chapter 2 in this book relates how several households have recalled family experiences over one or more generations.

2. Boorstin, *op. cit.,* p. 105.

3. *Ibid.,* p. 530.

4. U.S. Bureau of Census, Census of Population, 1970, Vol. 1, Part 1, *Characteristics of the Population,* U.S. Summary (Washington, D.C.: U.S. Government Printing Office, 1972), p. 46.

5. U.S. Bureau of the Census. *Statistical Abstract of the United States, 1973* (Washington, D.C.: U.S. Government Printing Office, 1973) Table 2, p. 5 and Table 900, p. 547.

6. U.S. Department of Labor, *How American Buying Habits Change* (Washington, D.C.: U.S. Government Printing Office, 1959) p. 182.

7. U.S. Bureau of the Census, *Historical Statistics of the U.S., Colonial Times to 1957* (Washington, D.C.: U.S. Government Printing Office, 1961) Series Q252, p. 458.

8. U.S. Bureau of the Census, *Statistical Abstract of the United States 1973* (Washington, D.C.: U.S. Government Printing Office, 1973) Table 2, p. 5 and Table 900, p. 547.

9. *Merchandising Week,* February 28, 1972, p. 22.

10. *Ibid.*

11. United Nations, Statistical Office, Department of Economic and Social Affairs. *United Nations Statistical Yearbook 1972* (New York: United Nations, 1973), pp. 353–356.

12. Joel Darmstadter, "Appendix: Energy Consumption Trends and Patterns," in Sam H. Schurr, ed., *Energy, Economic Growth, and the Environment* (Baltimore, Md.: Johns Hopkins Press, 1972).

13. Anthony Astrachan, "Problems Behind the Population Boom," *The Washington Post,* August 21, 1974, p. A-14.

14. U.S. Department of the Interior Release, "Energy Use Up Nearly 5 Percent in 1973," March 13, 1974, p. 1.

15. Geoffrey H. Moore and Janice Neipert Hedges, "Trends in Labor and Leisure," *Monthly Labor Review* 94 (February 1971), Table 5, and U.S. Bureau of Labor Statistics, *Employment and Earnings* (January 1974), Table 25, p. 157.

16. Moore and Hedges, *op. cit.,* p. 7.

17. John P. Robinson, "Historical Changes in How People Spend Their Time," in Andrée Michel, ed., *Family Issues of Employed Women in*

Europe and America (Leiden, Netherlands: E. H. Brill, 1971), p. 148, cited in an unpublished paper "U.S. Energy Use in Historical Perspective, 1900-1970" (Washington, D.C.: Energy Policy Project, November 1973).

18. Joann Vanek, *Keeping Busy: Time Spent in Housework, United States, 1920-1970* (Ph.D. dissertation, University of Michigan, 1974).

Notes to Chapter Three

1. U.S. Bureau of the Census, 1970 Census of Housing, *Detailed Housing Characteristics,* U.S. Summary, HC(1)-B1 (Washington, D.C.: U.S. Government Printing Office, 1972), Table 22, p. 1-242.

2. U.S. Bureau of the Census, *Construction Reports*—Series C25-72-13, "Characteristics of New One-Family Homes: 1972," Table 2, p. 2, and U.S. Bureau of the Census, 1970 Census of Housing, *Detailed Housing Characteristics,* U.S. Summary, HC(1)-B1 (Washington, D.C.: U.S. Government Printing Office, 1972), Table 22, p. 242.

3. For a discussion of building design and energy use see American Institute of Architects, *Energy Conservation in Building Design* (Washington, D.C., 1974).

4. Eric Hirst and John C. Moyers, "Efficiency of Energy Use in the United States," *Science* 179 (March 30, 1973), p. 1301.

5. R. D. Doctor and K. P. Anderson, *California's Electrical Quandary III: Slowing the Growth Rate* (Santa Monica, Calif.: Rand Corp., September 1972), p. 55.

6. Hirst and Moyers, *loc. cit.*

7. The analysis of trends in new one-family homes is taken from an article by Nancy F. Rytina and William R. Beachy. "Energy-Using Features Increase in New One-Family Houses," *Metropolitan Bulletin,* No. 11 (June-July 1973), (Washington, D.C.: Washington Center for Metropolitan Studies), pp. 4-5, and U.S. Bureau of the Census, *Construction Reports*—Series C25, "Characteristics of New One-Family Homes, 1971" (Washington, D.C.: U.S. Government Printing Office, 1972).

8. U.S. Bureau of the Census, *Construction Reports*—Series C20, "Housing Starts: May 1974" (Washington, D.C.: U.S. Government Printing Office, 1974), Table 9, p. 12.

9. U.S. Bureau of the Census, *Construction Reports*—Series C25-72-13, "Characteristics of New One-Family Homes, 1972" (Washington, D.C.: U.S. Government Printing Office, 1973), Table 4, p. 15.

10. U.S. Bureau of the Census, *Statistical Abstract of the United States 1973* (94th ed.) (Washington, D.C.: U.S. Government Printing Office, 1973), p. 37.

11. U.S. Bureau of the Census, Census of Population: 1970, Subject Reports Final Report PC(2)-2B, *Mobility for States and the Nation,* (Washington, D.C.: U.S. Government Printing Office, 1973), Tables 17 and 18, pp. 171-73 and pp. 177-78.

12. Tersh Boasberg and James Feldesman, *Coping with the Energy Crisis,* (Washington, D.C.: Office of Economic Opportunity, May 1974), p. 51.

13. Consolidated Edison, "Portable Electric Heaters No Solution to the Energy Crisis," *Customer News* (January 1974), p. 1.

14. The estimate of energy consumption by pilot lights (800 Btu per hour) is from "Gas Pilots—Useful Ignition Device With Fringe Benefits, Says AGA," *Air Conditioning, Heating, and Refrigeration News* (October 29, 1973), Figure 1, p. 21.

15. Electric Energy Association, *Annual Energy Requirements of Electric Household Appliances* (New York, 1973, pamphlet).

16. U.S. Department of Commerce, National Bureau of Standards, *Energy Labeling of Household Appliances* (Washington, D.C.: National Bureau of Standards, 1974, pamphlet).

17. Others have used appliance saturation data to gauge energy consumption. For example, see a paper by Thomas E. Browne, "Appliance Saturation and Load Data—A Forecasting Tool" (Albany, N.Y.: New York Public Service Commission, January 1972) (unpublished). Saturation refers to the proportion of households which have a particular appliance.

18. Supplied to the authors by a specialist at the U.S. Bureau of Labor Statistics.

19. Eric Hirst and John C. Moyers, "Efficiency of Energy Use in the United States," *Science* 179 (March 30, 1973), p. 1303.

20. U.S. Department of Commerce, National Bureau of Standards, *Energy Efficiency in Room Air Conditioners* (Washington, D.C.: National Bureau of Standards, 1974, pamphlet).

21. "19-Inch Color TV," *Consumer Reports* (January 1973), p. 8, and "19-Inch Black and White TV," *Consumer Reports* (March 1973), p. 158.

22. "How to Save Fuel at Home," *U.S. News and World Report* (December 17, 1973), p. 20.

23. F. DeLeeuw and Nkanta F. Ekanem, "The Supply of Rental Housing," *American Economic Review* 61 (December 1971), pp. 806–817; Arthur Kartman, "Demand for Housing: The Neglected Supply Side," *University of Washington Business Review* 30 (Spring 1971), pp. 59–64; and Nelson H. Foote, Janet Abu-Lughod, Mary Mix Foley, and Louis Winnick, *Housing Coices and Housing Constraints* (New York: McGraw-Hill, 1960).

24. National Bureau of Standards, *Seven Ways to Reduce Fuel Consumption in Household Heating Through Energy Conservation* (Washington, D.C.: U.S. Government Printing Office, 1972).

25. Eric Hirst, *Electrical Utility Advertising and the Environment* (Oak Ridge, Tenn.: Oak Ridge National Laboratory, April 1972), p. 15.

Notes to Chapter Four

1. For another set of estimates of energy efficiency by transportation mode see W. P. Goss and J. G. McGowan, "Transportation and Energy—A Future Confrontation," *Transportation* 1 (3) (November 1972), pp. 265–289.

2. The figure for 1940 women drivers is from Motor Vehicle Manufacturers Association, *1972 Automobile Facts and Figures* (Washington,

D.C., 1972), p. 42. The figure for 1972 women drivers is from U.S. Department of Transportation, Federal Highway Administration, *Drivers Licenses–1972* (Washington, D.C., 1973), p. 6.

3. U.S. Bureau of the Census, *Statistical Abstract of the United States, 1973* (Washington, D.C.: U.S. Government Printing Office, 1974), Table 888, p. 539.

4. *Ibid.,* Table 939, p. 567.

5. U.S. Environmental Protection Agency, *A Report on Automotive Fuel Economy* (Washington, D.C.: U.S. Government Printing Office, October 1973), p. 4.

6. Data on 1973 car weight and mileage from U.S. Environmental Protection Agency, *1974 Gas Mileage Guide for Car Buyers: Fuel Test Results for Automobiles and Light-Duty Trucks* (Washington, D.C., February 1974).

7. U.S. Environmental Protection Agency, *A Report on Automotive Fuel Economy* (Washington, D.C., October 1973), p. 3.

8. This historical summary is developed in detail in an unpublished paper by Walter D. Velona, "Urban Growth and New Technology for Transportation" (Washington, D.C.: Office of the Secretary of the U.S. Department of Transportation, October 15, 1971). See also U.S. Department of Labor, *How American Buying Habits Change* (Washington, D.C.: U.S. Government Printing Office, 1959), pp. 180–182; and J. R. Meyer, J. F. Kain, and M. Wohl, *The Urban Transportation Problem* (Cambridge, Mass.: Harvard University Press, 1966).

9. John B. Lansing and Gary Hendricks, *Automobile Ownership and Residential Density* (Ann Arbor, Mich.: Institute for Social Research, 1967).

10. U.S. Department of Transportation, Federal Highway Administration, "Household Travel in the United States," *Report No. 7* by Beatrice Goley, Geraldine Brown, and Elizabeth Samson (December 1972), p. 4.

11. U.S. Bureau of the Census, Censuses of Population: 1960 and 1970, *General Social and Economic Characteristics,* U.S. Summary, PC (1)-1C, (Washington, D.C.: U.S. Government Printing Office, 1962 and 1972), 1960, Table 94, p. 224 and 1970, Table 98, p. 404.

12. U.S. Bureau of the Census, Censuses of Population: 1970, *General Social and Economic Characteristics,* Final Report, PC (1)-1C, U.S. Summary, Table 78, p. 372; and *Detailed Characteristics* Final Report PC (1)-1D, U.S. Summary (Washington, D.C.: U.S. Government Printing Office, 1972), Table 242, p. 830.

13. Colin Walters, *Travel Growth in Washington Region Highlights Need for More Small Vehicle Transit* (Washington, D.C.: Washington Center for Metropolitan Studies, August 1974).

14. David Tillotson, "Consumer Routes for Bicycles," Letter to the Editor of the *Washington Post,* June 20, 1974.

Notes to Chapter Five

1. Ford Foundation Energy Policy Project, *A Time to Choose: America's Energy Future* (Cambridge, Mass.: Ballinger 1974), Chapter 5.

2. Frank Ackerman, Howard Birnbaum, James Wetzler, and Andrew Zimbalist, "Income Distribution in the United States," *Review of Radical Political Economics* 3 (3) (Summer 1971), pp. 20–43. Also, *Economic Report of the President, 1974* (Washington, D.C.: U.S. Government Printing Office, 1974), p. 140; Dorothy S. Projector and Gertrude Weiss, *Survey of Financial Characteristics of Consumers* (Washington, D.C.: Federal Reserve System, 1966); James D. Smith and Stephan D. Franklin, "The Concentration of Personal Wealth, 1922–1969," *American Economic Review* (May 1974), pp. 162–167.

3. In car ownership, mileage, and gasoline consumption, there is the work of Lansing and Hendricks, Houthakker, Verleger and Sheehan and a Data Resources study. In electricity consumption, there is the work of Chapman, Tyrrell and Mount; Halvorsen; Wilson; two Rand Corporation studies; and Houtthaker, Verleger, and Sheehan.

See especially, John B. Lansing and Gary Hendricks, *Automobile Ownership and Residentail Density* (Ann Arbor, Michigan: Institute for Social Research, 1967); H. S. Houthakker, Philip K. Verleger, and Dennis P. Sheehan, "Dynamic Demand Analyses for Gasoline and Residential Electricity," paper presented at the December 1973 meetings of the American Economic Association and available from Data Resources, Inc., 29 Hartwell Ave., Lexington, Mass. 02173; Data Resources, *A Study of the Quarterly Demand for Gasoline and Impacts of Alternative Gasoline Taxes* (Lexington, Mass., 1973); Duane Chapman, Timothy J. Tyrrell and Timothy D. Mount, "Electricity and the Environment: Economic Aspects of Interdisciplinary Problem Solving," paper presented at the December 1971 meetings of the American Association for the Advancement of Science and available from Duane Chapman at Cornell University, Ithaca, New York; Chapman and others, "More Resistance to Electricity," *Environment* 15 (8) (October 1973), pp. 19–20; Robert Halvorsen, "Demand for Electric Power in the United States," paper presented at the December 1973 meetings of the Econmetric Society and available from the Institute for Economic Research, University of Washington, Seattle, Washington 98195; John W. Wilson, "Electricity Consumption: Supply Requirements and Demand Electricity and Rate Design," unpublished paper available from author at 6425 Belleview Drive, Columbia, Md. 21046; M. B. Berman, M. J. Hammer, and D. P. Tihansky, *The Impact of Electricity Price Increases on Income Groups: Western United States and California* (Santa Monica, Calif.: Rand Corp., 1972); and M. B. Berman and M. J. Hammer, *The Impact of Electricity Price Increases on Income Groups: A Case Study of Los Angeles* (Santa Monica, Calif.: Rand Corp., 1973).

4. Wilbur Smith and Associates, *On-Bus Origin-Destination Survey* (Washington, D.C.: Washington Metropolitan Area Transit Authority, April 1974), pp. 50–68.

5. Carl B. Stokes, "On Reordering the Priorities of the Planning Profession," *Planning 1971* (Chicago: American Society of Planning Officials, 1971), as quoted in Russell W. Thibeault, Edward J. Kaiser, Edgar W. Butler, and Ronald J. McAllister, "Accessibility Satisfaction, Income, and Residential Mobility," *Traffic Quarterly* 27 (April 1973): 290.

6. For materials on lower middle income Americans, see Arthur B.

Shostak, *Blue-Collar Life* (New York: Random House, 1969); Jerome M. Rosow, *The Worker and the Job* (Englewood Cliffs, N.J.: Prentice-Hall, 1974); U.S. Bureau of Labor Statistics, *Employment and Earnings* (see establishment data and hours and earnings data, any current monthly issue); James W. Rinehart, "Affluence and the Embourgeoisement of the Working Class: A Critical Look," *Social Problems* 19 (Fall 1971), pp. 149–162; Martin Oppenheimer, "What Is the New Working Class?" *New Politics* 10 (Fall 1972), pp. 29–43; and John C. Raines, "Middle America: Up Against the Wall and Going Nowhere," *Christian Century* (May 2, 1973), pp. 504–507.

7. See "Cost of Operating An Automobile," *Family Economic Review* (September 1972), p. 17.

8. U.S. Department of Labor, *How American Buying Habits Change* (Washington, D.C.: U.S. Government Printing Office, 1959) and U.S. Bureau of Labor Statistics, *Consumer Expenditures and Income*, Supplement 3–Part A to BLS Report No. 237-93 (May 1966), T29A, pp. 2–15.

9. Neil Fabricant and Robert M. Hallman, *Toward a Rational Energy Policy: Energy, Politics and Pollution* (New York: George Brazillen, 1971), pp. 15–16.

10. Barbara Epstein, "A Proposal to Modernize Electricity Tariffs," *Public Utilities Fortnightly* (August 30, 1973), p. 26. For other materials on this topic, see the chapter on electric utility regulation in Ford Foundation, Energy Policy Project, *A Time to Choose: America's Energy Future* (Cambridge, Mass.: Ballinger, 1974).

11. Unpublished correspondence from Joseph R. Rensch, President, Pacific Lighting Corporation, dated May 9. 1974.

12. John J. Musial and Edward M. Mayers, *Brief of Michigan UAW-CAP and Consumer Alliance of Michigan,* case No. U-3910 before the Michigan Public Service Commission (May 17, 1971), p. 9 (attorneys Daniel P. Dozier and V. Paul Donnelly).

13. B. Epstein, *op. cit.,* p. 28.

14. Thomas O'Toole, "FEA Raps Oil Firms' 'Hard Sell,' " *The Washington Post,* August 6, 1974, p. A15.

15. Eric Hirst, *Electric Utility Advertising and the Environment* (Oak Ridge, Tenn.: Oak Ridge National Laboratory, 1972), p. 6.

16. For a recent study of promotional practices among electric utilities, see Sandra Jerabek, "A Survey of State Utility Regulatory Commissions: Initiatives Taken to Affect the Growth in Demand for Electric Power," (Washington, D.C.: Environmental Action Foundation, 1973, unpublished); and Eric Hirst, *op. cit.,* p. 30.

17. "Travel Stamps Get U.S. Funding," *The Washington Post,* June 14, 1974, p. A24.

18. Eric Hirst, *op. cit.,* p. 30.

Notes to Chapter Six

1. U.S. Council on Environmental Quality, *Environmental Quality: The Fourth Annual Report of the Council on Environmental Quality* (Washing-

ton, D.C.: U.S. Government Printing Office, September 1973), p. 266 (hereafter cited as *CEQ 1973*).

2. **Emission of Pollutants at Electric Power Plants—Average Rate by Type of Fossil Fuel**

Pollutant	*Coal lb/ton*	*Oil lb/1,000 gal.*	*Gas lb/10⁶ ft³*
Nitrogen dioxide	20	104	390
Sulfur dioxide	38.5[a]	157S[a]	b
Carbon monoxide	.5	b	b
Hydrocarbons as methane	.2	3.2	b
Particulates	17A[c]	10.0	15

Btu equivalent: 25,000,000/ton, 150,000,000/1,000 gal., 1,044,000,000/10^6 ft^3

[a]S equals percent sulfur in the fuel. For example, coal with 2 percent sulfur will emit 76 lbs. of SO_2 per ton of coal burned.

[b]Less than .05.

[c]Emissions of fly ash are a function of the ash content of the fuel and type of furnace. For a dry bottom pulverized coal unit, fly ash emissions in pounds per ton of coal burned would be 17 A where A is the ash content of the coal expressed in percent.

3. *CEQ 1973*, p. 267.

4. Ian T. T. Higgins and Benjamin G. Ferris, "Epidemiology of Sulphur Oxides and Particles," in National Academy of Sciences–National Research Council, *Proceedings of the Conference on Health Effects of Air Pollutants,* prepared for the U.S. Congress, Senate, Committee on Public Works pursuant to S. Res. 135, 93rd Congress, 1st Session (Washington, D.C.: U.S. Government Printing Office, 1973), p. 252 (hereafter cited as *Conf. on Health Effects of Air Pollutants*).

5. *Federal Register,* V. 36, No. 84 (April 30, 1971), p. 8187.

6. Donald J. Bartlett, Jr., "Effects of Carbon Monoxide on Human Physiological Processes," *Conf. on Health Effects of Air Pollutants,* p. 116.

7. U.S. Department of Health, Education, and Welfare, National Air Pollution Control Administration, *Air Quality Criteria for Carbon Monoxide* (Washington, D.C., March 1970), p. 10-6.

8. *Federal Register,* V. 36, No. 84 (April 30, 1971), p. 8187.

9. U.S. Department of Health, Education, and Welfare, National Air Pollution Control Administration, *Air Quality Criteria for Hydrocarbons* (Washington, D.C., March 1970), pp. 8-4 and 8-15.

10. Oscar J. Balchum, "Toxicological Effects of Ozone, Oxident and Hydrocarbons," *Conf. on Health Effects of Air Pollutants,* p. 497.

11. *Ibid.*

12. *Federal Register,* V. 36, No. 84 (April 30, 1971), p. 8187. The standard in 1974 was 160 ug/m^3 for the three-hour period 6 a.m. to 9 a.m. The standard is not to be exceeded more than once per year.

13. For a full discussion of this method and results, see Lyndon R. Babcock, Jr., "A Combined Pollution Index for Measurement of Total Air Pollution," *Journal of the Air Pollution Control Association* 20 (October 1970): 653–59, and Lyndon R. Babcock Jr. and Niren L. Nagda, "Cost Effectiveness of Emission Control," *Journal of the Air Pollution Control Association* 23 (March 1973): 173–79.

14. *CEQ 1973,* pp. 267 and 271. The figure below illustrates Babcock's adjustment from emissions to effects of emissions.

1971 Air Pollution Emissions, Percentage by Pollutant, Un-adjusted and Adjusted for Effects

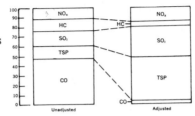

Source: U.S. Environmental Protection Agency, Office of Air and Water Programs and Office of Air Quality Planning and Standards, *Compilation of Air Pollutant Emission Factors,* 2nd ed. (Research Triangle Park, N.C., April 1973), Figure 3.1.1-1.

15. Thomas E. Waddell, *The Economic Damages of Air Pollution* (Washington, D.C.: Environmental Protection Agency, 1974), p. 131.

16. The definition of poverty used by the Census Bureau is complex. It produces a range of income cutoffs that take into account factors such as family size, sex and age of the family head, and farm-nonfarm residence. The income cutoff for a nonfarm family of four was $3,743 in 1969. For a detailed exposition of the poverty definition, see U.S. Bureau of the Census, *Current Population Reports,* Series P-23, No. 28, "Revisions in Poverty Statistics, 1959 to 1968" (Washington, D.C.: U.S. Government Printing Office, August 1969).

17. The following graph shows the relationship between vehicle speed and emission:

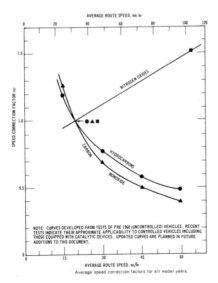

Source: U.S. Environmental Protection Agency, Office of Air and Water Programs and Office of Air Quality Planning and Standards, *Compilation of Air Pollutant Emission Factors,* 2nd ed. (Research Triangle Park, N.C., April 1973), Figure 3.1.1-1.

18. TRW, Inc., *Prediction of the Effects of Transportation Controls on Air Quality in Major Metropolitan Areas* (McLean, Va., November 1972), pp. 4-1 and 4-3.

19. The model used for carbon monoxide and hydrocarbons is the Gifford-Hanna model. The model states that the concentration of a pollutant is essentially a function of the speed and direction of the wind and the strength of the source of the pollutant in question. Specifically,

$$X = \sqrt{\frac{2}{\pi}} \; \frac{1}{u} \; \frac{(\Delta x/2)^{1-b}}{a(1-b)} \; \left\{ Q_o + \sum_{i=1}^{N} Q_i \; [(2i+1)^{1-b} - (2i-1)^{1-b}] \right\}$$

Where X = concentration (mg/m^3)

u = wind speed (m/sec)

x = grid side length $(m \times 10^3)$

Q_o = central grid source strength $(g/m^2 - sec)$

$N = 10$

a and b = empirical constants of urban stability averaging 0.15 $(meters^{1-b})$ and 0.75, respectively

For a complete discussion of the diffusion model and the results for the National Capital Air Quality Control Region, see TRW Systems Group. *Air Quality Implementation Planning Program, Vol. 1, Operator's Manual* (Springfield, Va.: U.S. Department of Commerce, National Technical Information Service, November 1970), Chapters 3 and 4; also Department of Environmental Services, Government of the District of Columbia, *Proposed Air Quality Standards for the District of Columbia* (Washington, D.C., October 1971), pp. 3-15 and 3-16, and Appendices A & B.

20. *Federal Register,* V. 36, No. 84 (April 30, 1971), p. 8187.

21. The federal standard for non-methane hydrocarbons is 160 ug/m^3 for the three-hour period 6 a.m. to 9 a.m. Our hydrocarbon measurement includes both methane and nonmethane hydrocarbons and relates to the eight-hour period 11 a.m. to 7 p.m.

22. For a complete discussion of diffusion models and results for the National Capital Air Quality Control Region, see TRW Systems Group, *loc. cit.;* also, Department of Environmental Services, Government of the District of Columbia, *loc. cit.*

23. *CEQ 1973,* p. 273.

24. Traffic count data were supplied by the District of Columbia Department of Highways and Traffic for 1968 and 1972. The avenues surveyed were Constitution Ave., Massachusetts Ave., Connecticut Ave., New York Ave., Pennsylvania Ave., Rhode Island Ave., and North Capital Street. In 1968 an average of 28,400 vehicles traveled on a typical block on these avenues, while in 1972 the total was 27,900 per block.

25. U.S. Bureau of the Census, *Current Population Reports,* Series P-60, No. 90, "Money Income in 1972 of Families and Persons in the United States," (Washington, D.C.: U.S. Government Printing Office, 1973), Table 62.

26. U.S. Bureau of the Census, *Current Population Reports,* Series P-60, No. 88, "Characteristics of the Low Income Population: 1972" (Washington, D.C.: U.S. Government Printing Office, June 1973), Table 3.

27. Jeffrey M. Zupan, *The Distribution of Air Quality in the New York Region* (Baltimore, Md.: Johns Hopkins University Press for Resources for the Future, Inc., 1973), p. 49.

28. *Ibid.*

29. *Ibid.,* see especially pp. 33–50. Zupan, for example, calculated vehicle miles traveled and speeds on a county basis. He also used residential and nonresidential density estimates and emissions rather than actual concentration of pollutant estimates.

30. A. Myrick Freeman, III, "The Distribution of Environmental Quality," in Alan V. Kneese and Blair T. Bower (Eds.), *Environmental Qualtiy Analysis* (Baltimore, Md.: Johns Hopkins University Press for Resources for the Future, Inc., 1971), p. 265.

31. Reproduced in Council on Environmental Quality, *Environmental Quality: The Second Annual Report of the Council of Environmental Quality,* (Washington, D.C.: U.S. Government Printing Office, August 1971), p. 193.

32. Jeffrey M. Zupan, *The Distribution of Air Quality in the New York Region* (Baltimore, Md.: Johns Hopkins University Press for Resources for the Future, Inc., 1973), pp. 18–21. Zupan's data are limited to New York City proper. If he had included the rest of New York SMSA and northeastern New Jersey—all parts of the New York Standard Consolidated Area—the relationship would probably have been much stronger. For example, according to the 1970 Census, Manhattan and its immediately adjacent counties had median family incomes of between $8,308 (Bronx) and $11,894 (Richmond). The next "layer" of counties, including Nassau and Westchester, N.Y., and Bergen, Essex, and Union, N.J., had median family incomes from $10,685 (Essex) to $14,632 (Nassau) in 1970. U.S. Bureau of the Census, 1970 Census of Population: *General Social and Economic Characteristics,* New York [PC(1)-C34] and New Jersey [PC (1)-C32] (Washington, D.C.: U.S. Government Printing Office, 1972), Table 124.

33. A. Myrick Freeman, III, "The Distribution of Environmental Quality," *Environmental Quality Analysis,* p. 265; Council on Environmental Quality, *Environmental Quality: The Second Annual Report of the Council on Environmental Quality,* p. 194; and Jeffrey M. Zupan, *The Distribution of Air Quality in the New York Region,* pp. 18–21.

34. District of Columbia, *Code* (1970), Sect. 8-2: 709, "Incinerators." Particulate information supplied by David DiJulio of the Health and Environmental Protection Department of the Washington Area Council of Governments.

35. Washington Center for Metropolitan Studies' Lifestyles and Energy Surveys.

36. *Ibid.*

Notes to Chapter Seven

1. See especially 1960 and 1970 Censuses of Population, Subject Reports, *Nonwhite Population by Race,* PC (2)-1C, and *Negro Population,* PC(2)-1B (May 1973), p. 207 plus appendixes; U.S. Bureau of Labor Statistics, *The Negroes in the United States, Their Economic and Social Situation,* BLS Bulletin No. 1511 (June 1966), p. 241; U.S. Bureau of Labor Statistics and U.S. Bureau of the Census, *Social and Economic Conditions of Negroes in the U.S.,* Series P-23, No. 24 and BLS Report No. 332 (Washington, D.C., October 1967), p. 97. Three subsequent annual reports are by the Bureau of Labor Statistics and Bureau of the Census; later editions are by the Bureau of the Census only.

2. Roxanne Hiltz, "Black and White in the Consumer Financial System," *American Journal of Sociology* 76 (May 1971), pp. 987–998; Marjorie Balenson, "Do Blacks Save More?" *American Economic Review* 62(1) (March 1972), p. 211–215, and see especially p. 215.

3. U.S. Bureau of the Census, *Current Population Reports,* Series P-60, No. 91, "Characteristics of the Low-Income Population 1973," (Washington, D.C.: U.S. Government Printing Office, December 1973), Table H for number in poor families by race; and U.S. Bureau of the Census, *Current Population Reports,* Series P-60, No. 90, "Money Income in 1972 of Families and Persons in the United States," (Washington, D.C.: U.S. Government Printing Office, December 1973), Table 18, pp. 48–50.

4. See D. Parke Gibson, *The $30 Billion Negro* (Toronto: Collier-Macmillan Canada, 1969) and in this book, the "Recommended Reading on the Negro Market," pp. 271–279, which includes over 100 references on the black consumer. Also, note the special report *Profile on the Black Consumer* by Daniel Starch and Staff Inc., (Mamaroneck, N.Y., 1973), p. 485, based on a national probability sample of black households interviewed in 1971–72 and describing their specific household and personal buying habits.

5. U.S. Bureau of the Census, *Current Population Reports,* Series P-60, No. 90, "Money Income in 1972 of Families and Persons in the United States" (Washington, D.C.: U.S. Government Printing Office, December 1973), Table 45, pp. 108–109.

6. U.S. Bureau of the Census, *Current Population Reports,* Series P-23, No. 48, "The Social and Economic Status of the Black Population in the United States, 1973" (Washington, D.C.: U.S. Government Printing Office, August 1974), Table 6, p. 17.

7. John F. Kain and John M. Quigley, "Housing Market Discrimination, Homeownership and Savings Behavior," *American Economic Review* 62 (June 1972), pp. 263–277. This article has a bibliography of many related studies that further document the discussion here.

8. Daniel Starch and Staff, Inc., *op. cit.,* p. 66ff. Data on appliance ownership by income class and race is not available in precise statistics from the WCMS study, but can be deduced. The Starch report documents these statements; it shows data by age and income class.

9. Motor Vehicle Manufacturers Association of the U.S. Inc., *1973 Motor Truck Facts* (Washington, D.C., 1973), pp. 16–17; also, Recreational

Vehicle Institute, *Recreational Vehicle Industry Facts and Figures* (Bulletin 6-750, 1974), pp. 4 and 14, and National Recreation and Park Association, *Parks and Recreation* (August 1971), "Special Issue: Leisure–A New Dawn in America."

10. Donald R. Deskins, Jr., "Race, Residence and Workplace in Detroit, 1880 to 1965," *Economic Geography* 48 (January 1972), pp. 79–94; Samuel J. Bernstein, "Mass Transit and the Urban Ghetto," *Traffic Quarterly* 27 (July 1973), pp. 431–449; John F. Kain, *The Effect of the Ghetto on the Distribution and Level of Nonwhite Employment in Urban Areas* (Santa Monica, Calif.: Rand Corp., May 1965), p. 18; Dorothy K. Newman, "The Decentralization of Jobs," *Monthly Labor Review*, 90(5) (May 1967), pp. 7–13; Wilfred Owen, "Urban Housing and Transportation: A New Partnership," *Current History* 59 (351) (November 1970), pp. 290–310; Esther Piovia, Robert B. Hill, and Wilhelmina Leigh, *Journey to Work Patterns of Transportation Consumers Among the Urban Disadvantaged* (Washington, D.C.: Department of Transportation, September 1973), p. 179; and Wilbur Smith and Associates, *WMATA 1972 On-Bus Origin-Destination Survey* (Washington, D.C.: Washington Metropolitan Area Transit Authority, 1973), Chapter 6, pp. 50–67.

11. See, among others, National Commission on Urban Problems, *Building the American City: Report of the National Commission on Urban Problems* (New York: Praeger, 1972), pp. 211–222; Lawrence Sager, "Tight Little Islands," *Stanford Law Review* 21 (1969), p. 767; Lawrence Sager, "Exclusionary Zoning: Constitutional Limitations on the Power of Municipalities to Restrict the Use of Land," *Land Use Control Annual* (Chicago: American Society of Planning Officials, 1972), pp. 153–176; Daniel Lauber, "Recent Cases in Exclusionary Zoning," Report No. 292 (Chicago: American Society of Planning Officials, Planning Advisory Service, June 1973), p. 33; National Committee on Discrimination in Housing (NCDH) and Urban Land Institute (ULI), *Fair Housing and Exclusionary Land Use: Historical Overview and Summary of Litigation* (Washington, D.C.: NCDH and ULI, 1974); Urban Land Institute, *Management and Control of Growth: Issues, Techniques, Problems, Trends*, 3 vols. (Washington, D.C.: ULI, 1974); Mary E. Brooks, *Exclusionary Zoning* (Chicago: American Society of Planning Officials, 1970), p. 42; Richard F. Babcock and Fred P. Bosselman, *Exclusionary Zoning: Land Use Regulation and Housing in the 1970s* (New York: Praeger, 1973); U.S. Commission on Civil Rights, *The Federal Civil Rights Enforcement Effort–A Reassessment* (Washington, D.C.: U.S. Commission on Civil Rights, 1973), pp. 98–186; and U.S. Civil Rights Commission, *Equal Opportunity in Suburbia* (Washington, D.C.: U.S. Commission on Civil Rights, July 1974). See also, Washington Post editorial, "Seton Bell Village," August 4, 1974.

12. National Commission on Urban Problems, *Building the American City: Report of the National Commission on Urban Problems* (New York: Praeger, 1969), pp. 211–222.

13. *Ibid.*, p. 212.

14. U.S. Commission on Civil Rights, *Mortgage Money: Who Gets It? A Case Study in Mortgage Lending Discrimination in Hartford, Connecticut* (Washington, D.C.: U.S. Commission on Civil Rights, June 1974), pp. 11–32.

15. Richard F. Babcock and Fred P. Bosselman, *Exclusionary Zoning: Land Use Regulation and Housing in the 1970s, (New York: Praeger, 1973),* p. 210

Notes to Chapter Eight

1. Current issues of *Construction Review* (U.S. Department of Commerce) and of *Current Population Reports* (U.S. Bureau of the Census).

2. Most of the analysis on this page is from data in U.S. Bureau of the Census, *Construction Reports,* "Characteristics of New One-Family Homes: 1972," Series C25-72-13, August 1973; "Price Index of New One-Family Houses Sold, Fourth Quarter 1973", Series C27-73-4, 1974; and News Releases, "May 1974 Sales of New One-Family Homes at an Annual Rate of 601,000," July 12, 1974; "Price Index of New One-Family Houses Sold: First Quarter 1974, Series C27-74-1, 1974; News Release, "Housing Starts and Building Permits in June 1974," Series CB74-171, July 17, 1974; *Current Housing Reports Pt. II,* "Housing Vacancies: Vacancy Rates and Characteristics of Housing in the United States—Annual Statistics 1973," Series H-111-73-5, 1974; U.S. Bureau of the Census in U.S. Department of Commerce and U.S. Department of Housing and Urban Development, *Current Housing Reports,* "Market Absorption of Apartments Annual," Series H-130-72-B, August 1973, and "Market Absorption of Apartments, First Quarter 1974," Series H-130-74-1, June 1974; and U.S. Department of Housing and Urban Development, *1972 HUD Statistical Yearbook* (Washington, D.C.: U.S. Government Printing Office, 1974), especially Tables 345–348.

3. Ben J. Wattenberg, *The Forming Families* (New York, Ziff-Davis, 1974), p. 5.

4. U.S. Office of Management and Budget, *Appendix to the Budget for Fiscal Year 1975,* (Washington, D.C.: U.S. Government Printing Office, 1974), p. 475.

5. U.S. Office of Management and Budget, *The United States Budget in Brief,* Fiscal Year 1975, p. 37.

6. U.S. Treasury Department and Joint Committee on Internal Revenue Taxation, *Estimates of Federal Tax Expenditures* (Washington, D.C.: U.S. Government Printing Office, June 1, 1973), Table 1.

7. *Ibid.,* Table 2, p. 8.

8. Randall W. Scott, "A Comment and Research Bibliography," in Urban Land Institute, *Management and Control of Growth: Issues, Techniques, Problems, Trends,* 3 vols. (Washington, D.C.: Urban Land Institute, 1974).

9. *Ibid.*

10. U.S. Office of Management and Budget, *The United States Budget in Brief,* Fiscal Year 1975, p. 39.

11. Henry C. Wallich, "The Materialistic Society: Its Achievements and the Social Costs," *America and the Future of Man: Lectures for the First Courses by Newspaper* (Solana Beach, Calif.: Publishers Inc., 1974), p. 20.

Notes to Appendix A2

1. Preliminary Results from the Nationwide Personal Transportation Survey, 1969–70, U.S. Department of Transportation, Federal Highway Administration, as published in *1972 Automobile Facts and Figures* (Detroit: Motor Vehicle Manufacturers Association of the U.S., 1972), p. 35.

2. U.S. Bureau of the Census, *Current Population Reports,* Series P-60, No. 91, "Characteristics of the Low Income Population, 1972" (Washington, D.C.: U.S. Government Printing Office, 1973).

3. Hittman Associates, *Residential Energy Consumption, Single-Family Housing,* Final Report (Columbia, Md.: January 1973), p. 12, Table 2.

4. U.S. Department of Commerce, Environmental Data Service, *Climatic Atlas of the of the U.S.* (Washington, D.C.: U.S. Government Printing Office, June 1968); U.S. Department of Commerce, National Oceanic and Atmospheric Administration, Environmental Data Service, *Local Climatological Data, Annual Summary with Comparative Data* (Washington, D.C.: U.S. Government Printing Office, 1973).

5. *1972 Gas Facts* (Arlington, Va.: American Gas Association, 1973), pp. 195; 198; 204.

6. U.S. Department of Commerce, Environmental Data Service, *Climatic Atlas of U.S.,* 1968.

7. U.S. Federal Power Commission, *Glossary of Important Power and Rate Terms, Abbreviations, and Units of Measurement* (Washington, D.C.: U.S. Government Printing Office, 1965), p. 27.

Bibliography

Abe, Masatoshi A. "Pricing and Welfare in Urban Transportation." *Urban Studies* 10 (June 1973): 419-449.

Achenback, Paul, Joseph Davis, and William Smith. *Analysis of Electrical Energy Usage in Air Force Homes Equipped with Air-to-Air Heat Pumps.* National Bureau of Standards, Department of Commerce. Washington, D.C.: U.S. Government Printing Office, Monograph No. 51, 1972.

Ackerman, Frank, Howard Birnbaum et al. "Income Distribution in the United States." *Review of Radical Political Economics* 3 (3) (Summer 1971): 20-43.

American Gas Association. *American Gas Association Rate Service.* Arlington, Va., 1972.

_____. *Gas Facts 1971: A Statistical Record of the Gas Utility Industry in 1970.* Arlington, Va., 1972.

_____. *Gas Facts 1972: A Statistical Record of the Gas Utility Industry in 1972.* Arlington, Va., 1973.

_____. *Gas Rate Fundamentals,* rev. ed. New York, 1969.

_____. *Single Family Residential Gas Appliance Usage, 1971.* Arlington, Va. 1971.

American Institute of Architects. *Energy Conservation in Building Design.* Washington, D.C., 1974.

American Petroleum Institute. *Annual Statistical Review–U.S. Petroleum Industry Statistics.* Washington, D.C., May, 1972.

_____. *Annual Summary of Disabling Work Injuries in the Petroleum Industry for 1971.* New York, 1972.

_____. "Dealer Turnover at Service Stations." *Report No. 18.* Washington, D.C., 1971.

_____. *Petroleum Facts and Figures.* Washington, D.C., 1971.

American Society of Planning Officials. *Land Use Control Annual.* Chicago, 1972.

American Society of Heating, Refrigerating and Air Conditioning

Engineers. *ASHRAE Guide and Data Book Applications for 1966 and 1967.* 2nd rev. New York, 1966.

American Transit Association. *'71–72 Transit Fact Book.* Washington, D.C., 1972.

Anderson, Kent P. *Residential Demand for Electricity: Econometric Estimates for California and the U.S.* Santa Monica, Calif.: Rand Corporation, 1972.

Anderson, W.T. "Identifying the Convenience-Oriented Consumer." *Journal of Marketing Research* 8 (May 1971): 179–183.

Annual Energy Requirements of Electric Household Appliances. New York: Electric Energy Association, 1972.

Annual Report, 1971. Washington, D.C., Potomac Electric Power Company, 1971.

Astrachan, Anthony. "Problems Behind the Population Boom." *The Washington Post,* August 21, 1974, A-14.

Atkinson, A.B. "The Distribution of Wealth and the Individual Life Cycle." *Oxford Economic Papers* 23 (July 1971): 239–254.

Babcock, Lyndon R., Jr. "A Combined Pollution Index for Measurement of Total Air Pollution." *Journal of the Air Pollution Control Association* 20 (October 1970): 653–659.

Babcock, Lyndon R., Jr. and Niren L. Nagda. "Cost Effectiveness of Emission Control." *Journal of the Air Pollution Control Association* 23 (March 1973): 173–179.

Babcock, Richard F. and Fred P. Bosselman, *Exclusionary Zoning: Land Use Regulation and Housing in the 1970's.* New York: Praeger, 1973.

Bacon, Edmund N. "Energy and Land Use." *Urban Land* 32 (7) (July–Aug. 1973): 13–21.

Baldwin, Malcolm F. "Public Policy on Air—An Ecological Perspective." *Ecology Law Quarterly* 1 (Spring, 1971): 245–303.

Balenson, Marjorie. "Do Blacks Save More?" *American Economic Review* 62 (1) (March 1972): 211–215.

Baron, S. "Options in Power Generation and Transmission." *Public Utilities Fornightly* 90 (July 20, 1972): 22–31.

Becker, Gary, *The Economics of Discrimination.* Chicago: University of Chicago Press, 1971.

Becker, Theodore, Lewis and Vernon G. Murray, eds. *Government Lawlessness in America.* New York: Oxford University Press, 1971.

Bell, Daniel. "Occupational Discrimination as a Source of Income Differences: Lessons of the 60's" *Public Interest* 29 (Fall 1972): 29–68.

Bellman, James R. and J. Morgan Jones. "Formal Models of Consumer Behavior: A Conceptual Overview." *Journal of Business* 45 (Oct. 1972): 544–562.

Berman, M. B. and M. J. Hammer. *The Impact of Electricity Price Increases on Income Groups: A Case Study of Los Angeles.* Santa Monica, Calif.: Rand Corp., 1973.

Berman, M. B., M. J. Hammer, and D. P. Tihansky. *The Impact of Electricity Price Increases on Income Groups: Western United States and California.* Santa Monica, Calif.: Rand Corp., 1972.

Bernstein, Samuel J. "Mass Transit and the Urban Ghetto," *Traffic Quarterly* 27 (July 1973): 431-449.

Berry, R. Stephen. "Recycling, Thermodynamics and Environmental Thrift." *Bulletin of the Atomic Scientists* (May 1972): 8-15.

Berry, R. Stephen, M. F. Fels, and H. Makino. "A Thermodynamic Valuation of Resource Use: Making Automobiles and Other Processes." Chicago, University of Chicago. (Unpublished.)

Boasberg, Tersh and James Feldesman. *Coping with the Energy Crisis.* Washington, D.C.: U.S. Office of Economic Opportunity, 1974.

Boorstin, Daniel J. *The Americans—The Democratic Experience.* New York: Random House, 1973.

Borukhov, Eli "Diseconomics of Scale in Urban Transportation." *Southern Economic Journal* 38 (July 1971): 79-82.

Boulding, Elise. "Orientation Toward Achievement or Security in Relation to Consumer Behavior." *Human Relations* 13 (4) (November 1960): 365-383.

Boyd, Alan S. "Electricity: Answer to Transportation Energy Riddle." *Edison Electric Institute Bulletin* 41 (May-June 1973): 99-102.

Bradley, Paul G. "Increasing Scarcity: The Case of Energy Resources." *American Economic Review* 63 (May 1973): 119-128.

Britt, Steuart Henderson. *Consumer Behavior in Theory and Action.* New York: John Wiley & Sons, 1970.

Brooks, Mary E. *Exclusionary Zoning.* Planning Advisory Service Report No. 254. Chicago: American Society of Planning Officials, 1970.

Brown, Keith, ed. *Regulation of the Natural Gas Producing Industry.* Baltimore: Published for Resources for the Future by Johns Hopkins University Press, 1970.

Brown, Lester R. *World Without Borders.* New York: Random House, 1972.

Browne, Thomas E. "Appliances Saturation and Load Data—A Forecasting Tool." Albany, N.Y.: New York Public Service Commission, January 1972. (Unpublished.)

Buel, Ronald A. *Dead End.* Baltimore: Penguin Books, 1973.

Burk, Marguerite C. *Consumption Economics: A Multidisciplinary Approach.* New York: John Wiley & Sons, 1968.

Cabinet Task Force on Oil Import Control. *Oil Import Question.* Washington, D.C.: U.S. Government Printing Office., 1970.

California Institute of Technology. "People, Power, Pollution." *Technology Report #1* (September 1971): 13-14.

Cambel, Ali Bulent. Socio-Political Aspects of Energy. *National Goals Symposium: Energy Policy and National Goals, Pt. 1,* pp. 3-36. Testimony before U.S. Senate Committee on Interior and Insular Affairs, 92nd Cong., 1st sess., Washington, D.C.: U.S. Government Printing Office, 1971.

Campbell, Earl. "The Energy Outlook for Transportation in the United States." *Traffic Quarterly* 27 (April 1973): 183-209.

Caplovitz, David. *The Poor Pay More.* Glencoe, Ill.: Free Press, 1963.

Chapman, Duane and Tim Tyrrell. "Alternative Assumptions About

Life Style, Population, and Income Growth: Implications for Power Generation and Environmental Quality." Paper prepared for Sierra Club Power Policy Conference, January 1972. (Mimeograph.)

Chapman, Duane, Timothy Mount and Tim Tyrrell. "Electricity and the Environment: Economic Aspects of Interdisciplinary Problem Solving." Paper presented at the December 1971 meetings of the American Association for the Advancement of Science and available from Chapman at Cornell University, Ithaca, New York.

———. "Electricity Demand Growth: Implications for Research and Development." Paper prepared for U.S. House, Subcommittee on Science, Research, and Development of the Committee on Science and Astronautics. (Mimeograph.) no date.

———. "Predicting the Past and Future in Electricity Demand." Paper prepared for the National Science Foundation Workshop on Energy and the Environment, February 22–24, 1972, San Juan, Puerto Rico. (Mimeograph.)

Chase, Richard. "Unrelated Individuals: A Back Wash Poverty Population." *American Journal of Economics and Sociology* 27 (October 1968): 337–346.

Chicago Tribune. *1970 Appliance Study.* Chicago: 1970.

Christ, Carl F., ed. *Measurements in Economics: Studies in Mathematical Economics and Econometrics in Memory of Yehuda Grunfeld.* Stanford, Calif.: Stanford University Press, 1963.

Christian, Virgil L., Jr. and Claude M. Vaughan. "Some Aspects of Cost and Demand in the Pricing of Electric Power." *Land Economics* 47 (August 1971): 281–288.

Citizens Advisory Committee on Environmental Quality. *Citizens Action Guide to Energy Conservation.* Washington, D.C., 1973.

Cochran, S. and D.E. Eldridge. "Employment and Personal Consumption Expenditures." *Monthly Labor Review* 61 (December 1971): 932.

Coleman, Richard and Bernice Neugarten. *Social Status in the City.* San Francisco: Jossey-Bass, 1971.

Commoner, Barry. "Power Consumption and Human Welfare." Paper presented at Symposium on the Energy Crisis, at the annual meeting of the American Association for the Advancement of Science, Philadelphia, December 1971.

Commoner, Barry. *The Closing Circle.* New York: Bantam Books, 1971.

Construction Review. Current Issues.

Cook, Earl. "The Flow of Energy in an Industrial Society." *Scientific American* 224 (September 1971): 134–148.

Cooper, Tom. "Fuel Oil Crisis Hits the Cities." *Nation's Cities* 11 (June 1973): 22 and 63.

"Cost of Operating an Automobile." *Family Economic Review* (September 1972): 17.

Cottrel, Frank. *Energy and Society.* New York: McGraw-Hill 1955.

Culberson, Oran L. *Consumption of Electricity in the United States.* Oak Ridge, Tenn.: Oak Ridge National Laboratory, 1971.

Dalvi, M.O. and N. Lee. "Variations in the Value of Travel Time: Further Analysis." *Manchester School of Economic Social Studies* 39 (September 1971): 187–204.

Daly, Herman E. "Electric Power, Employment, and Economic Growth." Paper presented at the annual meeting of the American Association for the Advancement of Science, Philadelphia, December 1971.

Darmstadter, Joel. "Appendix: Energy Consumption Trends and Patterns." In Sam H. Schurr, ed. *Energy, Economic Growth and the Environment.* Baltimore: Published by Johns Hopkins University Press for Resources for the Future, 1972.

Data Resources. *A Study of the Quarterly Demand for Gasoline and Impacts of Alternative Gasoline Taxes.* Lexington, Mass., 1973.

David, Martin. "Family Composition and Consumption." *Economic Analysis* 25 (May 1971): 12–14.

deLeeuw, F. "The Demand for Housing: A Review of Cross-Section Evidence." *Review of Economic Statistics* 53 (February 1971): 1–10.

deLeeuw, F. and Nkanta F. Ekanem. "The Supply of Rental Housing." *American Economic Review* 61 (December 1971): 806–817.

Deskins, D. R. "Race, Residence, and Workplace in Detroit 1880–1965." *Economic Geography* 48 (January 1972): 79–94.

District of Columbia. *Code.* (1970).

———. Department of Environmental Services. *Proposed Air Quality Standards for the District of Columbia.* Washington, D.C., 1971.

Doctor, R. D. *The Growing Demand for Energy.* Santa Monica, Calif.: Rand Corp., 1972.

Doctor, R. D. and K. P. Anderson. *California's Electrical Quandry III: Slowing the Growth Rate.* Santa Monica, Calif.: Rand Corp., 1972.

Duker, Jacob M. "Housewife and Working-Wife Families: A Housing Comparison." *Land Economics* 46 (May 1970): 138–145.

Edison Electrical Institute. *Statistical Year Book of the Electric Utility Industry for 1972.* New York, 1973.

Electric Energy Association. *Annual Energy Requirements of Electric Household Appliances.* New York, 1973. (Pamphlet.)

Electricity: How to Get the Most for the Least. Washington, D.C.: Potomac Electric Power Company, 1971.

Elifson, Kirk W. and Francis P. Noe. "Leisure Lifestyles 1929–1960: Effects of Employment, Cost and Time." Paper presented at the Annual American Sociological Association Conference, New York City, 1973.

Employment and Earnings 20 (January 1974): 157.

Energy Policy 1 (June 1973).

Environment 14 (June 1972).

Epstein, Barbara. "A Proposal to Modernize Electricity Tariffs." *Public Utilities Fortnightly* (August 30, 1973): 26; 28.

Erber, Ernest. "Jobs Go Where the Poor Can't." *Manpower* 2 (September 1970): 2-7.

Fabricant, Neil and Robert M. Hallman. *Toward a Rational Energy Policy: Energy, Politics and Pollution.* New York: George Braziller, 1971.

Federal Register 36 (84) (April 30, 1971): 8187.

Ferber, Robert. "Consumer Economics, A Survey." *Journal of Economic Literature* 11 (4) (December 1973): 1303-1342.

_____. "Family Decision-Making and Economic Behavior." Paper presented at the Institute of Life Insurance Conference, 1971.

"Fifty Years of Statistics and History." *Merchandising Week* 104 (February 1972): 22-27.

Foote, Nelson H., Janet Abu-Lughod, Mary Mix Foley, and Louis Winnick. *Housing Choices and Housing Constraints.* New York: McGraw-Hill, 1960.

Ford Foundation Energy Policy Project. *A Time to Choose: America's Energy Future.* Cambridge, Mass.: Ballinger, 1974.

Fourastié, Jean. *The Causes of Wealth.* Glencoe, Ill.: The Free Press, 1960.

Frankel, Martin R. *Inference from Survey Samples.* Ann Arbor: Institute for Social Research, University of Michigan, 1971.

Freeman, S. David. Statement before the House Committee on Antitrust and Monopoly, June 27, 1973. (Mimeograph.)

_____. "Toward a Policy of Energy Conservation." *Bulletin of the Atomic Scientists* 17 (October 1971): 8-13.

Friedlander, S. K. "Small Particles in Air Pose a Big Control Problem." *Environmental Science and Technology* 7 (12) (December 1973).

Friedman, Milton. *Theory of the Consumption Function.* Princeton, N.J.: National Bureau of Economic Research, 1957.

_____. "Windfalls, the 'Horizon,' and Related Concepts in the Permanent-Income Hypothesis." In Carl F. Christ et al. *Measurement in Economics; Studies in Mathematical Economics and Econometrics in Memory of Yehuda Grunfeld.* Stanford, Calif.: Stanford University Press, 1963.

Fuchs, Victor. "Redefining Poverty and Redistributing Income." *Public Interest* 8 (Summer 1967): 88-95.

Gans, Herbert J. "The Positive Functions of Poverty," *American Journal of Sociology* 78 (September 1972): 175-189.

Garvey, Gerald. *Energy, Ecology, Economy.* New York: W. W. Norton, 1972.

"Gas Pilots—Useful Ignition Device with Fringe Benefits." *Air Conditioning, Heating, and Refrigerating News* (October 29, 1973).

Gelfand, J. E. "Mortgage Credit and Lower Middle Income Housing Demand." *Land Economics* 94 (October 1971): 21-32.

Ginsburg, Helen, ed. *Poverty, Economics, and Society.* Boston: Little, Brown, 1972.

Gibson, D. Parke. *The $30 Billion Negro.* Toronto: Collier-Macmillan, 1969.

Goldblatt, Abraham and Charles B. Pitcher. "Mobile Homes—A

Growing Force in the Housing Sector." *Construction Review* 18 (September 1972): 4–9.

Goodwin, Leonard. "Middle-Class Misperceptions of the High Life Aspirations and Strong Work Ethic Held by the Welfare Poor." *American Journal of Orthopsychiatry* 43 (July 1973): 554–563.

Goss, W. P. and J. G. McGowan. "Transportation and Energy—A Future Confrontation." *Transportation* 1 (3) (November 1972): 265–289.

Grier, Eunice. *Characteristics of Black Suburbanites.* Washington, D.C.: Washington Center for Metropolitan Studies, 1973.

Halverson, James T. Statement before the Senate Subcommittee on Antitrust and Monopoly, June 27, 1973. (Mimeographed.)

Halvorsen, Robert. "Demand for Electric Power in the United States." Paper presented at the December 1973 meeting of the Econometric Society. Available from the Institute for Economic Research, University of Washington, Seattle, Washington.

———. "Residential Electricity: Demand and Supply." Unpublished paper for Environmental Systems Program, Oak Ridge National Laboratory, December 1971.

Hannon, Bruce. "Bottles, Cans, Energy." *Environment* 14 (March 1972): 11–21.

———. "Options for Energy Conservation." Urbana, Ill. Center for Advanced Computation, University of Illinois, Urbana-Champaign, Document #63, February 1973.

———. "Systems Energy and Recycling: A Study of the Beverage Industry." Urbana, Ill.: Center for Advanced Computation, University of Illinois, Urbana-Champaign, Document #23, January 1972.

Hannerz, Ulf. *Soul Side: Inquiries into Ghetto Culture and Community.* New York: Columbia University Press, 1969.

Hardy, Vance. "Analysis of Residential Energy Consumption and Disposable Personal Income." Beaumont, Tex.: Lamar University, 1972. (Unpublished.)

Harrison, B. "Human Capital, Black Poverty, and 'Radical' Economics." *Industrial Relations* 10 (October 1971): 277–286.

Haug, Marie R., Marvin B. Sussman. "The Indiscriminate State of Social Class Measurement." *Social Forces* 49 (June 1971): 549–569.

Hayghe, Howard. "Labor Force Activity of Married Women." *Monthly Labor Review* 96 (April 1973): 31–36.

Heien, Dale. "Demographic Effects and the Multiperiod Consumption Function." *Journal of Political Economics* 80 (January–February 1972): 125–138.

Heller, Walter, "Economics of the Race Problem." *Social Research* 37 (Winter 1970) 495–510.

Hickel, Walter J. *Geothermal Energy.* Fairbanks, Alaska: University of Alaska, 1972.

Hill, Christopher T. "Thermal Pollution and Its Control." *Electric Power Consumption and Human Welfare* (August 11, 1972): I-7–31.

Hiltz, Roxanne. "Black and White in the Consumer Financial

System." *American Journal of Sociology* 76 (6) (May 1971): 987-998.

Hirst, Eric and Robert Henderson. "A Diet Guide for Chronic Energy Consumers." *Saturday Review Science* 55 (October 28, 1972): 64-66.

Hirst, Eric and John C. Moyers. "Efficiency of Energy Use in the U.S." *Science* 179 (march 30, 1973): 1299-1304.

———. "Potential for Energy Conservation Through Increased Efficiency of Use." *Energy Conservation, Pt. 1*, pp. 155-176. Testimony submitted to the U.S. Senate, Committee on Interior and Insular Affairs, 93rd Cong., 2nd sess. Washington, D.C.: U.S. Government Printing Office, March 1973.

Hirst, Eric. *Electric Utility Advertising and the Environment.* Oak Ridge, Tenn.: Oak Ridge National Laboratory, April 1972.

———. *Energy Consumption for Transportation in the U.S.* Oak Ridge, Tenn.: Oak Ridge National Laboratory, March 1972.

———. *Energy Intensiveness of Passenger and Freight Transportation Modes, 1950-1970.* Oak Ridge, Tenn.: Oak Ridge National Laboratory, 1973.

Hittman Associates, Inc. *Residential Energy Consumption Single-Family Housing.* Final Report, Columbia, Md.; 1973.

Holdren, J. and P. Herrera. *Energy: A Sierra Club Battlebook.* San Francisco: Sierra Club, 1971.

Holmes, J. M. "A Direct Test of Friedman's Permanent Income Theory." *Journal of American Statistical Association* 65 (September 1970): 1159-1162;

Honeywell, Inc. *Reducing Fuel Consumption by Dialing Down the Thermostat.* Minneapolis, 1973. (Pamphlet.)

Houthakker, H. S. and Lester D. Taylor. *Consumer Demand in the United States, Analyses and Projections.* Cambridge, Mass.: Harvard University Press, 1970.

Houthakker, H. S., Philip K. Verleger et al. "Dynamic Demand Analyses for Gasoline and Residential Electricity." Paper presented at the American Economic Association Conference, December 1973. Available from Data Resources, Inc., 19 Hartwell Ave., Lexington, Mass. 19173.

"How to Save Fuel at Home." *U.S. News and World Report* (December 17, 1973): 20.

Jerabek, Sandra. "A Survey of State Utility Regulatory Commissions: Initiative Taken to Affect the Growth in Demand for Electric Power." Washington, D.C.: Environmental Action Foundation, July 1973. (Unpublished.)

Kain, John F. *The Effects of the Ghetto on the Distribution and Level of Nonwhite Employment in Urban Areas.* Santa Monica, Calif.: Rand Corp., 1965.

Kain, John F. and John M. Quigley. "Housing Market Discrimination, Homeownership, and Savings Behavior." *American Economic Review* 62 (June 1972): 263-277.

Kartman, Arthur. "Demand for Housing: The Neglected Supply Side." *University of Washington Business Review* 30 (Spring 1971): 59-64.

Katz, M. "Decision-Making in the Production of Power." *Scientific American* 224 (September 1971): 91-200.

Kaun, D. E. and W. Lentz. "Occupational Migration and the Central City Labor Force." *Monthly Labor Review* 94 (December 1971): 57-61.

Kiker, B. F., ed. *Investment in Human Capital.* Columbia, S.C.: University of South Carolina Press, 1971.

Kirkwood, John B. "Cash Deposits—Burdens and Barriers in Access to Utility Services." *Harvard Civil Liberties Law Review* 7 (May 1972): 630-650.

Klausner, Samuel. "Energy Rationing." Paper presented at the 139th Meeting of the American Association for the Advancement of Science, December 1972. (Unpublished.)

Klein, William. "Familial Relationships and Economic Well-Being." *Harvard Journal on Legislation* 8 (March 1971): 361-405.

Kneese, Alan V. and Blair T. Bower, eds. *Environmental Quality Analysis.* Baltimore: Published by Johns Hopkins University Press for Resources for the Future, 1971.

Kosobud, Richard F. and James N. Morgan, eds. *Consumer Behavior of Individual Families Over Two and Three Years.* Ann Arbor: Institute for Social Research, University of Michigan, 1964.

Kreps, Juanita. *Sex in the Market Place: American Women at Work.* Baltimore: Johns Hopkins University Press, 1971.

Kurchara, K., ed. *Post-Keynesian Economics.* New Brunswick, N.J.: Rutgers University Press, 1954.

Kyrk, Hazel. *The Family in the American Economy.* Chicago: University of Chicago Press, 1953.

Landsberg, H. H. and S. H. Schurr. *Energy in the United States.* New York: Random House, 1970.

Lansing, John B. and Gary Hendricks. *Automobile Ownership and Residential Density.* Ann Arbor: Institute for Social Research, University of Michigan, 1967.

Lansing, John B. and Leslie Kish. "Family Life Cycle as an Independent Variable." *American Sociological Review* 22 (5) (October 1957): 512-519.

Lansing, John B., Stephen B. Withey, and Arthur C. Wolfe. *Working Papers on Survey Research in Poverty Areas.* Ann Arbor: Institute for Social Research, University of Michigan, 1971.

Large, David B. " 'Energy Crisis' A Synopsis and Summary of the Issues." Washington, D.C., May 1972. (Unpublished.)

Lauber, Daniel. "Recent Cases in Exclusionary Zoning." *Report No. 292.* Chicago: American Society of Planning Officials, June 1973.

Laumas, P. S. and K. A. Mohabbat. "The Permanent Income Hypothesis: Evidence from Time Series Data." *American Economic Review* 62 (4) (September 1972): 730-734.

Lee, F. Y. "Estimation of Dynamic Demand Relations from a Time Series of Family Budget Data." *Journal of American Statistical Association* 65 (June 1970): 586-597.

Levinson, Alfred L. "Reducing Residential Demand for Electric Power." Paper presented at the Sierra Club Conference on Electric Power Industry, Johnson, Vermont, January 15, 1972.

Levitan, S. A. and R. Taggart. "Has the Blue-Collar Worker's Position Worsened?" *Monthly Labor Review* 94 (September 1971): 23-29.

Linden, Fabian. "Consumer Markets: The Pattern of Demand for Household Durables." *Conference Board Record* 8 (December 1971): 35-37.

_____. *Expenditure Patterns of the American Family.* New York: The National Industrial Conference Board, Sponsored by *Life,* 1965.

_____. "The Family Market—Young and Old." *Conference Board Record* 7 (August 1970): 26-30.

"The Geography of Consumer Demand: Consumer Markets." *Conference Board Record* 6 (December 1969): 45-48.

Lipset, Seymour M. "Social Mobility and Equal Opportunity." *Public Interest* 29 (Fall 1972): 90-108.

Lobel, Martin. "Red, White, Blue and Gold: The Oil Import Quotas." *Washington Monthly* 2 (August 1970): 8-19.

Luten, D. B. "The Economic Geography of Energy." *Scientific American* 224 (September 1971): 164-175.

McFall, John. "Priority Patterns and Consumer Behavior," *Journal of Marketing* 33 (October 1969): 50-55.

Makhijani, A. B. and A. J. Lichtenberg. *An Assessment of Energy and Materials Utilization in the U.S.A.* Berkeley: University of California Electronics Research Laboratory, 1971.

_____. *An Assessment of Residential Energy Utilization in the U.S.A.* Berkeley: University of California Electronics Research Laboratory, 1972.

_____. "Energy and Well-Being." *Environment* 14 (June 1972): 10-18.

Mandle, J. "Some Notes on the American Working Class." *Review of Radical Political Economics* 2 (Spring 1970): 48-68.

Martineau, Pierre. "Social Classes and Spending Behavior." *Journal of Marketing* 23 (2) (October 1958): 121-130.

Meadows, Donella H., Dennis L. Meadows, Jorgen Randers, and William W. Behrens, III. *The Limits to Growth.* New York: Universe Books, 1972.

Metcalf, L. and V. Reinemer. *Overcharge.* New York: David McKay, 1967.

Metropolitan Washington Council of Governments. *Air Quality on the National Capital Air Quality Control Region—1972.* Washington, D.C., 1973.

Meyer, J. R., J. F. Kain, and M. Wohl. *The Urban Transportation Problem.* Cambridge, Mass.: Harvard University Press, 1966.

Michael, Robert T. *The Effect of Education on Efficiency on Consumption.* New York: Columbia University Press, 1972.

Michel, Andrée, ed. *Family Issues of Employed Women in Europe and America.* Leiden, Netherlands: E. H. Brill, 1971.

Mincer, Jacob. "The Distribution of Labor Incomes: A Survey With Special Reference to the Human Capital Approach." *Journal of Economic Literature* 11, (4) (December 1973): 1303-1342.

Modigliani, Franco. "The Life Cycle Hypothesis of Saving, the Demand for Wealth and the Supply of Capital." *Social Research* (Summer 1966): 160-217.

———. "Utility Analysis and the Consumption Function: An Interpretation of Cross-Section Data." *In* K. Kurchara, ed. *Post-Keynesian Economics*. New Brunswick, N.J.,; Rutgers University Press, 1954.

Mohl, Raymond A. "Poverty, Pauperism, and Social Order in the Preindustrial American City 1780–1840." *Social Science Quarterly* 7 (March 1972): 934–948.

Moore, G. H. and J. M. Hedges. "Trends in Labor and Leisure." *Monthly Labor Review* 94 (February 1971): 3–11.

Morgan, David. "Community, Social Rank, and Attitudes Toward Suburban Living." *Sociological and Social Research* 55 (July 1971): 401–413.

Morgan, James E. et al. *Five Thousand American Families—Patterns of Economic Progress*. Ann Arbor: Institute for Social Research, University of Michigan, 1974.

Motor Vehicle Manufacturers Association of the U.S., Inc. *1972 Automobile Facts and Figures*. Washington, D.C., 1972.

———. *1973 Motor Truck Facts*. Washington, D.C., 1973.

Moyers, John C. *Value of Thermal Insulation in Residential Construction: Economics and the Conservation of Energy*. Oak Ridge, Tenn.: Oak Ridge National Laboratory, December 1971.

Musial, John J. and Edward M. Mayers. *Brief of Michigan UAW-CAP and Consumer Alliance of Michigan.* Case No. U-3910 before the Michigan Public Service, May 19, 1971.

Myrdal, Gunnar. *Objectivity in Social Research*. New York: Pantheon, 1969.

Nagatani, Keizo. "Life Cycle Savings: Theory and Fact." *American Economic Review* 62 (3) (June 1972): 344–353.

National Academy of Sciences. *Proceedings of the Conference on Health Effects of Air Pollution*. Washington, D.C.: U.S. Government Printing Office, 1973.

National Association of Motor Bus Owners. *Bus Facts*. Washington, D.C., 1971.

National Commission on Urban Problems. *Building the American City: Report of the National Commission on Urban Problems*. New York: Praeger, 1972.

National Committee on Discrimination in Housing and Urban Land Institute. *Fair Housing and Exclusionary Land Use. Historical Overview and Summary of Litigation*. Washington, D.C., 1974.

National Science Foundation. *Cornell Workshop on Energy and the Environment*. Washington, D.C.: U.S. Government Printing Office, 1972.

Netschert, Bruce, "The Energy Company: A Monopoly Trend in the Energy Markets." *National Goals Symposium: Energy Policy and National Goals, Pt. 2*, pp. 429–433. Submitted statement to the U.S. Senate, Committee on Interior and Insular Affairs, 92nd Cong., 1st. sess. Washington, D.C.: U.S. Government Printing Office, 1971.

Newman, Dorothy K. "The Decentralization of Jobs." *Monthly Labor Review* 90 (5) (May 1967): 7–13.

———. *Let Them Freeze in the Dark*. Washington, D.C.: Washington Center for Metropolitan Studies, 1974.

———. "Middle Income Black Families, Are They Middle-Class?"

Tuesday at Home, Chicago Sunday Sun-Times, October, 1971, pp. 8–9; 10; 23.

Newman, Joseph W. "A Look at the American Consumer." In *On Knowing the Consumer.* New York: John Wiley & Sons, 1966.

"19-Inch Black and White TV." *Consumer Reports* (March 1973): 158.

"19-Inch Color TV." *Consumer Reports* (January 1973): 8.

1973 Platts Oil Price Handbook and Oilmanac. New York: McGraw-Hill, 1974.

Oppenheimer, Martin. "What Is the New Working Class?" *New Politics* 10 (Fall 1972): 29–43.

O'Toole, Thomas. "FEA Raps Oil Firms' Hard Sell." *Washington Post,* August 6, 1974, p. A15.

Owen, Wilfred. "Urban Housing and Transportation: A New Partnership." *Current History* 59 (351) (November 1970): 290–310.

Pacific Lighting Corporation. Personal correspondence between Joseph R. Rensch, President, and the writers, May 9, 1974.

Parks and Recreation. August 1971. (entire issue.)

Pascal, Anthony. *Racial Discrimination in Economic Life.* New York: Lexington Books, 1972.

Pennock, Jean L. "Planning Ahead for the Buying of Major Equipment." Paper presented at the U.S. Department of Agriculture 40th Annual Outlook Conference, Washington, D.C. November 15, 1962.

Perrella, Vera C. "Young Workers and Their Earnings." *Monthly Labor Review* 94 (July 1972): 19–33.

Pifer, Howard William, III. Testimony before the Senate Subcommittee on Antitrust and Monopoly, Washington, D.C., June 26, 1973. (Mimeographed.)

Pinkerton, James. "City-Suburban Residential Patterns by Social Class." *Urban Affairs Quarterly* 4 (June 1969): 499–519.

Piovia, Esther, Robert B. Hill, and Wilhelmina Leigh. *Journey to Work—Patterns of Transportation Consumers Among the Urban Disadvantaged.* Washington, D.C.: U.S. Department of Transportation, 1973.

Plessas, Demetrius J. "Airplane Noise: Some Analytic and Policy Perspectives." *Land Economics* 49 (February 1973): 14–21.

"Portable Electric Heaters No Solution to the Energy Crisis." *Customer News* (January 1974): 1.

Projector, Dorothy S. and Gertrude Weiss. *Survey of Financial Characteristics of Consumers.* Washington, D.C.: Federal Reserve System, 1966.

"Race and Social Stratification," *Race* 13 (April 1972): 385–495.

Raines, John C. "Middle America: Up Against the Wall and Going Nowhere." *Christian Century* (May 2, 1973): 504–507.

Rall, D. P. "A Review of the Health Effects of Sulfur Oxides." Paper submitted to the Office of Management and Budget at the request of Roy Ash, October, 1973.

Reardon, W. A. *An Input/Output Analysis of Energy Use Changes from 1947 to 1958 and 1958 to 1963.* Richland, Wash.: Pacific Northwest Laboratories, a Division of Battelle Memorial Institute, June 1972.

Recreational Vehicle Institute. *Recreational Vehicle Industry Facts and Figures.* Bulletin 6-750, 1974.

Reissman, Leonard. "Readiness to Succeed: Mobility Aspirations and Modernism Among the Poor." *Urban Affairs Quarterly* 4 (March 1969): 379-395.

Residential Energy Use by Appliance in the TVA Area. Oak Ridge, Tenn.: Tennessee Valley Authority, May 12, 1972.

Resources for the Future. "Poverty and Pollution." *Resources for the Future Annual Report.* Baltimore: Published for Resources for the Future by Johns Hopkins Press, 1972.

Rinehart, James W. "Affluence and the Embourgeoisement of the Working Class." *Social Problems* 19 (Fall 1971): 149-162.

Roberts, Marc J. "Economic Consequences of Energy Costs." Paper presented at 139th Meeting of American Association for the Advancement of Science, Washington, D.C. December 29, 1972.

——. "Energy Supply and Demand and the Environment." *Fuel and Energy Resources, Pt. 2,* pp. 449-465. Testimony before the Committee on Interior and Insular Affairs, 92nd Congress, 2nd sess. Washington, D.C.: U.S. Government Printing Office, 1971.

Robinson, John P. "Historical Changes in How People Spend Their Time." *In* Andrée Michel, ed. *Family Issues of Employed Women in Europe and America.* Leiden, Netherlands: E. H. Brill, 1971.

Rosow, Jerome M. *The Worker and the Job.* Englewood Cliffs, N.J.: Prentice-Hall, 1974.

Rothschild, Emma. "Illusions About Energy." *New York Review of Books* 20 (13) (August 9, 1973):

——. "What Is the 'Energy Crisis'?"*New York Review of Books* 20 (12) (July 19, 1973):

Rytina, Nancy F. and William R. Beachy. "Energy-Using Features Increase in New One-Family Houses." *Metropolitan Bulletin* 11 (June-July 1973). Washington, D.C.: Washington Center for Metropolitan Studies.

Sager, Lawrence. "Exclusionary Zoning: Constitutional Limitations on the Power of Municipalities to Restrict the Use of Land." *Land Use Control Annual.* (1972), pp. 153-176.

——. "Tight Little Islands." *Stanford Law Review* 21 (1969): 767.

Schnore, Leo F. and L. Z. Klaff. "Suburbanization in the Sixties: A Preliminary Analysis." *Land Economics* 48 (February 1972): 23-33.

Schultz, Theodore. *Investment in Human Capital—The Role of Education and of Research.* New York: The Free Press, 1971.

Schurr, Sam H. *Energy in the American Economy 1850-1975.* Baltimore: Johns Hopkins Press, 1973.

Schurr, Sam H., ed. *Energy, Economic Growth, and the Environment.* Baltimore: Published by Johns Hopkins Press for Resources for the Future, 1972.

Selltiz, Claire, Marie Jahoda, Morton Deutsch, and Stuart W. Cook. *Research Methods in Social Relations.* New York: Holt, Rinehart, and Winston, 1959.

"Seton Bell Village." *The Washington Post,* August 4, 1974, p. C-6.

Sherman, Roger. "The Design of Public Utility Institutions." *Land Economics* 46 (February 1970): 51-58.

Smith, James D. and Stephen D. Franklin. "The Concentration of Personal Wealth, 1922–1969." *American Economic Review* 64 (2) (May 1974): 162–167.

Shostak, Arthur B. *Blue-Collar Life.* New York: Random House, 1969.

Simon, Julian and Carl B. Barnes. "The Middle-Class U.S. Consumption Function: A Hypothetical Question Study of Expected Consumption Behavior." *Oxford Institute of Economics and Statistics Bulletin* (February 1971): 73–80.

Spilerman, S. and D. Elesk. "Alternative Conceptions of Poverty and Their Implications for Income Maintenance." *Social Problems* 18 (Winter 1971): 358–373.

Stanford Research Institute. *Patterns of Energy Consumption in the U.S.* Stanford, Calif., 1972.

Starch, Daniel and Staff, Inc. *Profile of the Black Consumer.* Mamaroneck, New York, 1973.

Starr, Chauncey. "Energy and Power." *Scientific American* 225 (September 1971): 37–49.

Stein, Bruno. *On Relief: The Economics of Poverty and Public Welfare.* New York, Basic Books, 1973.

Stein R. L. and J. N. Hedges. "Earnings and Family Income." *Monthly Labor Review* 94 (June 1971): 13–24.

Stein, Richard G. "Spotlight on the Energy Crisis: How Architects Can Help." *American Institute of Architects Journal* 57 (6) (June 1972): 18–23.

Steiner, Henry M. and Christopher S. Davies. "The Transportation Efficiency of Disadvantaged Blacks." *Traffic Quarterly* 27 (April 1973): 255–268.

Sternlieb, S. and A. Bauman. "Employment Characteristics of Low-Wage Workers." *Monthly Labor Review* 95 (July 1972): 19–21.

Stokes, Carl B. "On Reordering the Priorities of the Planning Profession." *Planning 1971.* Chicago: American Society of Planning Officials, 1971.

Suits, Daniel B., ed. *Impacts of Monetary Policy.* Englewood Cliffs, N.J.: Prentice-Hall, 1963.

Sullivan, J. "Pollution: Discrimination in Center City." *Environmental Action* 3 (February 19, 1972): 3–5.

Summers, Claude M. "The Conversion of Energy." *Scientific American* 225 (September 1971): 148–160.

Sundquist, James. *On Fighting Poverty: Perspectives from Experience.* New York: Basic Books, 1969.

Szalai, Alexander, ed. *The Use of Time: Daily Activities of Urban and Suburban Population in Twelve Counties.* The Hague, Netherlands: Mouton, 1972.

Tallman, Irving and Ramona Mergner. "Life-Style Differences Among Urban and Suburban Blue-Collar Families." *Social Forces* 48, (March 1970): 334–348.

Thibeault, Russell, Edward J. Kaiser, Edgar W. Butler, and Ronald J. McAllister. "Accessibility Satisfaction, Income, and Residential Mobility" *Traffic Quarterly* 27 (April 1973): 289–305.

Thurow, Lester. "The Optimum Lifetime Distribution of Consumption Expenditures." *American Economic Review* 59 (3) (June 1969): 324–330.

Tillotson, David. "Commuter Routes for Bicycles." *Washington Post,* June 20, 1974, p. A-15.

"Travel Stamps Get U.S. Funding." *The Washington Post,* June 14, 1974, p. A-24.

TRW, Inc. *Prediction of the Effects of Transportation Controls on Air Quality in Major Metropolitan Areas.* McLean, Va., 1972.

TRW Systems Group. *Air Quality Implementation Planning Program,* Vol. 1, *Operator's Manual.* Springfield, Va.: National Technical Information Service, 1970.

United Nations. Statistical Office. Department of Economic and Social Affairs. *United Nations Statistical Yearbook 1972.* New York, 1973.

U.S. Bureau of Labor Statistics. *City Workers Family Budget, Pricing, Procedures, Specifications, and Average Prices.* Bulletin No. 1570–3. Washington, D.C.: U.S. Government Printing Office, 1966.

_____. *Consumer Expenditures and Income 1960–61.* BLS Reports 237–1. Washington, D.C.: U.S. Government Printing Office, 1964.

_____. *Consumer Expenditures and Incomes.* BLS Report 237–93. Supplement 3, part A. Washington, D.C.: U.S. Government Printing Office, 1966.

_____. *Consumer Expenditures and Income.* Bulletin No. 1684. Washington, D.C.: U.S. Government Printing Office, 1971.

_____. *Handbook of Labor Statistics,* Washington, D.C.: U.S. Government Printing Office, 1973.

_____. *The Negroes in the United States, Their Economic and Social Situation.* Bulletin No. 1511. Washington, D.C.: U.S. Government Printing Office, 1966.

_____. *Three Budgets for an Urban Family of Four Persons.* Bulletin No. 1570–5. Washington, D.C. U.S. Government Printing Office, 1967.

_____. *Three Budgets for an Urban Family of Four Persons, 1969–70.* Supplement to Bulletin No. 1570–5. Washington, D.C.: U.S. Government Printing Office, 1971.

_____. "Urban Family Budget and Comparative Indexes for Urban Areas, Autumn 1973" News Release. U.S.D.L. 1974–304, June 16, 1974.

U.S. Bureau of Outdoor Recreation. *Selected Outdoor Recreation Statistics.* Washington, D.C., 1972.

U.S. Bureau of the Census. Census of Housing. *1970 Detailed Housing Characteristics,* HC(1)–B1, U.S. Summary. Washington, D.C.: U.S. Government Printing Office, 1972.

_____. Census of Housing. *1970 General Housing Characteristics of the Population* Final Report HC(1)–A1, U.S. Summary. Washington, D.C.: U.S. Government Printing Office, 1972.

————. Census of Housing. *1960 Census of Housing, States and Small Areas,* vol. 1, U.S. Summary, Final Report, HC(1)-1. Washington, D.C.: U.S. Government Printing Office, 1962.

————. Census of Housing, *1950 Census of Housing, General Characteristics,* vol. 1, U.S. Summary. Washington, D.C.: U.S. Government Printing Office, 1952.

————. Census of Housing: *1940 Census of Housing, General Characteristics,* vol. 2, part 1, U.S. Summary. Washington: U.S. Government Office, 1942.

————. Census of Population, 1970. vol. 1. *Characteristics of the Population.* Part 1, U.S. Summary. Washington, D.C.: U.S. Government Printing Office, 1972.

————. Census of Population, 1970, vol. 1 *Characteristics of the Population.* Part 1, U.S. Summary. Washington, D.C.: U.S. Government Printing Office, 1972.

————. Census of Population, 1960, vol. 1 *Characteristics of Population.* Part 1, U.S. Summary. Washington, D.C.: U.S. Government Printing Office, 1962.

————. Census of Population, 1970 Subject Reports, PC(2)-2B. *Mobility for States and the Nation.* Washington, D.C.: U.S. Government Printing Office, 1973.

————. Census of Population, 1970 Subject Reports, PC(2)-1B. *Negro Population.* Washington, D.C.: U.S. Government Printing Office, 1973.

————. Census of Population, 1960 Subject Reports, PC(2)-1C. *Nonwhite Population by Race.* Washington, D.C.: U.S. Government Printing Office, 1963.

————. Census of Population and Housing, 1970 Census Tracts. Final Report PHC(1)-226. Washington, D.C., Md., Va. Washington, D.C.: U.S. Government Printing Office, 1972.

————. *Census of Transportation Travel Survey 1957.* Washington, D.C.: U.S. Government Printing Office, 1957.

————. *Census of Transportation 1963, Passenger Transportation Survey.* Washington, D.C.: U.S. Government Printing Office, 1963.

————. *Census of Transportation 1967, National Travel Survey.* Washington, D.C.: U.S. Government Printing Office, 1967.

————. *Construction Reports.* "Characteristics of New One-Family Homes": 1972, '71; '70; '69; '68; '67; '66. Washington, D.C.: U.S. Government Printing Office, 1966-1972.

————. *Construction Reports.* Series C20. "Housing Starts: May, 1974." Washington, D.C.: U.S. Government Printing Office, 1974.

————. *Construction Reports.* Series C27-74-1. "Price Index of New One-Family Houses Sold: First Quarter 1974." Washington, D.C.: U.S. Government Printing Office, 1974.

————. *Construction Reports,* Series C27-73-4. "Price Index of New One-Family Houses Sold: Fourth Quarter 1974." Washington, D.C.: U.S. Government Printing Office, 1974.

————. *Current Housing Reports.* Series H-111-73-5, Part II.

"Housing Vacancies: Vacancy Rates and Characteristics of Housing in the United States: Annual Statistics 1973." Washington, D.C.: U.S. Government Printing Office, 1974.

_____. *Current Housing Reports.* Series H-130-72-B, "Market Absorption of Apartments Annual." Washington: U.S. Government Printing Office, August 1973.

_____. *Current Housing Reports.* Series H-130-74-1. "Market Absorption of Apartments, 1st Quarter 1974." Washington: U.S. Government Printing Office, 1974.

_____. *Current Population Reports.* Series P-20, No. 218. "Household and Family Characteristics: March 1970." Washington: U.S. Government Printing Office, 1971.

_____. *Current Population Reports.* Series P-20, No. 246. "Household and Family Characteristics: March 1972." Washington: U.S. Government Printing Office, 1973.

_____. *Current Population Reports.* Series P-20, No. 262. "Mobility of the Population of the United States, March 1970 to March 1973." Washington: U.S. Government Printing Office, March 1974.

_____. *Current Population Reports.* Series P-23, No. 28. "Revisions in Poverty Statistics, 1959 to 1968." Washington: U.S. Government Printing Office, August 12, 1969.

_____. *Current Population Reports.* Series P-23, No. 48. "The Social and Economic Status of the Black Population in the United States, 1973." Washington: U.S. Government Printing Office, 1974.

_____. *Current Population Reports.* Series P-60, No. 87. "Money Income in 1972 of Families and Persons in the United States." Washington, U.S. Government Printing Office, June 1973.

_____. *Current Population Reports.* Series P-60, No. 88. "Characteristics of the Low Income Population, 1972." Washington: U.S. Government Printing Office, June, 1973.

_____. *Current Population Reports.* Series P-60, No. 89. "Household Money Income in 1972 and Selected Social and Economic Characteristics of Households." Washington: U.S. Government Printing Office, July 1973.

_____. *Current Population Reports.* Series P-60, No. 90. "Money Income in 1972 of Families and Persons in the U.S." Washington: U.S. Government Printing Office, 1973.

_____. *Current Population Reports.* Series P-60, No. 91. "Characteristics of the Low-Income Population, 1972." Washington: U.S. Government Printing Office, 1973.

_____. *Current Population Reports.* Series P-60, No. 93. "Money Income in 1973 of Families and Persons in the United States. Washington: U.S. Government Printing Office, July 1974.

_____. *Current Population Reports.* Series P-65, No. 18. "Special Report on Household Ownership and Purchases of Automobiles and Selected Household Durables; 1960-1967." Washington: U.S. Government Printing Office, 1967.

_____. *Current Population Reports.* Series P-65, No. 28. "Special

Report on Household Ownership and Purchases of Cars, Homes and Selected Household Durables: 1968 and 1969." Washington, D.C.: U.S. Government Printing Office, 1969.

――――. *Current Population Reports.* Series P-65, No. 33. "Special Report on Household Ownership of Cars, Homes and Selected Household Durables: 1970, 1969, and 1960." Washington: U.S. Government Printing Office, 1970.

――――. *Current Population Reports.* Series P-65, No. 40. "Household Ownership and Availability of Cars, Homes, and Selected Household Durables and Annual Expenditures on Cars and Other Durables: 1971." Washington: U.S. Government Printing Office, 1972.

――――. *Current Population Reports.* Series P-65, No. 41. "Recent Purchase of Cars, Houses, and Other Durables and Expectations to Buy in the Months Ahead: Survey Data Through April, 1972." Washington: U.S. Government Printing Office, 1972.

――――. *Current Population Reports.* Series P-65, No. 45. "Household Ownership of Cars and Light Trucks, July 1972." Washington: U.S. Government Printing Office, February 1973.

――――. *Historical Statistics of the U.S., Colonial Times to 1957.* Washington: U.S. Government Printing Office, 1961.

――――. *Historical Statistics of the U.S., Colonial Times to 1951, Continuation to 1961 and Revisions.* Washington: U.S. Government Printing Office, 1965.

――――. *Housing Construction Statistics 1889 to 1964.* Washington: U.S. Government Printing Office, 1966.

――――. *Revised Study Plan for the Consumer Expenditure Survey.* Washington: U.S. Government Printing Office, 1971.

――――. *Statistical Abstract of the United States.* 1972 and 1973 eds. Washington: U.S. Government Printing Office, 1972 and 1973.

――――. *U.S. Department of Commerce News.* CB74-171. "Housing Starts and Building Permits in June 1974. Washington: U.S. Government Printing Office, July 17, 1974.

――――. *U.S. Department of Commerce News.* CB74-169. "May 1974 Sales of New One-Family Homes at an Annual Rate of 601,000." Washington: U.S. Government Printing Office, July 12, 1974.

U.S. Bureau of Mines. *Bureau of Mines Minerals Yearbook 1971.* Washington: U.S. Government Printing Office, 1971.

――――. *Natural Gas Production and Consumption: 1972.* Washington: U.S. Government Printing Office, 1973.

――――. *Sales of Fuel Oil and Kerosene in 1972.* Washington: U.S. Government Printing Office, October 10, 1973.

U.S. Commission on Civil Rights. *Equal Opportunity in Suburbia.* Washington, D.C.: 1974.

――――. *The Federal Civil Rights Enforcement Effort–A Reassessment.* Washington, D.C., 1973.

――――. *Mortgage Money: Who Gets It? A Case Study in Mortgage Lending Discrimination in Hartford, Connecticut.* Washington, D.C., 1974.

U.S. Congress. Joint Economic Committee. *The Economy, Energy and the Environment,* by Legislative Reference Service of the Library of Congress. Joint Committee Print, 91st Congress, 2nd sess. Washington: U.S. Government Printing Office, 1970.

U.S. Congress. Senate. Committee on Commerce. *The Inner City Environment and the Role of the Environmental Protection Agency.* Hearings before the Subcommittee on the Environment, on inner-city environmental problems with emphasis on health hazards to ghetto children. 92nd Congress, 2nd session. Washington: U.S. Government Printing Office, 1972.

U.S. Congress. Senate. Select Committee on Nutrition and Human Needs. *Fuel Crisis Impact on Low Income and Elderly.* Hearings before the Select Committee on Nutrition and Human Needs, 93rd Congress, 2nd sess. Washington, D.C.: U.S. Government Printing Office, 1974.

U.S. Congressional Research Service. *Conservation of Energy.* Washington, D.C.: U.S. Government Printing Office, 1972.

U.S. Council on Environmental Quality. *Environmental Quality: The Second Annual Report of the Council on Environmental Quality.* Washington: U.S. Government Printing Office, 1971.

_____. *Environmental Quality: The Fourth Annual Report of the Council on Environmental Quality.* Washington, D.C.: U.S. Government Printing Office, 1973.

U.S. Department of Commerce. Bureau of Competitive Assessment and Business Policy. "New Construction, Housing and Mobile Homes—A Look Ahead." *Construction Review* 17 (9) (September 1971).

_____. Environmental Data Service. *Climatic Atlas of the U.S.* Washington: U.S. Government Printing Office, 1968.

_____. National Air Pollution Control Administration. *Air Quality Criteria for Hydrocarbons.* Washington: U.S. Government Printing Office, 1970.

U.S. Department of Commerce and U.S. Department of Housing and Urban Development. "Sales of New One-Family Homes Totals 620,000 in 1973." *Press Release,* June 10, 1974.

U.S. Department of Health, Education and Welfare. National Air Pollution Control Administration. *Air Quality for Carbon Monoxide.* Washington: U.S. Government Printing Office, 1970.

U.S. Department of Housing and Urban Development. *1972 HUD Statistical Yearbook.* Washington, D.C.: U.S. Government Printing Office, 1974.

U.S. Department of Interior. "Energy Use Up Nearly 5 Percent in 1973." *U.S. Department of Interior Release,* March 13, 1974.

U.S. Department of Labor. *Black Americans—A Decade of Occupational Change.* Washington, D.C., U.S. Government Printing Office, 1972.

_____. *How American Buying Habits Change.* Washington, D.C., U.S. Government Printing Office, 1959.

_____. *Manpower Report of the President.* Washington, D.C., U.S. Government Printing Office, 1972, 1973, 1974.

U.S. Department of Transportation. *1972 National Transportation Report.* Washington, D.C.: U.S. Government Printing Office, 1972.

U.S. Department of Treasury and the Joint Committee on Internal Revenue Taxation. *Estimates of Federal Tax Expenditures.* Washington, D.C.: U.S. Government Printing Office, June 1, 1973.

U.S. Environmental Protection Agency. Office of Air and Water

Program and the Office of Air Quality Planning and Standards. *Compilation of Air Pollutant Emission Factors.* Research Triangle Park, N.C., 1973.

————. *1974 Gas Mileage Guide for Car Buyers: Fuel Test Results for Automobiles and Light-Duty Trucks.* Washington, D.C.: U.S. Government Printing Office, 1974.

————. *A Report on Automobile Fuel Economy.* Washington, D.C.: U.S. Government Printing Office, October 1973.

U.S. Federal Highway Administration. Bureau of Public Roads. *Highway Statistics Summary to 1965.* Washington, D.C.: U.S. Government Printing Office, 1967.

————. *Drivers License–1972.* Washington, D.C., 1973.

————. *Nationwide Personal Transportation Study (Annual Miles of Automobile Travel).* Washington, D.C.: U.S. Government Printing Office, 1972.

————. *Report No. 7.* "Household Travel in the United States." Washington, D.C., 1972.

U.S. Federal Power Commission, Office of Economics. *Promotional Practices of Public Utilities: A Survey of Recent Actions by State Regulatory Commissions.* Washington, D.C.: U.S. Government Printing Office, 1970.

U.S. Federal Power Commission. *All Electric Homes in the U.S. Annual Bills–Cities 50,000 or More.* Washington: U.S. Government Printing Office, June 1972.

————. *Glossary of Important Power and Rate Terms, Abbreviations, and Units of Measurement.* Washington, D.C.: U.S. Government Printing Office, 1965.

————. *Statistics of Privately Owned Electric Utilities in the U.S.* Washington, D.C.: U.S. Government Printing Office, December 1970.

————. *Statistics of Publicly Owned Electric Utilities in the U.S.* Washington, D.C.: U.S. Government Printing Office, February 1970.

————. *The 1970 National Power Survey.* Washington, D.C., U.S. Government Printing Office, 1970.

————. *Typical Electric Bills, 1971.* Washington, D.C.: U.S. Government Printing Office, 1971.

————. *Energy Efficiency in Room Air Conditioners.* Washington, D.C.: U.S. Government Printing Office, 1974.

————. *Eleven Ways to Reduce Energy Consumption and Increase Comfort in Household Cooling.* Washington, D.C.: U.S. Government Printing Office, 1971.

————. *Seven Ways to Reduce Fuel Consumption in Household Heating Through Energy Conservation.* Washington, D.C.: U.S. Government Printing Office, 1972.

————. *Technical Options for Energy Conservation in Buildings.* NBS Technical Note 789. Washington, D.C.: U.S. Government Printing Office, 1973.

————. *Energy Labeling of Household Appliances.* Washington, D.C.: U.S. Government Printing Office, 1974.

U.S. National Laboratory. Oak Ridge, Tenn. *An Inventory of Energy Research.* Prepared for the Task Force on Energy of the Subcommittee on Science, Research and Development of the Committee on Science and Astronautics, U.S. House of Representatives, 92nd Congress, 2nd sess. Washington, D.C.: U.S. Government Printing Office, 1972.

U.S. Office of Emergency Preparedness. *The Potential for Energy Conservation*. Washington, D.C.: U.S. Government Printing Office, 1972.

U.S. Office of Management and Budget. *The Budget of the United States Government, 1975–Appendix*. Washington, D.C., U.S. Government Printing Office, 1974.

_____. *The United States Budget in Brief, 1975*. Washington, D.C.: U.S. Government Printing Office, 1974.

U.S. Office of Science and Technology. The Energy Policy Staff. *Electric Power and the Environment*. Washington, D.C., U.S. Government Printing Office, 1970.

U.S. President. *Economic Report of the President, 1974*. Washington, D.C.: U.S. Government Printing Office, 1974.

Urban Land Institute. *Management and Control of Growth: Issues, Techniques, Problems, Trends*. 3 vols. Washington, D.C., 1974.

Vanek, Joann. "Keeping Busy: An Historical Analysis of Time Spent in Housework Over Five Decades." Ann Arbor: University of Michigan, 1974. (Ph.D. dissertation.)

Velona, Walter D. "Urban Growth and New Technology for Transportation." Washington: Office of the Secretary of the U.S. Department of Transportation, October 15, 1971. (Unpublished.)

Wachtel, Dawn Day. "Lower-Income Households Use Little Gas, Travel Mainly for Essentials, Nationwide Survey Shows." *Metropolitan Bulletin*, No. 13, August 1974. Washington: Washington Center for Metropolitan Studies.

Wachtel, Howard M. "Statistical Noise and the Voices of the Poor." *Review of Radical Political Economics* 2 (Spring 1970): 87–89.

_____. "Looking at Poverty From a Radical Perspective." *Review of Radical Political Economics* 3 (Summer 1971): 1–19.

Waddell, Thomas E. *The Economic Damages of Air Pollution*. Washington, D.C.: Environmental Protection Agency, 1974.

Wallace, P. A. "Economic Position and Prospects for Urban Blacks." *American Journal of Agricultural Economics* 53 (May 1971): 316–318.

Wallich, Henry C. "The Materialistic Society: Its Achievements and the Social Cost." *America and the Future of Man: Lectures for the First Courses by Newspaper*. Solana Beach, Calif.: Publishers Inc., 1974.

Walters, Colin. *Travel Growth in Washington Region Highlights Need for More Small Vehicle Transit*. Washington, D.C.: Washington Center for Metropolitan Studies, 1974.

Wattenberg, Ben J. *The Forming Families*. New York: Ziff-Davis, 1974.

Wilbur Smith and Associates. *On-Bus Origin–Destination Survey*. Washington, D.C.: Washington Metropolitan Area Transit Authority, April 1974.

_____. *WMATA 1972 On-Bus Origin–Destination Survey*. Washington, D.C.: Washington Metropolitan Area Transit Authority, 1973.

Wilson, John W. "Electricity Consumption: Supply Requirements and Demand Electricity and Rate Design." Unpublished paper available from author at 6425 Belleview Drive, Columbia, Md. 21046.

————. "Residential Demand for Electricity." *Quarterly Review of Economics and Business* 10 (Spring 1971): 7–22.

Weiss, L. and J. G. Williamson. "Black Education, Earnings, and Interregional Migration: Some New Evidence." *American Economic Review,* 62 (June 1972):

Young, Anne M. "Children of Working Mothers." *Monthly Labor Review* 96 (April 1973): 37–40.

Zupan, Jeffrey M. *The Distribution of Air Quality in the New York Region.* Baltimore: Published for Resources for the Future by Johns Hopkins Press, 1973.

Reviewer Comment

What seems to me to be missing in this discussion of energy and the way people live is an account of the many serious experiments now under way to develop new life styles which conserve energy and other resources. Professor Sim Van Der Ryn of the University of California, Berkeley, has been a leader in this area. Some of the people interviewed in the chapter on "The Way Some People Live" seem to want to practice energy conservation but don't quite know how to go about it. Van Der Ryn and others are doing the kind of thinking and experimenting that will make meaningful change possible.

—Alfred Heller

Index

About the Authors

Dorothy K. Newman, a Yale University Ph.D in Sociology, directed the study of the American energy consumer while a Senior Associate at the Washington Center for Metropolitan Studies. She is a member of the Research Council on Environmental Impact Analysis of the American Society of Civil Engineers. Among her numerous publications are many on construction and housing. For much of the past three decades, Dr. Newman served as an economist in the U.S. Department of Labor, responsible for research on construction, housing, employment, prices, the consumer, and minorities. In 1968 she left to set up the National Urban League's Department of Research, and was its head for four years. She is currently directing a major study of Black Americans and governmental policy, with the support of the Carnegie Corporation of New York.

Dawn Day is a teacher of sociology at Brooklyn College of the City University of New York. She has served with the Washington Center for Metropolitan Studies and for the New York State Legislative Institute as a consultant on social aspects of energy. Her research has focused on social issues relating to poverty and discrimination. Her educational background includes a Ph.D in sociology from the University of Michigan, a master's degree in social work from the University of Michigan and a bachelor's degree in economics from Oberlin College. She was raised in North Dakota, a state where winter brings a long heating season and glistening landscapes.